From Black
to African American

From Black
to African American

A New Social Representation

Gina Philogène

Foreword by Serge Moscovici

Westport, Connecticut
London

305.896073
P56 f

Library of Congress Cataloging-in-Publication Data

Philogène, Gina, 1961–
    From Black to African American : a new social representation /
Gina Philogène : foreword by Serge Moscovici.
        p.   cm.
    Includes bibliographical references.
    ISBN 0–275–96284–9 (alk. paper)
    1. Afro-Americans—Race identity.   2. Afro-Americans—Psychology.
3. Afro-Americans—Attitudes.   4. Blacks—United States—Race
identity.   5. Blacks—United States—Attitudes.   6. Black
nationalism—United States.   7. United States—Race relations.
I. Title.
E185.625.P47   1999
305.896073—dc21   99–21594

British Library Cataloguing in Publication Data is available.

Library of Congress Catalog Card Number: 99–21594
ISBN: 0–275–96284–9

First published in 1999

Praeger Publishers, 88 Post Road West, Westport, CT 06881
An imprint of Greenwood Publishing Group, Inc.
www.praeger.com

Printed in the United States of America

The paper used in this book complies with the
Permanent Paper Standard issued by the National
Information Standards Organization (Z39.48–1984).

10 9 8 7 6 5 4 3 2 1

JK

This book is dedicated to the memory of Leon Festinger (1919–1989), a genius of great originality whose ideas, scholarship, and critical intelligence represent what is best in social psychology.

Contents

Foreword

There is no goal more important today than to create the conditions for the eradication of racism. For there to be democratic politics, a democratic culture, anything democratic, the first step has to be cultural, to create the kind of cultural source that would inexorably eliminate all those things undermining democracy as well as human dignity.

As a social psychologist I can recognize that two circumstances have rendered this goal so important, even radical. I am using the word radical not in the sense of a rise to extremes, but in the sense given to it by Marx, as a return to the roots of the human being. First, the holocaust showed the length to which obscure racial sentiments can go in nations which have worked so hard for their own grandeur, yet have done nothing or next to nothing for the value of humans. And then there were those circumstances which have propelled forward human rights, proclaimed by both the American and the French Revolutions as the criteria and bedrock for relations between nations and individuals, hence our culture of today in the making. And among these rights, the one of resisting oppression is the heart, as numerous thinkers have declared.

Any observer can recognize that the introduction of human rights has had the effect of activating passive minorities, of sparking energy and movement. This is advantageous, since it ends stagnation and thus prepares the ground for a reaction capable of producing something better and more elevated from the point of view of culture. As the great Portuguese poet Fernando Pessoa has written: "When disorder takes hold, a healthy society responds right away—not to maintain order which can only be provisional, but to attack the evil that has caused this disorder."

Proof? Anyone who has witnessed the changes during our last half-century or read the pages of its history should not need any.

What I just wrote has been lived and is sincere, but probably not very original. Still, it's a fact that throughout my professional life I have unconsciously eluded any research on racism, even avoided directing theses on that subject, which occupies such a prominent place in social psychology. Recently I happened to become aware of the reasons responsible for this evasion. It was above all due to the experience of a sort of ancestral discrimination as a Jew and as a foreigner. The word "discrimination" is in any case not strong enough to express what I lived through in my childhood, then during the war, and what I have seen and felt in the displaced-persons camps after the war. First of all, I did not feel capable of fulfilling the sine qua non conditions of scientific counterpoint: a certain detachment vis-à-vis one's subjective experience and a controlled reflection concerning its significance. Moreover, the specialized work I found in this domain did not seem to come close to what I intuitively thought regarding the nature of racism. I admire all those ingenious studies on prejudice, stereotypes, group categorization, and cognitive biases. What more can be added, once we have come to understand the logic, so dominant, used to justify their repetition throughout so many years? Still, I have a sense of a disproportion between the causes—let's risk the term "individual causes"—and the consequences, so shocking, so tragic throughout history. Instead let us say: Violence, once beyond the control of reason, no longer constrained by concern with appearance, supported by religions and shared ideologies, penetrates even the most inaccessible parts of the human soul and existence. Maybe I am still too attached to a classical view of these phenomena—one that we can see, for instance, in the works of W.E.B. Du Bois or Max Weber.

We can endlessly debate the relationship between race and class, or the nature of the dual consciousness, but not their relevance. Like many other American students at the beginning of the century Du Bois went to Germany, where he established many intellectual links, with Max Weber among others. Weber in turn travelled to America, from where he brought back numerous precious observations concerning the life of sects and the economic situation there. The volatile atmosphere during those years of industrial boom, the enthusiasm he sensed among the Americans, did not prevent him from having the premonition that their future, as he wrote in 1904, is "clouded only by the negro question and the terrible immigration." His comments on that question were shaped more than one would think by Du Bois, but that is not the point I wish to discuss here.

Donc veniamus ad rem. Why have I mentioned the relationship between those two thinkers or, shall we say, sociologists? Above all, because at the time several scientists confused ethnic group and race, explaining them with a biological determinism hidden beneath a scientific vocabulary. And during a debate (in which he mentioned Du Bois) Weber continued a more humanistic tradition, pointing out to his colleagues that race is a cultural category and that prejudices are "the product not of fact and empirical experience, but of mass beliefs." That is exactly the conclusion I reached over all those years during which I was subjected to prejudices as a personified abstraction, as well as later on. A system of mass beliefs augments the terrible loneliness of the discriminated group, which, put through quarantine, has to go through the labyrinths of the absurd while trying to find peace within and give meaning to something devoid of hope.

In other words, since prejudices result neither from facts nor empirical experience, it is difficult to look for reason in terms of automatic thought processes, mistakes in judgment, lack of contact, or even the education of children, since everything depends on the old question: who educates the educators? Prejudices always seem to result from mass beliefs, whose presence can be seen in language, artwork, philosophical writings, or scientific works which justify and amplify them. Stereotypes are, for that matter, an extreme and non-institutional possibility of these mass beliefs in the conditions of ordinary life.

There are moments when, by observing closely their use, one can ask whether these discriminatory prejudices do not have as their primary purpose the valorization of one's ingroup, the "us," and the devalorization, even exclusion, of "them," the others belonging to what we call the outgroup. One only needs to read the descriptions of far-away populations and the traits attributed to the savages by certain writers to be amazed by the similarity of these descriptions and traits to those we attribute to the country folk close to home, whom we treated as savages and pagans and who were thus lowered by the sheer fact of comparison. And what could be said of Frazer's *Golden Bough*, whose minute detail in the recounting of legends, beliefs, and rituals among numerous primitive peoples has evoked the admiration of many generations? Of course, those far away from Western civilization may appear at the same time far away from reason, as drowning in ignorance, the dream, and the trance of millenary phantasms: a stupefying melange which Frazer said at one point we can find not far away from Europe, even in Europe itself if we scratch just a bit below the surface of the masses. He believed in this way to have established the proof of intellectual inferiority, of cognitive deficiencies in groups constituting the amorphous majority of our societies, while reason remained the realm of an elite.

These prejudices try to create and legitimize, by indirect means, a state of superiority which valorizes one part of the group at the expense of another. In other words, they have as their function to create a line of demarcation between those one actually knows and those one merely resembles. Prejudices are unforgiving reminders of who one is and wishes not to be. By the same token, they project a similarity between devalorized individuals or subgroups within one's own group, and external groups—for example, by associating the peasant with the savage, women with primitives, and so on. The power of prejudices derives, perhaps, from this contrast, this mixture of similarity and difference projected onto the other but also felt within oneself. That is why it would be useful to understand better what people believe they may have in common with the group from which they try to differentiate themselves, against which they discriminate, and on whom they impose stereotypes—as two aspects of the same prejudice.

I am afraid I have moved a bit away from my starting point, which consisted of trying to explain why I had never participated in works on racism, despite its eminent place in social psychological research. My reluctance was such that, when Gina Philogène, then a young student at the New School for Social Research in New York, came to propose a thesis subject on that topic, I refused. But she showed herself stubborn enough, which eventually forced me to reflect on my own experience, obviously, as well as on those mass beliefs which are, by all evidence, the background for what we call prejudice or stereotype. It was easy to see that race is a cultural category inscribing itself in the two fundamental opposites, nature/culture and animal/human, which form the basis for these beliefs. But those beliefs are much more difficult to understand.

Hence, while having neither a theory nor a concept that seemed adequate, it appeared not unreasonable to think that the theory of social representations could provide us with a satisfactory approximation. It is true that this approach explores in a more heuristic manner phenomena *in statu nascenti*, in the making, than phenomena already made, thus crystallized and normalized. This is simply to underline that the questions to be asked by theory, the enigmas to be looked at, are different when studying beliefs in motion within a society rather than beliefs that remain static and are internalized by the individuals making up that society.

To my knowledge, Gina Philogène is the first researcher to have extended the theory of social representations to the realm of racism. The way in which she has done this is unexpected. To begin with, she undertook a reinterpretation of classical works from Katz and Braly on, putting them into a new perspective. Then she broadened her field of investigation by a means that at first sight seemed surprising, namely that of the reference, of the name assigned to a group, a name which underscores the significance of the judgment applied to that group.

There is apparently nothing more evident, more tangible and palpable than a proper name. Yet we have not given names the same attention in social psychology as in anthropology, where they are considered one of the keys to understanding the classification of groups in a society. We know, nevertheless, in what manner these names serve to denigrate or insult a discriminated group and how, in turn, a discriminated group seeks to change its name to escape such discrimination. Before the Second World War, in France, the term *Juif* (Jew) had a pejorative meaning which the common term Israelite did not have: the second was used in official documents, newspapers, and so on, while the first was used in anti-Semitic remarks. More recently, in Eastern Europe, the gypsy communities have tried to rid themselves of their old denomination in order to call themselves Rom. All the sadness in the lives of discriminated groups can be seen here: their exclusion, or inclusion, depends on a name. And each name represents a particular universe which has to be continually reconstituted in a broader universe filled with threats. Between a name, which changes, and the group adopting that name, a fissure opens.

Gina Philogène uncovers in great detail the emergence of "African American" and the meaning taken by this term, the fusion of contrasts between the first part of the word combination, emphasizing the difference between Blacks and Whites, and the second part, which highlights what they have in common as Americans. But there is more to the story, and this concerns social representations. One may ask how these representations are formed, and on what occasion. Well, often an insignia or a name emerges which attracts and encompasses numerous partial representations circulating in society. These are attractors (almost in the sense given to the term in physics) which hold or repeat, among the mass of concepts and images available to individuals or present in the media of mass communication, certain ones which they order swiftly to constitute a new representation. The latter is, by definition, unstable, even improbable, and it is only through the efforts and under the influence of the group that it comes to replace the old one. But Gina Philogène managed to focus her great conceptual microscope precisely on that fugitive moment when such a representation emerged, and to make us see how that happened. It is the representation pushed forward by a subgroup of those referring to themselves as African Americans, in the quest for an identity which defines them neither by their physical appearance, by their propensity to obey, nor by memories of exclusion, so as to open a field to free their energy, their vitality, after touching the depth of racial discrimination and after the efforts of the last twenty years. More and more, I find the pages devoted to this quest, the examination of specific names, the most passionate and rich in the book.

This leads to me insist: the genesis of social representations is above all found in some proper names which are at the same time both attractors and social references. Representations are built on these names, like a house on its pillars. But at the same time, by linking the social representation *in statu nascenti* to the collective movement spreading it, Gina Philogène discovers something new. Or more precisely, she endows one of Max Weber's notions with a new significance. The Weberian concept is that of anticipatory representations, which are not something calculated, but invented so as to allow a transformation of the amalgam of desires and disparate ideas into a real unity. Activating the future in the present, an anticipatory representation shifts the center of gravity of the group from the old identity to the new, from Black to African American. I wish to bring attention to one last point that I have already mentioned: the categories of nature and culture. The shift from the old identity to the new identity, contrary to the shift from Negro to Black, for example, implies a shift from nature to culture, and an anticipated reshuffling of the meaning of racism, of the similarities and the differences with the other groups shaping American society.

It is often at the very end, at the end of a friendship, at the end of an existence, that the past abruptly unfolds itself like a whole, with everything taking clear shape and mastered significance. It is often the same with the end of a thesis, of a book. It is in reading the end of this work that I have come to understand the goal pursued by Gina Philogène during all these years, the originality of her accomplished work, and the novelty as well as the vigor she brings to the theory of social representations by taking the latter for granted, if I may say so. From the theoretical observatory that she conceived, Gina Philogène designed methodologies which allowed her to follow a concrete movement in the United States, the outcome of which may be judged in different ways, but the historic importance of which no one can deny. And in this way she may have allowed us to improve our understanding of racism, this pathology of our societies, this stain on democracy, on the values of all civilizations and on human rights altogether.

I have rarely had occasion to write such a long foreword. But I have also rarely read theses and books of such novelty and originality. I wish her a large number of readers. They will be enchanted by the intelligence of her writing and the clarity of the ideas, which follow one another in the mind of the author, becoming her own adventure. It is she one follows from chapter to chapter, from the first page to the last.

Serge Moscovici
Paris, July 1998

Acknowledgments

First of all I want to thank Serge Moscovici for his involvement in this project. The book grew out of my doctoral thesis at the Ecole des Hautes Etudes en Sciences Sociales in Paris, and Moscovici's masterful direction allowed that thesis to become an important catalyst for my transformation into a social psychologist. I also wish to express my gratitude for his having given us the theory of social representation, a "good" theory in the Lewinian sense of being practical. It is a theory that provides us with a synthesis between the world of the individual and the dynamic of social life. As such it has repositioned social psychology at the center of the social sciences, as the nodal point for many possible interdisciplinary avenues of research. My collaboration with him will forever remain a highlight in my life.

My sincere appreciation goes to Kay Deaux, who has through the course of this project given me support, advice, and the opportunity to participate in her famous seminar on "Social Identity" at the Graduate Center of CUNY. It was above all that seminar which gave me a sense of the best statistical approaches to my material.

I would also like to thank Denise Jodelet for encouraging me to pursue my research and for having helped me considerably in clarifying the cultural and anthropological dimensions of social representations.

Jean-Claude Abric, who has given us the extremely useful concept of the central core, invited me at a crucial stage of my work to Aix-en-Provence for a presentation at his seminar, and in the process helped me comprehend a key aspect of African American as social representation in the making: its anticipatory qualities. For this I wish to express my gratitude.

No acknowledgment would be complete without expressing my greatest appreciation to Praeger Publishers and Nita Romer as well as Marcia Goldstein, my editors at Praeger, for the opportunity to publish this book.

Last, but not least, I wish to thank my family for showing such patient and loving support. My parents, Camille and Lucas Philogène, have given me the values and wisdom to face the challenges of life. Robert Guttmann, my husband, was always there when I needed support. Our son, Alexandre, and daughter, Maxine, besides being for me daily fountains of joy, represent the hope in a better future that motivated this work.

Introduction

In the United States the use of "African American" as a new denomination has rapidly become common practice in social interactions. The emergence of the term in everyday conversation, mediatic communications, or symbolic exchanges makes clear and explicit the elaboration of a new social reality. Barely a decade after its introduction this denomination has not only become the most acceptable and positive term to refer to Americans of African descent, but it has also been adopted as the preferred self-designation by one out of three black Americans.

This books aims to show the extent to which the switch from Black to African American signals a transformation in the social representation of black Americans. The new term is positive, and this particular characteristic gives it a projective quality which redefines the group in a more inclusive light. Not yet fully concretized into our reality, this new representation is kept alive through a collectively defined repertoire of symbolic references and through its contradistinction to Black.*

To illustrate our phenomenon, the study is framed within the dynamic and polemical relation African American has with the term Black. The focus is twofold here. For one, an onomastic investigation will focus on the convergence of attributes concerning African American and how they contrast with those of Black. In addition, this book examines various cultural markers in search of the topoi of our culture, to understand how

*I have capitalized the terms Black(s) and White(s) in the text whenever they are to be read as names Americans use to designate groups on the basis of racial differentiation. The word black is used in lower case to delineate a group comprising Americans of African descent, as for instance in "black Americans." I have left the questionnaires in the appendix as originally distributed to subjects.

the emergence of African American as a new social representation of a
group hitherto referred to as Blacks does in fact change our ways of
perceiving and evaluating Americans of African descent.

By redirecting attention away from race, the term African American
has created a vacuum which is being filled with notions of culture, ethnicity, and multiculturalism that stress the common destiny of all Americans. It appears that the new denomination offers a more flexible
perspective on the newly redefined group, as opposed to the rigid racial
perception. Consequently, this representation signals greater inclusion of
the group in American culture, and makes its interactions with others
more permeative.

Chapter 1

Defining the Problem

Significant changes in race relations occurred with the post–World War II wave of "Black" collective movements over a span of three decades. These social movements, culminating in the Civil Rights movement of the early 1960s, not only affected legal and political processes in the United States, but also had a strong impact on black Americans themselves. While these movements were primarily responses to openly manifest racism, their social mobilization and political action transformed black Americans at several levels. Individual as well as collective identity was modified. Moreover, a sense of group cohesion developed. The Negro became Black, and in the process the new name for the group became for the first time a catalyst for a positive group identity as crystallized in the "Black is Beautiful," "Black Power," and "I am proud to be Black" slogans of the 1960s. Finally, legal provisions for more equality, in particular the right to vote, did open the American political system to greater participation by black Americans, while also allowing many members of that group to move into the middle class.

However, while gradually moving toward greater integration, the black middle class is today still facing some limits imposed by new forms of exclusion and alienation. These contemporary manifestations of racism are harder to confront directly, because they are by and large no longer overt and explicit. Instead they have shifted their social expression toward the covert and subtle, such as "racial steering" by real estate agents or the implicit biases found in SAT tests for college applicants. Following the legislative achievements of the Civil Rights movement, race-based expressions of discrimination have been channeled into new institutionalized forms that are less obvious to the naked eye, and at the same time tend to be experienced in more individuated situations. Such conditions of atomization do not lend themselves as well to highly focused mass movements as did the conditions of uniform segregation in the 1950s and 1960s. What we have instead is an ongoing dialogue between and within the groups, driven by a collective effort to define a new America.

Despite the undeniable progress in race relations since the Civil Rights laws of the 1960s, the full integration of Americans of African descent into mainstream society has been prevented by deeply entrenched negative views of Blacks that even the positive redefinition of Black identity in the 1960s could not completely eliminate. Given the persistence of racial prejudice, a more radical break with the past may be necessary. To tackle the more subtle expressions of racial discrimination prevailing today, some black Americans are seeking to impact on a deeper system of perceptions, beliefs, attitudes, and opinions about people of African descent. It is against this background that the recent switch from Black to African American, far from being just a change in name, must instead be seen as a re-presentation of Blacks as something totally new, for which cognitive pathways shaping its interpretation are not yet elaborated.

In this chapter I will analyze the context from which the term African American has emerged by contrasting it to the context from which the "positivation" of Black evolved. These two redefinitions, from Negro to Black on the one hand, and from Black to African American on the other, were part of a response system black Americans developed to handle the crises they were facing. In both cases they tried to recreate a social representation.

The context that led to the use of Black as a positive term in the 1960s centered on a strong collective effort around the demand for the inclusion of black Americans in the rest of the American culture. This goal, reversing decades of exclusion, required a broad-based social movement. Its legislative successes notwithstanding, this movement failed to prevent continued exclusion and marginalization of many members of the group. Even those black Americans advancing into the middle class, while in their personal aspirations and values clearly identifying themselves as Americans, often find resistance concerning their recognition as such by the rest of the society (Cose, 1993; Gaiter, 1994; Staples, 1994; West, 1994).

The group denomination African American has evolved in an entirely different social context than the earlier effort to make Black a positive term. It emerged after the failure of Affirmative Action and following Jesse Jackson's presidential campaigns, when a subgroup of black Americans sought to be defined as African Americans, legitimizing their inclusion in America while assessing and expressing their group's position and progress in society.

To understand the formation, elaboration, and communication of these two social representations, it is important to begin with the positioning of race, a key structural element centrally located in American society to organize and direct interaction between the groups. By acknowledging race as a central component, it becomes possible to look meaningfully at the contexts out of which the terms Black and African American emerged, and to understand the major differences between these two representations.

RACE, RACIAL DYNAMICS, AND DESEGREGATION IN AMERICA

For over a century following the Civil War, intergroup relations between black and white Americans were defined by the notion of two separate societies in one country, organized around the legal paradigm of "separate but equal." Introduced as a system of exclusion and as the logical extension of slavery, segregation was at that time more than just black-white separation. It was a very pervasive social psychological condition of American society. Characterized as a state of mind as well as a constructed daily reality, this interdynamic around the issue of race was construed out of a social representation that not only gave meaning to social life by shaping perceptions, beliefs, opinions, and attitudes, but also clearly organized intergroup relations. So the reality of segregation went far beyond its initial conceptual definition, which suggests limits or restrictions upon contact between the groups, and impacted directly on more general communication and social relations (Rose, 1981). This allowed the maintenance of a well-structured and reified world.

As an extension of the earlier system of slavery, which was based on humans as property, with the implication of the human as a thing, segregation was founded on a similar basis of categorization. Once slavery became socially unacceptable and was gradually abolished, the notion of a subhuman-human dualism persisted and manifested itself in legislation and social practices of separation, exclusion, and segregation. This organized and institutionalized form of exclusion marked the core of America's history by centralizing the issue of race as a normative and prescriptive component of social life.

However, a growing sense of discontent and self-consciousness, similar to those sentiments that guided the overthrow of slavery, began to attack the organization of segregation. Black Americans, especially those sent abroad to fight for America and its ideals, found themselves after World War II returning to a system of repression and discrimination which they had helped to defeat overseas. Once they began to question the legitimacy of this normative system, mass mobilization toward change and militancy increased rapidly.

Yet changing the segregating patterns of intergroup dynamics was difficult because of deeply entrenched customs and conventions. The federal government, whose intervention capacity had dramatically increased in the wake of the New Deal and World War II, was expected—and it succeeded eventually in meeting this expectation—to become more responsive to the needs of those segregated, by denouncing practices of exclusion. From Roosevelt onwards, the role of the federal government became more and more important, to the point that government was perceived as the strongest factor capable of affecting the pace of change in race relations. As protector of the common citizen, the federal government was seen as a major force which could not only impact on the formation of generalized societal norms of civil rights and equal status, but also change racial dynamics.

It soon became clear that, once discontent became manifest, anything less than "full" integration would never resolve the contradiction between black inequality, segregation, and racial prejudice and the American ideals of equality and justice (Myrdal, 1944). So any effective alternative to the segregation system had to allow for total inclusion of black Americans in the mainstream of American life.

Although the social practice of segregation had indirectly come under challenge in the earlier part of the century, as more progressive views began to dislodge the biologistic paradigm which had justified the notion of racial inferiority as part of a natural order of mankind, these views never specifically addressed the issue of race. Instead, the Progressives introduced the concepts of cultural pluralism (Kallen, 1924) and assimilationism (Park, 1950). Both theories focused primarily on the concept of culture as the key basis for group formation processes and were not explicitly concerned with racial minorities. In that context both variants looked at race as a social category and as one determinant, among many, of ethnic group identity. However, the two views diverged quite fundamentally on whether any group could maintain its own distinct ethnic identity over time. The cultural pluralists and the assimilationists disagreed as to the possibility of maintaining ethnic differentiation in a society that appeared dominated by the presence of a "majority culture," the Anglo culture (Gordon, 1964).

The impact of these two views was consequently limited to specific groups; they did not attempt to resolve racial matters. Whatever the extent of discrimination and prejudice other immigrant groups experienced in the United States, mainstream society always offered them a sort of social contract. For those who could assimilate, this contract centered around such issues as language, deinstitutionalization of religion, and above all sharing of the "American Dream." Adopting these norms from the Anglo culture was the price of becoming American. This kind of social contract represented a synthesis of two different visions of a society made up of multiple immigrant groups: assimilation ("melting pot") and pluralism ("mixed salad").

Unlike groups who had immigrated voluntarily, black Americans were institutionally marginalized based on their racial category, and therefore were unable to participate in the Anglo cultural conformity. It was Myrdal's study (1944) which for the first time specifically moved the question of black Americans' integration into mainstream American life to the center. Until then, black Americans had been prevented from assimilating and joining the mainstream in their pursuit of the "American Dream." Nor could they relate to any original culture, since slavery had erased that bridge to the past. This squeeze modulated black American culture as fundamentally shaped by the experience of slavery and then segregation in America.

Desegregation was supposed to have extended to black Americans the kind of social contract that allowed other groups to become American. The Supreme Court decision in May 1954 to outlaw segregation in schools, acknowledged as one of the most important decisions of our century, was based on the belief that increased contact between members of two groups would translate into overall improvements in intergroup attitudes and relations. The ruling of the Court in *Brown v. Board of Education* was motivated by an optimistic climate in the aftermath of desegregation in the military. It ignored the fact that the army's trend toward desegregation was mandated by the particular conditions of World War II (Davis, 1966) and was therefore a special case. Instead, the judicial decision of 1954 was made under the premise that, apart from being psychologically damaging to black American children, the doctrine "separate but equal" also perpetuated ethnic prejudice and racial intolerance (Cook, 1979).

In this context, mere contact was seen, simplistically, as a "quick fix" for two centuries of black American subordination and exclusion from most institutions of American society. Such a solution was firmly supported by Gordon Allport's influential publication *The Nature of Prejudice* (1954) which recommended contact as a means to reduce friction and tension between groups. This "quick fix" idea ignored the fact that the racial paradigm, omnipresent in people's minds, still represents one primary form of social organization in this country and therefore structures intergroup relations. So while school desegregation clearly marked the beginning of a changing dynamic between black and white Americans, it resulted in limited attitudinal change in intergroup relations. Desegregation—or the naive solution of mere contact—was only one step in the process of changing intergroup relations, and as such it was clearly insufficient.

The "summer camp" studies of Muzafer Sherif showed us clearly that the idea of contact alone would not necessarily assure better intergroup relations (Sherif et al., 1961; Sherif, 1966). Sherif concluded that mere contact is not only insufficient to reduce friction but, without a whole range of complex conditions required for positive outcomes in inter-group relations, would just serve to promote rivalry and antagonism between groups. In the face of centuries of exclusion, the naive contact approach to desegregation, Sherif correctly argued, could not transform a deeply rooted reality of separation. It did not take long for the limits of this approach to appear and dash hopes and expectations.

THE "BLACK POWER" MOVEMENT

The Civil Rights movement of the 1960s, supported by a broad seg-ment of American society, sought to transform social norms and values pertaining to race. To do this, and in the process break long-standing norms of exclusion, it had to address the overloaded issue of race di-rectly. Until then, black Americans had been excluded from full citizen-ship merely on the basis of their race. As Michael Omi and Howard Winant (1986) put it,

In its efforts to transform [the] social system, the black movement sought to expand the concerns of politics, without abandoning the earlier economically centered logic. This expansion of "normal" politics to include racial issues—this "common sense" recognition of the political elements at the heart of racial iden-tities and meanings—made possible the movement's greatest triumphs, its most permanent successes. These did not lie in its legislative accomplishments, but rather in its ability to create new racial "subjects." The black movement redefined the meaning of racial identity, and consequently of race itself, in American so-ciety. (p. 93)

In the context of a rapidly growing social movement, the black lead-ership could for the first time articulate goals that were specifically in the interest of black people. It was the socially shared sense of injustice that motivated the cohesiveness of the black American community. Since the entire group was discriminated against, its leaders could use this shared experience of marginalization to mobilize mass support for the objective of categorically overthrowing racial oppression (Omi & Winant, 1986). This mobilization resulted in an explicit and large-scale collective effort by the group to achieve greater inclusion and to fight racism.

The early phase of the movement, from the Montgomery bus boycott of 1955–1956 to Martin Luther King's "I Have a Dream" speech crowning the March on Washington in the summer of 1963, was propelled by an optimistic belief in the possibility of full integration, and was shaped by a series of successes. But by the end of 1963 a sense of disillusion had settled in. The new mood, which had built for some time below the surface in response to slow progress concerning school desegregation, con-tinued economic discrimination, and stiff resistance in Congress to Civil

Rights legislation, suddenly burst to the surface with the killings of Medgar Evers and James Meredith. These assassinations symbolized a violent backlash by Southern reactionaries against the movement, forcing its leaders to rethink their strategies and thus marking a turning point in the evolution of the struggle for racial equality (King, 1964).

New leaders emerged who acknowledged that the code of nonviolence characterizing the early phase of the Civil Rights movement was not sufficient. Pushing for a militant strategy, they followed the line of argument prescribed by Frederick Douglass a hundred years earlier. As Douglass had argued in 1857 when calling for mass resistance to slavery,

Those who profess to favor freedom yet deprecate agitation are men who want crops without plowing up the ground; they want rain without thunder and lightning. They want the ocean without the awful roar of its many waters. . . . Power concedes nothing without demand. It never did and it never will. Find out just what any people will quietly submit to and you have found out the exact measure of injustice and wrong which will be imposed upon them, and these will continue till they are resisted with either words or blows, or with both. (in Carmichael & Hamilton, 1967, p. x)

The threat of a violent backlash also convinced activists that they needed greater cohesion within the movement to succeed. Instead of emphasizing only the need to change the racial attitudes of Whites, movement leaders began to focus increasingly on self-conception and self-determination among Blacks (Carmichael & Hamilton, 1967). This reorientation crystallized around changing preferences in denomination, following growing criticism of using Negro, a term thought to be introduced by Whites to invoke negative images. As Stokely Carmichael and Charles Hamilton (1967) put it,

There is a growing resentment of the word "Negro," for example, because this term is the invention of the oppressor; it is *his* image of us that he describes. . . . When we begin to define our own image, the stereotypes—that is, lies—that our oppressor has developed will begin in the white community and end there. The black community will have a positive image of itself that it has created. This means we will no longer call ourselves lazy, apathetic, dumb, good-timers, shiftless, etc. Those are words used by white America to define us. If we accept these adjectives, as some of us have in the past, then we see ourselves in a negative way, precisely the way white America wants us to see ourselves. (p. 37)

By calling audaciously for "Black Power," the more militant segments of the leadership contended that Negro Americans should revert to the term Black, yet redefine its meaning and all that it symbolizes in order to associate this name with racial pride and dignity. When the Civil Rights movement decided to adopt Black in lieu of Negro, it consciously tried to turn a term inherently loaded with negative connotations into a positive identification. The slogans "Black is Beautiful" and "Black Power" managed for a while to transform an otherwise marginalizing term into an affirmation of strength for a political movement based on racial pride. The use of Black as the preferred denomination symbolized at that point the unity of black Americans in their struggle against racial intolerance in America.

In addition, from a linguistic point of view Black was seen as the best parallel and counterweight to White, as illustrated in Martin Luther King's famous "I Have a Dream" speech in 1963. At that point King still favored the term Negro, using it 15 times in the course of this particular speech. But he strategically mentioned Black four times as an adjective. Each time it appeared in parallel construction with White, such as "black men as well as white men" (Allen, 1990; Smith, 1992). By using Black in juxtaposition to White, proponents of the term emphasized the recognition and acceptance of skin color, therefore race, based on a new definition of the very category that until then had been used to justify abusive and repressive practices against them. In other words, people of African descent welcomed positive racial consciousness which the term Black, once it was redefined, was supposed to provide automatically.

While King focused primarily on the virtues of integration, as illustrated by his semantic tendency to use the terms Black and White jointly, those in the movement calling for "Black Power" stressed the need for maintaining the group's cultural uniqueness and finding fulfillment in it. The protagonists of "Black Power" coupled this appeal for self-love with a realization that they were part of America and therefore had to coexist with the rest of that society. Eventually, however, the reappropriation of the term Black into an expression of racial pride developed a more explicitly separatist dimension, especially among the followers of Malcolm X and the Black Panthers.

By the late 1960s Black had spread rapidly beyond its initial use by militant and radical members of the community and gained widespread acceptance in mainstream America. However, once established as the primary group denomination, the term also lost much of its original political force. Although the affirmation of Black in the late 1960s and early 1970s was very much aimed at changing images, attitudes, and opinions about the group, much like the introduction of African American attempts today, that earlier process of group positivation faltered with the end of the Civil Rights movement. Given the deeply entrenched symbolism of white as good and black as bad (Williams, 1966; Williams, Tucker, & Dunham, 1971), it proved difficult, if not impossible, to transform an inherently negative representation into a positive one. Ultimately Black remained a racial term which emphasized difference and division. Thus it could never escape the troubled legacy of a racially divided country.

The Civil Rights movement ended abruptly. By 1970 the country's attention had shifted to the Vietnam War and the rapidly growing antiwar movement. The struggle for racial equality, which had so dominated the preceding decade, left a mixed legacy. On the positive side, it accomplished major legislative achievements (e.g., the Civil Rights Act of 1964, the Voting Rights Act of 1965) which made it easier for many black Americans to enter the mainstream of American society. Paving the way for political participation and opening access to professional occupations, these laws helped create a sizeable black middle class. More importantly, black Americans, albeit still in very small numbers, have been able in recent years to enter high-visibility positions at the center of those institutions controlling this complex and diverse society—law, politics, academe, the media, and arts. Their presence has already made a profound impact by beginning a process of adjusting social relations to the multiethnic and multicultural reality of America.

On the negative side, the movement did not succeed in ending racial discrimination. Race remains a paramount issue, and the country continues to define itself on the basis of race—witness the controversies surrounding Clarence Thomas, Rodney King, and O.J. Simpson. The scandals involving these men profoundly reshaped the national debate on such contentious issues as sexual harassment, community relations, and domestic violence. Each case also served as a public forum, shaped by the national media's interpretations, to reexamine the issue of race. Issues of national concern thus came to be defined through the prism of race and to shape public opinion accordingly. That race-filtered context tended to polarize public opinion, with black Americans and white Americans looking at the same issue from very different angles.

The extent to which race still defines America and keeps its citizens from developing a common vision for their society can be seen in many instances. Race-based biases in the country's judicial system (e.g., disproportionately large numbers of black American males on death row), in education (where segregation and unequal treatment prevail), in housing (e.g., inequities in mortgage finance), or regarding access to health care continue to divide the society on the basis of race. A major reason for the persistence of race as a determining factor in social relations has been the failure of the Civil Rights movement to prevent a very large number of black Americans, possibly even a majority of the group, from being relatively worse off than in the darkest days of segregation. Urban ghettos, never rebuilt after the widespread riots of the 1960s (Watts, Newark, Detroit, etc.), have faced sustained decline and neglect, leaving most of their populations in desperate living conditions (Wilson, 1978).

It seems that the country cannot shake its legacy of racism (Bell, 1992) and its "obsession" with race (Terkel, 1992).

DUAL CONSCIOUSNESS

Since race has been such a dominant reality for so long, it forces black Americans to constantly rethink their identification with America. They live, and experience life, both inside and outside the culture. When Du Bois ([1903] 1965) talked of the Negro's dual consciousness, he was pointing to the dualistic existence of Americans of African descent. This two-ness is a constant tension contained in black American culture and gives the group a rather complex base for the establishment of its identities. Du Bois characterized this duality as follows:

One ever feels his two-ness—an American, a Negro; two souls, two thoughts, two unreconciled strivings; two warring ideals in one dark body, whose dogged strength alone keeps it from being torn asunder. . . . The history of the American Negro is the history of this strife, this longing to attain self-conscious manhood, to merge his double self into a better and truer self. In this merging he wishes neither of the older selves to be lost. He would not Africanize America, for America has too much to teach the world and Africa. He would not bleach his Negro soul in a flood of white Americanism, for he knows that Negro blood has a message for the world. He simply wishes to make it possible for a man to be both a Negro and an American, without being cursed and spit upon by his fellows, without having the doors of Opportunity closed roughly in his face. (pp. 3–4)

This dual consciousness has always created a rather broad spectrum of attitudes and opinions within the group, ranging from Black nationalism (as advocated by Marcus Garvey) to full assimilation (Mary McLeod Bethune). That reality belies a widely held, yet erroneous notion of homogeneity within the group. In the days of the Civil Rights movement the inherent duality found among Americans of African descent became more polarized, crystallizing around the conflict between the integrationist goals of Martin Luther King and the nationalist-separatist vision of Malcolm X. While the movement was concerned with black Americans challenging mainstream America for inclusion in the social contract that underlay the American Dream, the movement itself soon reflected the same dichotomy between assimilation and pluralism in the growing internal juxtaposition between Martin Luther King's "I had a dream" vision of integration and Malcolm X's militant separatism.

To the extent that the Civil Rights movement opened the way for some members of this hitherto excluded group into the mainstream of American society, it redefined the group experience of this dual consciousness by giving it a new material basis in the socioeconomic and political conditions of the group. The Civil Rights movement helped create a black middle class while at the same time setting the stage for a new kind of isolation among an even larger number of black Americans—an "underclass" crowded into the inner-city ghettos of urban America. The black middle class faces more subtle expressions of race-based discrimination, both covert and institutionalized on the basis of seemingly impersonal rules that govern access to the labor market, real estate, education, credit, and other necessities of life in an unequal fashion. Poor blacks continue to encounter overt, direct, and often violent expressions of racism.

Despite institutional barriers, those able to escape or to avoid ghetto life have had a chance to pursue the American Dream. Gradually, Americans of African descent have gained a significant presence in all major areas of public life. Yet the full Americanization of this subgroup clashes with the social expressions of an historically racist society. Many black Americans, even those reaching the highest echelons of their profession, still have to face discrimination and continue to feel unaccepted as equal. The daily reality of progress combined with persistent unfair barriers creates a great deal of internal tensions (Cose, 1993).

Dual racial consciousness is obviously also experienced by the other side, yet in an entirely different way. The tension many white Americans as well as other non-black Americans feel between the recognition of Americans of African descent as full Americans and the ongoing perception of them as a race apart has had various outlets. Two dimensions of that tension emphasize the inclusion of black Americans as an integral part of the culture. On the one hand, many non-black Americans basically do not admit that race still matters, preferring instead to believe in the notion of a color-blind society (Jones, 1986). For that matter, the diminution of overtly racist practices in the aftermath of the Civil Rights movement is frequently taken as welcome proof that racism has declined, if not altogether disappeared. In addition, a large segment of the majority wants to believe that America has met its greatest challenge, defined so eloquently first by French social philosopher Alexis de Tocqueville in the 1830s (de Tocqueville, [1869] 1966, chap. 10) and then again by the Swedish economist Gunnar Myrdal during World War II (Myrdal, 1944), namely to become a truly pluralistic society by extending the American Dream to black Americans.

Underneath that surface, however, race remains a core determinant defining the American culture, and continues to be the obsession it has always been. Whites acknowledge that Blacks are American and that in American society all members are to be treated as equal. Yet at the same time they cannot wish away the long history of racism and segregation which created such deeply rooted images of black Americans.

FROM "AFFIRMATIVE ACTION" TO "AFRICAN AMERICAN"

Following the Civil Rights movement, the white majority's desire to believe in a color-blind society expressed itself as a willingness to offer Blacks an opening for their participation (Glazer, 1995; Glazer & Moynihan, 1963; Gordon, 1964). Blacks, of course, had been waiting and struggling for such an opportunity. They were therefore quick to accept the compensatory social policies and laws of integration—voting rights, busing, and Affirmative Action. Voting rights, involving equal access to voter registration and the redrawing of districts, aimed at increasing the political representation of black Americans (Kinder & Sears, 1981). Busing was a federal policy imposed on recalcitrant local school districts in the North to force desegregation by transporting black children to and from schools in otherwise segregated white residential areas (Bobo, 1983; McConahay, 1982). Affirmative Action programs were directed at the hiring practices of American businesses, asking employers to set aside a certain number of job openings for minorities and women (Jacobson, 1985; Kinder & Sanders 1990; Kluegel & Smith, 1983).

All these federal policies proved controversial and were resisted on the state and local levels. Yet Affirmative Action was fundamentally different from the other two equal-opportunity policies in that it did not try to fight overtly racist practices, such as denial of the vote or segregation of public schools, with explicit measures of force. Affirmative Action depended instead on a degree of cooperation and interaction between the different groups, urging them to become a successful unit serving the marketplace, academe, and other unforgiving places. Moreover, its general design was such that it sidestepped the thorny issue of race. Affirmative Action programs addressed historic inequalities with regard to several groups, not just Blacks, and thus could claim legitimacy on the basis of an overarching principle of the American Dream, that of equal opportunity (Wilkins, 1995). By explicitly ruling out quotas based on demographic proportionality and instead preferring less ambitious numerical goals, these programs were designed to appear moderate, gradual, and reasonable. Their most difficult problem, that of a possible conflict between promotion based on merit and opportunity created by regulatory design, could be dealt with in an ideologically covenient fashion, by emulating the social benefits of education as a gradual social equalizer.

Most importantly, the implied logic of Affirmative Action programs corresponded to the pragmatic needs of both black and white Americans in their attempts to redefine intergroup relations after nearly two decades of conflict and debate. Members of the black middle class, for whom these programs held the promise of tangible advances, regarded Affirmative Action as a well-deserved result of their decade-long struggle against racism, and as a justified tool with which to rectify past wrongs of exclusion and segregation. Whites, to the extent that they accepted equal opportunity as a principle that should apply to all Americans (Rasinski, 1987), saw in Affirmative Action a reasonable way to affect a gradual change toward greater inclusion of "minorities" that had traditionally been treated unfairly. This new social policy, a direct application of the Civil Rights Act of 1964, thus enjoyed a fairly broad consensus at its inception in the late 1960s and following subsequent extensions during the 1970s.

Yet Affirmative Action ultimately proved a flawed policy. To begin with, it benefitted primarily those members of "minority" groups who were the least disadvantaged. It did very little for large numbers of black Americans and other minorities whose poor education and social isolation kept them shut out of the mainstream of American society. In other words, Affirmative Action was aimed at those who culturally, if not economically, belonged to the middle class (Rodriguez, 1982). The class-based aspect of this policy drove a wedge between upwardly mobile Blacks and those condemned to continued poverty, by helping to accentuate differences within the group (Deschamps, 1977). Moreover, the inclusion of a selected few was eagerly taken by the majority as a sign of progress towards integration, thus crowding out concern with the continued exclusion of many. In that sense Affirmative Action was a limited and narrowly targeted policy which took the place of more far-reaching reforms aimed at equalizing primary and secondary education, desegregating housing, and tackling other underlying causes of poverty.

Initially, the few beneficiaries of Affirmative Action accepted their selection as rightfully deserved retribution and welcomed it as an opening into the American mainstream. Gradually, as the policy took root in the late 1960s, black Americans with middle-class aspirations began to have more access to employment, and found college openings specifically set aside for them under these programs. The perception of improvement, reinforced by a long period of rapid economic growth and rising prosperity, nourished optimistic expectations about future progress.

In 1972 Congress amended the Civil Rights Act to expand the scope of Affirmative Action programs. But the implementation of this expansion coincided with the end of the postwar boom. Starting in 1973, socioeconomic deterioration in the United States endangered the social consensus underlying Affirmative Action. Whites became more insecure and less generous in response to intensifying competition in the labor market (Kluegel & Smith, 1983; Nosworthy, Lea, & Lindsay, 1995). Blacks, facing a general "last hired, first fired" rule in corporate America, found that the crisis hurt them disproportionately. This brought about disappointment and a heightened sense of relative deprivation among the black middle class (Pettigrew & Meertens, 1995).

As the economic crisis deepened, Affirmative Action became more controversial. Many white Americans, suddenly worried about their future outlook, began to denounce the policy as a "break" for less qualified and less able Blacks (Sears, 1988). That kind of attitude, of course, implied a notion of one's own superiority, emphasizing adherence to traditional American values which Blacks were presumed to lack (Kinder & Sears, 1981). At the same time, white Americans viewed the very existence of Affirmative Action as proof that racism was a matter of the past. Denying the persistence of racism and downplaying the need to correct decades of discrimination, a large segment of white Americans eventually began to question why they should continue to pay for the sins of their forefathers. From this position it was only a short way to the charge of "reverse discrimination," a complaint reinforced by tougher competition for good jobs amidst high unemployment.

Blacks, on other hand, could enter education and career positions through Affirmative Action programs, but only by being once again classified as a permanent "minority" whose numbers and relative status were now tightly controlled by seemingly impersonal rules. Moreover, black Americans aspiring to middle-class status had to embrace Affirmative Action as an escape from the potentially devastating misery experienced by other group members in the urban ghetto constantly held out to them as the inevitable alternative. Given the lingering legacy of segregation, Affirmative Action was often and for many the only way out. At the same time, many black beneficiaries of Affirmative Action could not avoid internalizing another aspect of "reverse discrimination," namely the feeling that they did not make it on their own and thus could not really prove themselves as equal in areas of competition. This leaves corrosive self-doubts (Carter, 1991).

Affirmative Action experienced a near-fatal setback with *Bakke v. University of California*, in which the Supreme Court affirmed in 1977 the claim of Allan Bakke that the University of California committed "reverse discrimination," and thus acted illegally, when it denied his application to medical school while accepting seemingly less qualified "minority" students (Lipset & Schneider, 1978). This judgment provided a legal basis for organized opposition to Affirmative Action, leading eventually to a full-blown attack on such programs by the Reagan Administration and its director of the Equal Employment Opportunity Commission, Clarence Thomas. The deeper reason for the failure of Affirmative Action was perhaps that it ended up pitting white Americans against black Americans, undermining the already precarious relations between the two groups instead of moving both sides closer to common ground (Bobo, 1983).

In addition, to the extent that Affirmative Action allowed some Blacks access to education and professional careers, it placed them in an essentially white world in which they had very few peers from their own group and in most instances lacked any support network. As Ellis Cose (1993) demonstrated through a large number of interviews, this isolation has the effect of pushing black professionals to act in ways they normally would not, in order to constantly reassure their colleagues that they differ from the media stereotype of the "angry Black man."

Negative attitudes about Affirmative Action programs are surely grounded in America's culture of individualism, reflecting a widely shared belief in the principle of merit and individual achievements that Affirmative Action was seen to violate (Rubin & Peplau, 1975). But an even more important factor for the declining level of support regarding Affirmative Action seems to have been a marked erosion of the commitment to equality in general during the Reagan era (Bobo, 1989). As Bobo's study demonstrated, many Whites felt threatened by the progress of another social group at a time when their own living standards faced multiple attacks. In an environment of heightened insecurity, they were more inclined to perceive any real or imagined advances of black Americans as tantamount to a loss of their own long-established superior group status.

This fear-inspired opposition to Affirmative Action as a vehicle of greater equality tends to invite a fundamental attribution error among many white Americans (Jones & Nisbett, 1972; Pettigrew, 1979). When they try to explain away the continued inequality between Blacks and Whites, the latter typically overestimate internal causes and systematically underestimate external causes. Blacks may absorb this bias in reverse, explaining their achievements as a result of outside help and not of their own merit. This propensity for self-doubt, which Affirmative Action tended to exacerbate, left many black beneficiaries of the policy with an internal imbalance (Rodriguez, 1982).

Souring attitudes toward Affirmative Action programs notwithstanding, they nevertheless managed to change, over the two decades of their brief existence, many of the normative dimensions in intergroup relations. The impact of these programs on race dynamics, and the increasingly bitter controversies surrounding them, provided an important background for Jesse Jackson's presidential campaigns of 1984 and 1988. With his "Rainbow Coalition" Jesse Jackson sought to fill the vacuum left behind by the Civil Rights movement and to exploit the permeability in race relations resulting from the integrationist programs of the 1970s and early 1980s, reviving the vision of a common destiny in the mind of Americans. By running for president Jackson pursued two objectives simultaneously. On the one hand, both times he ran an explicitly cross-cultural, class-based campaign centered on left-populist opposition to the

Reagan Right. And on the other hand he galvanized electoral participation of black Americans by organizing successful voter registration
drives in the rural South and urban centers of the North. The dichotomization of Jackson's campaign into two parallel objectives reflected the
same dual consciousness discussed earlier, that of American and African,
and was a decisive element in the significance attributed to both campaigns. His integrationist message accentuated the fact that Americans
of African descent were definitely American, and this message reached
a broad spectrum of Americans.

So Jesse Jackson's presidential campaigns set the stage for the emergence of the term African American as a new social representation. In
December 1988 Ramona H. Edelin, president of the National Urban Coalition, proposed at a meeting of Black leaders in New Orleans the use
of African American as the official designation of a group hitherto referred to as Black. The endorsement of the switch by many leaders
launched a successful campaign in favor of African American as the
group's newest denomination. Already by January 1990 approximately
one out of four black Americans had adopted this term as their preferred
name (Joint Center for Political and Economic Studies, 1990). The widespread use of African American by public-opinion makers has given the
name added weight, status, and significance. It has by now become the
most positive and acceptable term for non-black Americans to use in
public discourse when referring to black Americans.

Chapter 2

An Anticipatory
Social Representation

The emergence of African American in everyday conversations, its contradistinction to Black in mediatic communication, and its normative
qualities in symbolic exchanges (e.g., the "political correctness" movement) must be understood as the making of a new social representation.
Its creation reponds primarily to a crisis in the black American community which is related to a renewed tension in the "twoness," or dual
consciousness, of the group. Far from being a new state of affairs, this
duality has been a consistent source of conflict, and continues to define
the group. An earlier expression of this dilemma centered around the
Negro American as a hybrid belonging as much to Africa as to America.
It was around this conflict that Du Bois articulated his theory of "Dual
Consciousness" (Du Bois, [1903] 1965; Gaines & Reed, 1995). Later on,
during the Civil Rights movement, the same tension polarized black
Americans between the integrationist ideas of Martin Luther King (1964)
and the separatist views of Malcolm X (1965).

African American, as a denomination, is a new symbolic expression of
the duality between differentiation from and uniformity with the American culture. The use of the term is an attempt to modify cognitions and
attitudes concerning black Americans in the direction of inclusion and
equality. It also aims to reestablish an internal equilibrium within the
members of the group through association with positive images and attributes (Mugny et al., 1984). The term gains these transformatory powers because of an organized collective effort across traditional group
delineations, rendering the new denomination familiar by creating a normative context for its propagation. This effort explains in part why African American has infiltrated our lives at such a rapid rate that any

attempt to wish it away from our minds is no longer possible. More importantly, it is precisely through its collective elaboration that African American acquires enough significance to crystallize into a claimed identity for some and to provide a ground for interactions and symbolic exchanges. This is a social psychological phenomenon, expressed through the interplay of the individual mind and social life, a dynamic which allows a transformation in the social representation of black Americans. That dynamic turns the name itself into a new shared reality.

The term African American is a relatively new social representation, barely a decade old. As such it is a social representation in the making, involving processes of thought transformation in which new meanings are embedded into sets of projections that become actualized through people's expectations, interpretations, and actions. This projective force has added an anticipatory quality to the emerging social representation, implying a mixture of collectively shared notions of what is, what should be, and what should not be. Such an anticipatory representation is a particularly challenging and interesting object of analysis, because it highlights the dynamic qualities and the normative force of a collective effort aimed at changing our reality.

Expectation has always been an important regulator of social conduct, as an individual's perception, attitude, and indeed behavior appear to be controlled by such a superordinate system. For McDougall (1923) these regulatory forces, expressed by such phrases as "I must do this" or "I must not do that," were related to the expectation of social praise or blame. In the case of African American the projective force of this new denomination and the normative context of its use crystallize around anticipations, that is around expectations of a different future which force individuals to adjust what they think in the present. As the name becomes familiar and is given content, it effectively turns into a meta-system socially regulating how the individual mind functions. In that capacity the new term African American is changing much of our cognitions and attitudes concerning a group previously referred to as Black.

This social phenomenon provides us with an opportunity to look at the processes involved in the transformation of a social representation as they unfold. In this chapter I want to analyze the broader implications of African American as an anticipatory representation, in order to position it within the context of social representation theory. The arguments for an anticipatory representation add a new dimension to the theory of social representation developed by Moscovici (1961; 1976a), allowing us to study a phenomenon in the making. In this case the primary agent for the propagation of African American is a subgroup that emerged from the black American community. The innovative force of their influence impacts on the broader population. The process of minority influence carries, in this case, a new social representation which is embodied in the new group denomination.

Based on this preliminary description of African American, let us now examine the theory of social representation in order to contextualize, describe, and understand the emergence of such a new name. It is only as a social representation, as a process resulting from a societal effort, that African American can be seen as directly impacting on how we think, communicate, and share a certain understanding of the world.

THE PHENOMENON OF SOCIAL REPRESENTATION

> There is nothing so practical as a good theory.
>
> —Kurt Lewin

Social representations are socially elaborated and collectively shared. More specifically, they are public and collective creations of shared knowledge by a community (Doise, 1993; Jodelet, 1989; Moscovici, 1963, 1976a, 1984). As forms of social thinking, they are products as well as processes of mental activity (Jodelet, 1993). These forms of commonsense knowledge allow the interpretation of reality by guiding our relation to the social world. They originate in daily life, in the course of interindividual communication, directing and giving significance to the content of our beliefs, ideas, attitudes, and opinions. As Moscovici (1988b) states, they

concern the content of everyday thinking and the stock of ideas that gives coherence to our religious beliefs, political ideas and the connections we create as spontaneously as we breathe. They make it possible for us to classify persons and objects, to compare and explain behaviours, and to objectify them as parts of our social setting.

Rooted in our cultural background and permeating our social life, social representations emerge from communication processes and at the same time become the object of communication within and between groups. To the extent that these feedback dynamics allow them to establish an order within which individuals can orient their actions and communication, Moscovici (1984) adds, "they restore collective awareness and give it shape, explaining objects and events so that they become accessible to everyone and coincide with our immediate interest."

What is taken for granted by everyone in a culture fashions encounters between people. In this context, while reflecting on communication, Moscovici (1988b, p. 214) states, "we could reflect on social representations as being embedded in a kind of pragmatic inferences, namely presuppositions . . . best described here as relations between a speaker and the property of a sentence in a social context."

Social representations are everywhere. Their power resides precisely in their subversive modes of incorporation into a given culture. Any interaction, whether between two individuals or two groups of individuals, presupposes shared representations (Moscovici, 1984). Moscovici (1973) contends that social representations

are systems of values, ideas and practices with a two-fold function: first to establish an order which will enable individuals to orient themselves in and master their material world and second, to facilitate communication among members of a community by providing them with a code for naming and classifying the various aspects of their world and their individual and group history. (p. xiii)

In his definitions of social representations, Moscovici (1982, 1984, 1987) consistently emphasized the fact that the striking characteristic of modern society is the changing nature of our reality and the acceleration of these changes. Advances in communication have multiplied the instances and forms of interaction between social agents. For that reason our concerns should be primarily with the social nature of thought and the ways in which people change their societies. This perspective on social life goes beyond the concerns of traditional sociology, which has often denied the creative participation of individuals. It also goes beyond that of the cognitive approaches, dominant in current social psychology, which tend to focus solely on the processes of information (Neuberg & Fiske, 1987; Oyserman & Markus, 1995).

In Moscovici's theory, however, the interplay between internal mechanisms and the constantly changing social world is actualized through the interconnectedness of individuals. When an individual makes up his or her mind about something, this does not just reflect his or her ideas and images alone. Individuals do not form their thoughts in isolation; they influence one another, and therefore collectively share reifications of objects that make up our reality. In other words, we are interconnected through social representations, which act as the bridge between the individual world and the social world. Individuals elaborate those social representations in the course of exchanges, communication, or interactions in order to give a direction to their own thoughts and actions. It is precisely their public nature that has endowed representations with a holomorphic character, in which "the whole" or the collective, as in a superordinate structure, is fully integrated within an individually represented system of knowledge (Wagner, 1994).

The importance of social representation theory is precisely in its focus on developing a synthesis between the individual and the social (Fraser, 1994; Jaspars & Fraser, 1984). This is not an easy task, since most of the polemics in the social sciences have been between those emphasizing the individual and those stressing the social—a state of affairs that indicates the difficulty of properly integrating both dimensions of human existence. Notwithstanding the efforts of some "exceptional" social psychologists, who have consistently tried to reframe the individual member within his or her social group (Deaux, 1992; Lewin, 1935, 1948; Sherif, 1967), studies in social psychology have preferred to look at decontextualized and atomized individuals (Kelly & Thibaut, 1969).

The synthesis provided by social representation theory defines the theory as a sociological form of social psychology (Farr, 1984, 1987, 1993). This alternative to the dominant individualistic perspective of mainstream American social psychology, one that stresses how social influences shape the minds of individuals and orient their actions towards a particular interconnectedness, has the added advantage of being a theory that fits Lewin's characterization of a good theory: it is practical (Marrow, 1969). It is practical because it is a general theory of human behavior that applies to a broad range of concrete situations. It provides us with insights into key aspects of modern life. In their dialectical qualities social representations are especially well equipped to explain processes of change in a given place and time.

The theory is also practical because it can be applied, as a general theory, to specific situations, and can illuminate them in ways that other social psychological approaches fail to do. By focusing on various manifestations of interconnectedness in a specific setting, social representations capture the cultural specificities of social interaction. In contrast, most standard paradigms of social psychology (e.g., attribution, or social cognition as a whole) codify human behavior in such universal terms that they tend to reduce otherwise highly differentiated and complex situations to their lowest (and most abstract) common denominator. In that sense, social representation theory adds an indispensable dimension, that of an "anthropology of modern culture" (Moscovici, 1989).

Early European social scientists understood that the missing link in any general theory of society concerned the dynamic between the social and the individual. The French sociologist Emile Durkheim, whose notion of "representations collectives" was later adapted into "social representations" by Moscovici, played a crucial role in clarifying that dynamic to the extent that he delineated it and found in it the central explanation for a wide variety of phenomena in society (1953). In his theory Durkheim made a sharp distinction between individual representations, as the substract of the individual's mind, and collective representations, as that of society as a whole. The collective ones are exterior to individual minds in the sense that they do not derive from those minds alone, but are born out of associations between them. They surpass the individual as the whole surpasses the part (Durkheim, 1953).

The juxtaposition implied here, between sociology/anthropology and psychology, eventually found its synthesis in Moscovici's notion of social representations (Farr, 1984, 1987).

The precise nature of the interplay between the individual and the social is a key dividing point between Durkheim and Moscovici. The stable society of Durkheim is in sharp contrast to our modern and rapid pace of life, a central characteristic in Moscovici's argument. It is the fluid nature of our social world that lies at the heart of Moscovici's social representation theory. Since society changes all the time, he reintroduced social representations as the dynamic structures that allow society to evolve and be constantly transformed. Appropriately, social representations enable us to understand a social life in the making, rather than reflecting a preestablished, already made, and reified life, as in Durkheim's "collective representations."

For Lev Vygotsky (1978), Durkheim's notion of collective representations was an important theoretical advance in the interpretation of human cognition. However, Durkheim failed to explain how individuals acquire these representations and thus never fully completed the synthesis between the individual and the social. Correspondingly, he had a rather static view of society. Vygotsky resolved these issues by linking collective representations and their individuation to "higher mental processes" which are functions of socially meaningful and mediated activity (Kozulin, 1990; Yaroshevsky, 1989). Furthermore, Vygotsky adds that the locus of the mind is not to be found within the individual, but rather in meaningful action and interaction and in cultural artifacts which have a shared symbolic significance for individuals in a given society (Purkhardt, 1993). In this critique of the traditional rationalist approach, action precedes thought instead of the reverse, with higher mental functions being the objectivation of action.

Any higher mental function necessarily goes through an external stage in its development because it is initially a social function. This is the center of the whole problem of internal and external behavior. . . . When we speak of a process, "external" means "social." Any higher mental function was external because it was social at one point before becoming an internal, truly mental function. (Vygotsky [1931] 1978, p. 162)

Georg Simmel was among the first thinkers to disentangle completely the complex relationship between the individual and the collective by arguing that knowledge of psychic factors would inevitably lead to the explanation of historical and social facts (Simmel, 1950, 1955). The implication of such an argument, from which one can draw some similarities to Moscovici's theory, is that psychic activities find expression and significance in interactions between individuals. This bold position made him the only founding figure of sociology to endorse a psychological perspective publicly. For Simmel, the dynamic exchange of psychic factors and social facts results in what he termed "social ideas," which are a sort of operating agent structuring and crystallizing the reciprocal actions between individuals to form a higher superordinate unit (Moscovici, 1989).

Thus, Simmel emphasized the complementarity of individual phenomena and social phenomena in accounting for reality, much as the theory of social representations does today. In Moscovici's theory, however, these reciprocal actions have a mental character. They create social representations, with notions and images, that filter and orient our exchanges, communication, and actions. These representations allow a mental rehearsal of the outcomes of those reciprocal actions, anticipating their consequences.

Nevertheless, social representations are not mental creations with social effects; instead they are social creations that take shape in the mind. In other words, they do not emerge from within the individuals to be transformed into a sort of collective force. They are, a priori, of a social nature, and they fill in the minds of individuals to give meaning to their world. The synthesis underlying the relational dimension of the individual and the social is particularly well reflected in the dynamic nature of social representations. Moscovici's theory accords time and space, the historical context, a key position, allowing social reality to be reconstructed and recreated. Consequently, social representations are vectors of change with a forward-looking quality, in which imagination—of what is possible—as well as normative beliefs—of what should be (or should not be) valid—play a key role in orienting the social actions of individuals toward the future.

Max Weber ([1925] 1972) was concerned with similar issues. To a certain extent, an unorthodox interpretation of his sociology can point to social representations. They appear there as a frame of reference and a vector for the actions of individuals (Moscovici, 1989). Viewed as such, they may be seen as occupying a central position in Weber's work, playing an especially important role in his epistemology of sociology as the study of the meaning and interpretation of action.

In Weber's theory social representations are interpreted as structures "floating" in the heads of people, to orient their actions in a social context and posit possible outcomes (Moscovici, 1994). Examined from this perspective, according to Moscovici (1988a), Weber gives the notion of social representation a depth that it had lacked until then. As Weber explained in his famous preface to "Grundriss der Sozialökonomik" ([1925] 1976),

when we try to interpret the meaning of actions through sociology, these representations can only be seen as sequences and connections of specific actions by *individual* humans, because these are the only agents of meaningfully oriented action we can understand. Nonetheless, sociology should not *ignore* the "collective thought representations". . . . The interpretation of action must take account of the fundamentally important fact that those collective representations, which belong to our everyday thinking . . . are *representations* in the heads of real people of something that partly is and partly should be, on the basis of which their actions are *oriented*; and that as such these representations have a very powerful, often completely dominant, causal meaning for the specific ways in which these actions of real humans unfold. (6–7) (my translation)

Reinterpreting Weber in the framework of social representation theory points to a complex web of definitions and characteristics. He discussed an interconnecting network giving both individual thought and action a social dimension. In his aforementioned preface Weber seems to analyze social representations on three different levels. First, they crystallize around language, in the formation of a shared terminology for things and phenomena. By giving objects a name, words acquire specific meanings as collectively shared thought constructs. Second, social representations manifest themselves through the actions of individuals. By determining their connectedness and sequencing, social representations make these actions meaningfully oriented. Finally, social representations are dynamic in the sense that they are transformed over time. In their interactions, people anticipate outcomes, imagine future scenarios, and project normative structures of what is, could be, should be, and should not be valid. In the Weberian sense of *Vorstellungen*, social representations are important vectors of innovation in processes of change and transformation guiding the evolution of society.

SOCIAL REPRESENTATIONS AS VECTORS OF CHANGE

Reality constantly changes, as prevailing configurations break down and give rise to new forces. Often the process is driven by minority groups introducing new problems and engaging in conflictual relations with majority members. This results in the creation of a new social reality by challenging sets of social representations (which the majority maintains in preservation of the status quo) and by introducing alternative ones. Farr (1987) understood this quite clearly when he emphasized Moscovici's research on minority influence (Moscovici, 1976b, 1985; Moscovici & Faucheux, 1972; Moscovici, Lage, & Naffrechoux, 1969; Moscovici & Personnaz, 1980, 1991) as an integral part of his social representation theory, a point also argued by Doise (1985, 1989).

The entry of a new factor impacts on individuals by creating a conflict, decentralizing them from the majority norms as the ultimate point of reference (Moscovici, 1980). This decentralization alters the very nature of the underlying problem, or at least how it is perceived, by establishing within the individual a cognitive field composed of a bifocal point of anchoring (i.e., the minority norms and the majority norms). Such a process of innovation is only relevant if it is understood as a social phenomenon capable of changing what people see (Moscovici & Personnaz, 1980, 1991), what they think, and how they act. New information, ideas, or other forms of influence can only be effective if they transform existing social representations or give rise to new ones.

Thus one can say that innovation is the engine driving the formation of new social representations, while social representations in turn allow a new factor to move from the level of an idea to the level of action and reality. Putting the notion of social representations into this dynamic context gives them an inherently anticipatory quality, as people imagine solutions, project different outcomes, and come to associate a new situation with their own immediate interests.

Social representations play in this way a crucial role in the unfolding of change. They can assume this importance because they carry three characteristics that together make them ideally suited vectors of innovation. First of all, they are *prescriptive* and thus constraining in nature (Abric & Vergès, 1994; Flament, 1994; Moscovici, 1984). This means that any object, new or not, is understood through a socially created metasystem that regulates, controls, and directs individual minds (Doise, 1989, 1993; Moscovici, 1976a). That metasystem is a structure which interferes with us in ways we cannot control, guides us when we make up our minds about something, and forces us by means of conventions to take account of what others think. How an object is socially represented shapes what we think and how we act towards it.

Moreover, social representations are *consensual* in nature, and work to consolidate the group. Their implications for communication within and between groups are indeed fundamental inasmuch as they provide us with the basis for a shared understanding of objects, people, and events—an understanding structured by the implicit and explicit ideas and images accepted within groups. In this case consensus has to be understood not so much as a simple aggregate, but rather as a consensual universe with supra-individual qualities (Moscovici, 1985). Social representations create a structuring basis for our interactions and communication, which serve to define us as interconnected social agents. Individuals may still have very divergent views concerning any given object, but their differences are structured around shared representations of that object.

In fact, divergence is necessary for the continued existence of the representations in social life. But these divergencies make no sense unless they are relativized with each other for comparison and juxtaposition, so that we may understand the common organizing principle: the metasystem (Doise, 1985). And this relativation requires, within the divergent individual representations, a structuring core (Abric, 1984, 1994a) which presents the object in homogenizing fashion so that it can be conceptualized collectively as one and the same object. That consensual core is precisely what makes representations social and integrates divergencies into relative differences.

Once representations are created, they lead a life of their own. This characteristic allows them to evolve beyond the reach of individuals. Elaborated in interaction and refined by communication, the representations engage individuals as a social context shaping their minds and orienting their actions. It is precisely this extraneous quality of social representations which makes it possible for them to be linked with each other and, through synergy and synthesis, give rise to new representations. Purkhardt (1993), who clarified the prescriptive and consensual nature of social representations, failed to see that point when she concluded that they were not autonomous. Her characterization is only correct to the extent that social representations cannot be separated from the minds of the individuals which create and nourish them. But the same does not hold true in reverse. Social representations are *autonomous* to the extent that they are more and larger than what gets constructed in the minds of individuals.

Social representations thus assume a central role in processes of change. Their prescriptive, consensual, and autonomous nature enables them to shape the formation and orientation of our social life. Those same qualities also make social representations particularly effective vectors of innovation. As a source of prescription for normative beliefs, as the core of a consensual world, and as an autonomous force that individuals cannot escape, they give our heterogenous society a structuring context to contain the divergent forces of conflict around a core of agreements. That quality of cohesion is not at all static, since it accommodates change and, at times, even organizes it.

ANTICIPATORY REPRESENTATION: DEFINING A CONCEPT

Insofar as social representations play a central role in processes of change, they all possess an anticipatory quality (Abric, 1994b). As they affect change, they necessarily orient our actions towards the future and give our thoughts a forward-looking character. Those projections may be intensely conflictual and divergent. But their grounding in collectively elaborated representations of socially relevant objects gives the social actions of individuals a certain cohesion.

This grounding comes about to the extent that our actions and projections follow certain presuppositions, a set of pragmatic inferences we share automatically (Moscovici, 1994). In the shaping and reshaping of reality these presuppositions reinforce our interconnectedness by means of their prescriptive force, which propels individuals to adjust what they think about an object and how they act towards it. As individuals make these adjustments, they also allow the anticipated actions of others to guide their own decisions. Changes in the life conditions of a given society often result in an adjustment of the collective interpretations of social objects, and thus these social objects get redefined. Such a process re-constitutes the collectivity and makes sense of the world.

When adjusting to change and taking account of others, individuals must go beyond reflecting upon actual circumstances and consider alternative courses of action, new solutions to conflict. The choices we make, which come to determine our social actions, depend on the social representations we share. These are the driving force that carries us through processes of change in our society. They impose a structure on our social world, provide us with some collective basis for a consensual interpretation of social objects, direct our thoughts towards possible scenarios that correspond to our immediate interests, and orient our sequence of actions.

This anticipatory aspect of social representations, which shapes what people think about and how they imagine the future, is essential in processes of change and innovation. Because of their role in collective efforts to project a future together in the sense of Weber's *Vorstellungen*, social representations are the networks of interconnections between social agents, maintaining cohesion during periods of tumultuous change. As crises unfold, individuals as well as groups rethink their world together and communicate solutions to one another. In so doing, we recognize, reassert, and legitimize our collectivity by re-constituting our shared reality. Through this interplay, meaning is extracted from the world, and, in turn, the world is reproduced in our heads in a meaningful way (Moscovici, 1984).

This forward-looking quality of social representations is especially pronounced when crisis conditions force the emergence of new social representations. These are representations in the making; their very process of formation guides us through periods of change and in so doing reshapes our social reality. Their manifestations symbolize the extent to which society does actually think. At the point of crisis, when society is torn by conflict and confusion, social actors need to reconstitute a common understanding of the world in order to contemplate solutions and alternatives. New social representations satisfying this need—in other words *anticipatory representations*—are at the core of our social life, as they ascend from images in our heads to shared reality and ascribe new meaning to our world.

Anticipatory social representations carry presuppositions about a collectively imagined future. Those representations form an especially strong system of interconnectedness, because they reconstruct the collective mind before we become fully aware of it. They acquire their meaning in specific sequences of social actions by individuals, and in turn they render these actions meaningful. While still at a level of abstraction, they already manage to orient thought and direct action. In this sense, they make the thoughts and the actions of individuals social in terms of the outcomes which they presuppose. Since they are by definition not yet as stable and settled as an embedded representation of an already made object, they are particularly well suited instruments to carry us through periods of societal transformation. Their very elaboration is what transforms reality. In other words, as they get made, they create or remake the object that they will come to represent.

While all social representations are dynamic in nature, anticipatory representations are especially so. Since they must address conflict and are therefore, by definition, vectors of innovations, they possess special reality-transforming powers. As they circulate throughout society, they appear as a fluid phenomenon capable of adjusting quickly to changes in the social context and of accommodating internal contradictions.

ANTICIPATORY DIMENSION IN SOCIAL REPRESENTATION THEORY

Since social representations are an organizing principle for our social networks during periods of change, they all carry a degree of anticipation with them. This anticipation is the result of presuppositions that are floating in the heads of individuals, guiding the formation of a new representation or the transformation of a preexisting one. The floating dimension of these presuppositions reflects a phenomenon in the making. To some extent, all representations have that dimension—even those that are well established, since they must be constantly renewed in day-to-day conversations and other channels of public communication in order to persist and remain adapted to the ongoing transformations of modern life.

The varying degrees of anticipation attached to social representations emerge already clearly in the book which put social representation theory on the map, Moscovici's *La Psychanalyse: Son image et son public* (1961, 1976a). In this seminal work he analyzed how during an intense period of change in France, following the postwar chaos, the relocation of psychoanalysis from the scientific to the popular domain, as a social representation, became an organizing principle for people. In this study he was primarily concerned with the insertion of psychoanalysis as a new representation in everyday social discourse. In the process he endowed the new social representation with an anticipatory dimension that reflected a phenomenon in the making, one whose forward-looking quality served as a catalyst for crisis-driven change.

Moscovici's focus was twofold. On the one hand, he studied the transformation of a theory—thus far belonging to the scientific realm—into an object of everyday knowledge. As a newly appropriated substratum of common sense and an integrated part of everyday thinking, psychoanalysis impacted on many of our preexisting regulators of social interactions. The full understanding of these social normative structures, that is to say these social regulators, came through Moscovici's analysis of the assimilation, accommodation, and dissemination of this new knowledge. He studied the actual insertion of psychoanalysis by reviewing how newspapers of various ideological persuasions discussed it.

People obviously needed this popularization in order to explain problems and communicate them, as well as to search for solutions; they needed to accommodate psychoanalysis as an integral part of their cognitive functionings, one that would guide their thoughts and give direction to their action. After the war there was a great need to restore some internal equilibrium—especially in a time of accelerating technological, political, and cultural change. After World War II, at the end of a long cycle of war, depression, and revolution, people wanted something to pacify them. At that point, a generation after Freud, psychoanalysis had advanced enough to make this possible.

Chapter 3

African American
and Its Properties

The dynamic qualities of social representations discussed in the preceding chapter apply especially to anticipatory representations such as African American, where they appear in more pronounced fashion than in already well settled and established representations. To begin with, the new group denomination is in essence a social representation in the making, and thus a carrier of change in perception, cognition, and attitudes about black Americans. In this early phase of its evolution, when it is still being formed by continuous collective efforts, such an anticipatory representation must be viewed as a process of transformation of a shared reality. The key force behind this process is the denomination's prescriptive aspect, which provides a normative context for the elaboration of new rules and conventions in social exchange. As the new representation is being made, it reorients people's thoughts and actions towards a differently imagined future. This forward-looking characteristic allows an anticipatory representation to reshape the present in a way that affects all groups involved.

In this chapter we shall explore these underlying properties as they apply to African American. If we do not clearly understand the term's prescriptive and forward-looking properties, it becomes difficult to articulate important differences between Black and African American—as illustrated in several recent studies about Americans of African descent (Allen, Thornton, & Watkins, 1995; Jackson, McCullough, Gurin, & Broman, 1991; Oyserman, 1993). It is only by looking at such group denominations as social representations that one can go beyond considering those names merely as labels, a common practice among those studying Americans of African descent (Fairchild, 1985; Gordon, 1976; Hecht &

Ribeau, 1987, 1991; Larkey, Hecht & Martin, 1993; Smith, 1992), and view them instead as manifestations of change in self-perception, perceptions by others, and intergroup relations.

This chapter does three things. In the first section we explore the nature of African American as a representation in the making. The term is positive, and this particular characteristic gives it a projective quality which redefines the group in a more inclusive light. Then, in the second section, we look at the principal function of such an anticipatory representation: rendering the unknown familiar. The term becomes familiarized in different ways, depending on the group to which one belongs. In the last section, we examine the structural shifts in the makeup of African American, to see what allows this social representation to reconstruct and transform how the group is being perceived.

PROJECTIVE QUALITIES OF AFRICAN AMERICAN: THE NATURE

As argued in the last chapter, social representations play a central role in processes of change. Their emergence results from collective efforts by individuals to redefine their social world, and it guides these efforts in specific directions. African American as a new denomination for a group previously referred to as Black can be seen precisely in this context, as a new social representation whereby a specific group overcomes its hitherto marginalized position in American society. As Thelma Golden (1994) put it in *Black Male*, "One of the greatest inventions of the twentieth century is the African-American male—'invented' because black masculinity represents an amalgam of fears and projections in the American psyche which rarely conveys and contains the trope of truth about the black male's existence" (p. 19).

The new denomination (and this may well be typical of anticipatory representations) emerged in the context of a crisis which demanded change. During the late 1960s the Civil Rights movement had consciously tried to reappropriate the term Black and turn it into a positive group designation. By the late 1970s it had become clear that this earlier collective effort at group positivation had failed. The name Black, defining a group by skin color and thus on the basis of race, proved inherently too negative in its historic roots to be turned into something positive. The moment the term began to spread beyond the Civil Rights movement into the mainstream, replacing Negro, it lost its specific political context and became susceptible to reinterpretation along traditional lines. Ultimately Black implied the same racial polarization that Negro had in the era of segregation. The images associated with Black in the mainstream—as nourished and construed by the media—have by and large remained stubbornly negative (and, if anything, become progressively more so), even after thirty years of desegregation (Golden, 1994).

This failure to turn Black into a positive identity is surely not least due to the limited impact of desegregation itself. Many black Americans have remained shut out of participation in the American Dream. The urban ghetto—a product of local politics, federal policies, and institutionalized racism—persists, and living conditions in those marginalized areas of the cities are by any objective standard worse today than forty years ago. The combination of joblessness, neglect, and poverty there is very difficult to survive, as the sociologist William Julius Wilson argues:

Take a white or black middle-class family and strip them of all their resources to make them comparable to an inner-city family. Put them in one of those dangerous neighborhoods where the parents have to worry every day about what's going to happen to their children. Where they have to deal with the crime, the drugs, and the isolation. Where they can't depend on other families in the neighborhood, because they are also isolated. You put any family in that neighborhood, stick them there, let them be trapped, and see how successful they'll be over the long run in raising their children. (qtd. in Herbert, 1994)

Yet, at the same time, the Civil Rights movement has allowed some black Americans for the first time in the nation's history an entry into the mainstream. This opening has fostered middle-class aspirations among those fortunate enough to benefit from the dismantling of segregation in the 1960s and Affirmative Action policies of the 1970s. But prospects of full participation in the American Dream must remain elusive as long as those once-excluded Americans still have to live with a group designation that emphasizes their "otherness" in discriminatory fashion. The continuing presence of the term Black in day-to-day conversation, alongside an alternative designation that seems to resolve most of our racial tensions, points to a paradox well embedded in the American mind. This contradiction can be seen as a novel expression of Myrdal's "American Dilemma," a dilemma that arises inevitably when a society based on democratic ideals practices race-based exclusion of a particular group. The coexistence of both terms in current social exchanges has to be understood in terms of the persistence of race-based differentiation in our society. A reinterpretation of Myrdal's dilemma today has to include an analysis of the internalization of the same paradox in the black American mind.

This contradiction between apparent progress towards integration and continued discrimination plays itself out by exacerbating tensions among group members pertaining to their dual consciousness as part American and part African. One way to resolve this internal disequilibrium is to break away from being called Black in favor of a more neutral alternative. The term African American, officially introduced by a group of Civil Rights leaders in 1989 and propagated since then by precisely those black Americans able and willing to enter the mainstream, fits well in this regard. It deemphasizes race, focusing instead on culture and ethnicity. Structurally, it parallels those names used for all other groups comprising this multicultural society (Italian Americans, German Americans, Korean Americans, etc.). In that sense the term African American can be associated with inclusion and equality, in contrast to the polarizing implication of Black in juxtaposition to White. Finally, as a new term that breaks with the past, African American has the potential to redefine how the group perceives itself and is perceived by others.

This quality of transforming attitudes and perceptions concerning a specific group is precisely what makes the replacement term so relevant as an anticipatory representation. Unlike Black, the term African American is not wedded to the tragic past of a racially divided society. Instead, it is a new social representation that can be filled with positive images of equality, inclusion, and integration. And this collective effort to transform the past necessarily involves projections of a different future and appropriate changes in the normative context, both of which guide the collective thinking of our society.

That projective quality of the new group designation, as a vehicle for a redefinition of a group, is a representation in the making; its content is developed in the inter- and intragroup tensions it is designed to address. For the African Americans, an upwardly mobile subgroup propagating the term, this new group designation has the potential of resolving their dual-consciousness tension by moving the focus of their representation from race to culture. In addition, the term carries a strongly prescriptive dimension in terms of the treatment of African Americans and their participation in the making of America. This projection, of course, does not liberate them from continued racism, whose manifestations they continue to feel—a dissonance that parallels the coexistence of Black as a made representation and African American as one in the making. But the normative context, which the new term acquires with this projection, does allow African Americans to define themselves anew as a group and thereby create a certain permeability in their relationship with non-black Americans.

For Blacks the new term implies that some members of the group have been able to escape poverty. This realization proves fertile ground for ambivalence. On the one hand, it aggravates the Black's own sense of exclusion from middle-class life and professional careers. At the same time, it points to the possibility of exit from misery. African American as a new denomination is then a symbol of hope for those dis-abled by poverty and ghettoization. To the extent that Blacks internalize the American ethos just as other Americans do, their "pursuit of happiness" can once again be actualized into optimism, as a form of cognitive functioning. That optimism had been reawakened in 1963 when Martin Luther King's "I have a dream" speech presented America with a vision of integration, and in the process sensitized all segments of society to the destructive nature of racism. For the white majority he succeeded in projecting Blacks as human, as equal to the rest of America; for Blacks, he presented an image of America as an inclusive and fair society, his "promised land" of integration. Three decades later, the dream having proved possible for so few, disenfranchised Blacks can do little but "Keep Hope Alive," the slogan of Jesse Jackson's presidential campaign in 1988. Shortly thereafter, in 1989, Jackson gave this plea for hope a concrete direction when he launched a campaign for the propagation of African American as the official new group designation to replace Black.

For non-black Americans the new term serves in certain ways as a pacifier. To the extent that the continued legacy of racism breeds guilt, the new representation related to African American shifts the focus to the possibilities of a more egalitarian future and thus reinforces a "belief in a just world" (Lerner, 1980). As the term gets associated with the quintessential values of mainstream America, it also acquires a normative aspect that defines appropriate behavior. The implication is that if black Americans behave in certain generally accepted ways, they can be Americans like anyone else. White Americans and other non-black Americans can in this way continue to believe that the system works. What this belief also implies, of course, is that those black Americans not able to enter the mainstream only have themselves to blame. James Baldwin, in his dialogue on race with Margaret Mead (1971), made this point very clearly:

Alas, most white people until this hour, for a complex of reasons which there may be no purpose in going into, partly wilfully and partly out of genuine ignorance and a lack of imagination, really do not know why black people are in the street. And God knows, the mass media do not help to clarify this at all.

Everytime you see a riot, you see all these people stealing TV sets and looking like savages, according to the silent majority's optic. If you do not know why they are in the streets—especially with various ivy league colleges and Arrow-collar-ad men, and all the symbols and tokens of progress—there is a danger of another polarization, at least on the surface. Because then the world, the white American and the world, looks at, let us say Harry Belafonte, to use arbitrarily a famous public figure, and those people rioting on the South Side, and they conclude, as they are meant to conclude, really, that if those people on the South Side washed themselves and straightened up they could all be Harry Belafonte. There is nothing wrong with the system, so the American thinks; there is something wrong with the people. This is the greatest illusion, and the most dangerous delusion of all, because it exacerbates the rage of the people trapped in the ghettos. They know why they are there, even if America doesn't. (pp. 154–155)

Figure 3.1
The Triangular Model of African American

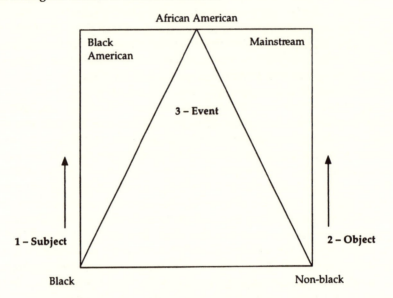

African American thus emerges in a triangular dynamic (see Figure 3.1) between Blacks, a new subgroup calling itself African American, and a combination of mainstream American culture and other minority groups. This new term is, in its nature, a social representation that connotes a people, an object, and an event (Breakwell, 1993; Jodelet, 1993). The tridimensionality of African American is what qualifies it as a total cultural phenomenon capable of reshaping contemporary America.

Figure 3.1 illustrates the triangular model by which African American is constituted. In the first dimension, that of a name for a specific group of people, the term African American refers to a subject which is defined in sociodemographic terms. In this sense, the switch in name denotes the historic appearance of an integrated professional middle class among black Americans in the aftermath of the Civil Rights struggles. For a majority of black Americans, especially those remaining disenfranchised and poor, the possibility of transforming into an "African American" and thus finding a certain measure of acceptance in society, is a beacon of hope for a different future. In its second dimension, the term African American evokes a new social object that finds its significance in contradistinction to the negative images associated with Black. For non-black Americans, in particular white Americans, the appearance of African American signals a certain resolution of America's dissonant history vis-à-vis Americans of African descent (Myrdal, 1944). This object, namely black Americans, can now be seen in two different ways—one positive, one negative. The final dimension closing the triangle relates to African American as an event, in the sense that it has, through communication, become part of our common sense, to the point that it infiltrates our daily lives in numerous exchanges and interactions. African American symbolizes, on the one hand, the transformation of our social reality from the divisiveness of race to coexistence in a multicultural society and, on the other hand, projections of a positive future.

The points of this triangle connect in dynamic fashion. These connections operate in both directions and at the same time affect one another. As the term African American circulates and becomes familiar, this new social representation of a minority group is elaborated and comes to be understood interdependently in each of its dimensions. The use of African American in current social discussions and everyday conversations is designed to become a carrier for transformations in perception as well as in interaction between different groups. In that sense the new term possesses a projective force as an anticipatory representation. The meanings elaborated for the new social creation are cast into a specific set of projections which are actualized through people's expectations about how the group is being perceived. The various ways in which the new term is used and interpreted provides direct and symbolic cues to guide behavior and communication attached to this new definition.

FAMILIARIZING A NEW SOCIAL OBJECT: THE FUNCTION

The creation of African American is a symbolic resolution of various dissonant cognitions; it is a synthesis of an otherwise contradictory dual consciousness for African Americans, a beacon of hope for Blacks, and a source of relief for Whites as well as other non-black Americans. These salutary effects can only come about to the extent that African American, as a representation in the making, settles in the minds of people as a projection of expectations (which in turn are shaped by the diverse experiences of each group). Even though the groups involved in its making approach the new term from different angles, there is a superordinate organizational structure to African American that homogenizes its interpretations. As an evolving social representation that points to a different future, the designation is consensual.

It is precisely this qualitative aspect of African American as an anticipatory representation which matters the most in the diffusion of the term. People, even those choosing not to use the new term, cannot escape its prescriptive force. They know, because of the normative and projective context of its social elaboration, that the new term means something quite different from Black. Everybody understands that African American constitutes a decisive break with the long tradition of racial classifications. Therefore we should not judge the term's "success" by what percentages of the different populations actually adopt the new term. Such a purely quantitative measue of usage fails to capture the forward-looking and positive imagery associated with the term; no one can escape this imagery not even those who until now have refrained from using the term.

It is, of course, not insignificant that in less than two years following its introduction nearly a quarter of all black Americans had already adopted the term African American. Such a rapid spread of its use confirms that the term had great appeal. But this ignores the deeper implications of the new term, as a collective effort by often antagonistic groups to redefine a social object. To emphasize the anticipatory qualities of social representations in the making is to comprehend how, as carriers of change and vectors of innovation, they transform a shared reality. We can then see how a new name for a group can radically alter how this group is perceived and perceives itself. In that context it becomes again highly relevant that so many black Americans began to identify themselves as African Americans in such a short period of time. Their identification as African Americans enables us to assimilate the new term and thereby define the new object in our minds. The unfamiliar thus becomes familiar. Any unfamiliar object of social relevance is by definition threatening to the extent that it disturbs preexisting conventions (Moscovici, 1984) while being at the same time still too vague to replace them. It is only when it acquires meaning that the new object can be assimilated and integrated into the social world of individuals.

Concerning African American, such meaning is derived in tripolar fashion, reflecting the triangular dynamic of this particular representation in its making (see Figure 3.2). In the first place, information about what the new social representation means and who it refers to originates with the salient characteristics of a subgroup claiming an identity as African Americans. This particular group has certain demographic characteristics, presenting a model of the mainstream (middle-class, hardworking) American, race apart. The term was created by this group. Therefore, how it is understood by anyone can never be completely detached from those having chosen the term for themselves. They are the primary source of its definition. They literally create and shape the new representation by what they project for themselves and about themselves, by what they demand from American society, by how they want the rest of America to view them and treat them. They personify the new name and give it its meaning.

On the receiving end of this collective triangular effort, from the points of view both of Blacks and of non-black Americans, the new social representation is a real phenomenon precisely because of its personification by a new group that calls itself African American. It cannot be ignored.

Figure 3.2
The Triangular Model in the Creation of Meanings

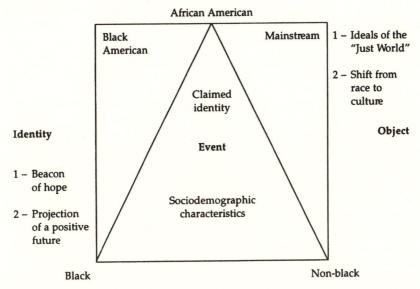

Equally importantly, the new representation breaks radically with past practice in two ways. For one, this particular term, uniquely among labels applied to the group, is consistent with the standard designation of other groups in a multicultural setting. Moreover, it is the first name change pertaining to black Americans that involves a collective effort by various groups. It thus shakes up the prevailing order of well-established representations about the group as Blacks. At the same time, the new social representation cannot immediately supplant those preexisting representations of the same object that had been dominant for so long. The social representations Black and African American coexist.

This coexistence impacts differently on Blacks than on the other groups. Despite the Civil Rights struggle and its legislation abolishing outright segregation, Blacks have seen their situation worsen in the past three decades. Their dreams of escaping poverty, discrimination, and isolation have been brutally dashed, a point reinforced, even symbolized, by the failure to turn Black into a positive representation. The difficult reality of their daily lives gives enough cause to lose all hope. The appearance of African American, and its personification by some black Americans claiming the term as a new identity, promise a way out of misery. There is once again reason for hope, irrespective of the actual probability of individual members of that group turning themselves into African Americans. For Blacks the new representation becomes a familiar focal point for projections of a different future, but at the same time also confronts them as an unattainable standard that can be used against them.

For non-black Americans, in particular White Americans (who as a group arguably still define the mainstream culture of their society), the assimilation of African American opens the possibility of moving away from the troubled past of a racially divided society. There is a collective interest for the group in doing so. Racism breeds guilt, which needs relief. Even more importantly, racist practices of discrimination and exclusion violate the fundamental moral notions of what America is all about, the American Dream of an equal-opportunity society. The integration of African American restores an internal equilibrium for non-black Americans, since it implies that a certain number of black Americans, namely those who play by the rules, can be accepted as Americans just like anyone else. Such selective inclusion also makes it easier for non-black Americans to shift the justification for continuing inequality from unfair societal practices to the victims themselves, a tendency described so well already a quarter of a century ago by James Baldwin in the quote above. In their opinion those black Americans unable to transform into African Americans only have themselves to blame for this failure, since the road to equality is no longer closed to all members of that group as was the case in the days of slavery and segregation.

These contradictory aspects of how the term African American becomes familiar among non-black Americans, as a normative context that signals acceptance of some black Americans as equal and at the same time justifies the exclusion of others as essentially self-inflicted, absolves the majority from any association with openly racist sentiments. This objective can only be achieved to the extent that the familiarization of African American manages to crowd out race as the central core of pre-existing social representations pertaining to black Americans, and replaces it with something qualitatively different, namely culture.

The persistent coexistence of Black and African American as two different representations of the same object, to the point that these terms may be used interchangeably in the same conversation, makes it clear that this transformation of the central core is not a straightforward process of substitution. Race remains a constant presence in the background, and even the most integrated African Americans still feel, at time, victimized by racism (Cose, 1993; Staples, 1994). Both sides, black Americans and non-black Americans, may suppress race to allow other factors to come forth, but this suppression is not the same as elimination.

TRANSFORMATION OF THE CORE: THE DYNAMIC STRUCTURE

The new social representation of black Americans, in contrast to any previous social representation held about the same group, is positive, and implies full integration and participation in the shaping of America. In light of the group's historically marginalized position, this new representation can only change perceptions if the object appears anew. Since the conceptual precursors of African American are deeply ingrained in our collective thoughts, African American must manage to transform something central and fundamental inside the object itself while maintaining its overall structure.

Precisely this aspect of social representation theory has been developed by several renowned social psychologists from the Laboratoire de Psychologie Sociale in Aix-en-Provence, France. This group has defined social representations "as socio-cognitive structures, with a specific organization, which are ruled by their own norms of functioning. The understanding of how these representations intervene in social practices implies that the internal organization of the representation is known." (Abric, 1994c, p. 8).

The internal organization of the social representation is built around a central core (Abric, 1984, 1987, 1989; Abric & Tafani, 1995; Abric & Vergès, 1994; Flament & Moliner, 1989; Moliner, 1989; Vergès, 1992) which contains an indispensable element or combination of elements giving the representation its meaning. It assumes two essential functions: a generative function in which the central element creates or transforms the significance of the other elements composing the representation; and an organizing function through which the central core, as a unifying and stabilizing factor, structures the links between those other elements of the representation.

Surrounding the central core is an organized constellation of peripheric elements (Flament 1987, 1989) which play an important role in concretizing the meaning of the representation. Those peripheric elements, which are only loosely connected with the central core, tend to be used to illustrate, explain, and justify that meaning (Abric, 1994b; Abric & Vergès, 1994). Both the primary and secondary elements of the periphery play an essential role in the representation. They are at the interface between the central core and the concrete situation within which the representation is elaborated and within which it operates. In that position they have three key functions: a concretizing function, which familiarizes the representation; a regulatory function, which allows adaption of the representation to a new context; and a protective function, defending the central core of the representation much like a shock absorber. With these functions the peripheric elements anchor the central core in reality.

This double system, comprising the central core and peripheric elements in interaction with each other, enables us to understand some seemingly contradictory characteristics of social representations. These representations are stable and rigid, because they are determined by the central core, which is profoundly crystallized in the value system shared by the members of a group (Abric, 1994b; Doise, 1985). Yet at the same time they are dynamic and fluid, since they integrate a wide variety of individual experiences with the social conditions that mark the evolution of the individuals or groups. In that adaptation and integration social representations connect individual agents to social norms and practices which guide intergroup relations (Abric, 1994b).

In this particular variant of social representation theory the notion of the central core provides an interesting answer to a key epistemological question concerning the link between individual representations and social reality. The central core is the organizing principle which makes the social representation stable, and this stability results from its objectification. This process creates a figurative nucleus, a core of images, which decontextualizes the principal elements of a representation to the point that they assume a life of their own as part of a social context shaping individual minds.

The central core elements of the representation are the ones most resistant to change. According to Abric (1994b), any change to the central core will bring about a complete change of the representation. Therefore, for two representations to be different, they must be organized around two different central cores. Any such difference is not confined to content alone. Equally important is the underlying organization of that content. Two representations defined by the same content can be radically different if their respective organization of that content, and therefore the centrality of certain elements, is different.

This differentiation applies in very relevant fashion to the emergence of African American. The elaboration of the new denomination into a distinct social representation is shaped by its contradistinction to Black, a competing representation with which it shares the same object. The new term becomes familiarized by association with a specific subgroup whose members call themselves African American, yet any African American is at the same time also a black American who might be referred to as Black. One representation of the object is in the making, while the other one is already made. The one in the making denotes culture, the other race. While the first one is positive and future-oriented, the other is negative and laden with a burdensome past. Both representations exist at the same time, struggling for the shaping of the present.

This coexistence of African American and Black posits an interesting theoretical question. If African American is to emerge fully as a new social representation, it will have to have transformed preexisting representations of the same object, in this case black Americans. Such a change can only come about to the extent that the central core of our preexisting representation has been transformed as well. The question is how such a transformation is possible if and when the principal core element, namely race, also applies to the newly (re)defined object—the African Americans who, after all, remain black Americans.

A possible answer to this question is to suggest a change of representation, rather than a change in the representation, to account for the contradistinction between the two terms. In other words, one may argue that the two group denominations constitute two distinct representations of the same object. The logical implication of this argument is that the two terms have two different central cores, each of which is made up of specific, uniquely organized elements. One core denotes culture, and the other race. These two "poles," while leading completely separate existences, may be connected through interaction in their respective peripheries. Within these constellations the two representations would share some common elements.

This argument, while clear and simple, does not address the anticipatory nature of African American. By omitting such a key aspect of the term, it obliterates the fact that our new representation is not only closely associated with Black, but at this point needs the existence of Black as a representation to sustain and validate its own existence. African American has its roots in Black, and the nature of the two denominations' coexistence in ordinary language illustrates a high degree of linkage and association between them. In this case, the dynamic contradistinction underlying their relationship is unlikely to allow for a stable and peaceful coexistence between the two terms. Their opposing valence, African American being positive while Black is negative, sets the ground for a rather polemical tension between them. Such a situation requires a more complex approach than the static dichotomy implied by two separate representations.

Our alternative interpretation centers around three key ideas. First, African American has its roots in Black. Second, the new denomination is an anticipatory representation that is still in the making. Finally, African American maintains a polemical relation to Black by evolving in contradistinction to this old name. Since an African American is someone who less than a decade ago would still have been identified as Black, the emergence of the new denomination in everyday conversations should be conceived as stemming from the use of the term Black. While it is already distinct enough from Black to evoke substantially different notions, perceptions, and even attitudes than those normally associated with the old name, African American is not yet fully independent from it.

In fact, this new denomination relates to Black like a branch to a tree. Such a duality of differentiation and connectedness between the two terms provides the base for their polemical relation. The expression of such a polemical relationship is found in the fact that the same object, the same person even, can be and is indeed addressed by others interchangeably as Black or as African American. The complexity in the nature of their relationship requires us to focus on the processes of change which are embedded in the switch of name. We also need to understand the innovation by which African American has come to emerge in public discussion and has established itself as a reconceptualization of Black.

Since the emphasis is on a cultural phenomenon which evolves within a historical context, we are much less concerned with making predictions about the future course of this denomination. Indeed, we do not know what African American will eventually evolve into and how different it will become from Black. We do know, however, that it has acquired some degree of autonomy, an existence outside our control, and can no longer simply be wished away. It also has a existence distinct from Black, sufficiently so to be used in conversations to evoke something quite different than Black. As a social representation, the new denomination has concretized itself within the culture and has acquired some specific and concrete meanings, different from those associated with Black.

As the term is endowed with meanings, it is transformed from a label into a social representation. According to Moscovici (1984), a social representation connects images to ideas as well as ideas to images, and projects the fusion of these associations into reality. Thus, a social representation has both iconic and symbolic facets. African American, however, as a social representation in the making, does not have a straightforward reciprocity between its iconic and its symbolic dimensions. On the one hand, the new denomination is clearly associated with images that are being created by those claiming the name. In this way the images are connected to an idea, and are validated in reality by being embodied in real people with public exposure in a growing number of fields. Turning these subjects into objects, on the other hand, the media and public opinion makers have facilitated the diffusion of the name by filling an idea with clear and concrete images. In this case the idea is defined by quintessential American values.

When the choice of a name conveys a social representation, it is through language that the dynamics between the iconic and the symbolic facets of such a representation are expressed. African Americans, representing the first post-segregation generation of black Americans, also symbolize the possibility of full integration, the possibility that the dream of a color-blind society may one day be realized. The term African American is therefore of direct relevance here as a group designation which, in its structure, equals those used for other groups in this multiethnic society, and which in addition puts the emphasis on American (Banton, 1988). Ideas of what African American means can take hold in the general public not least because of their roots in the social representation of the American. To some extent non-black Americans see themselves in African American.

The emphasis on American in the new denomination facilitates the collective effort in support of its elaboration. Unlike the positivation of Black in the 1960s, the circulation of African American involves all groups and is based on a triangular confluence of interests. Of course, this process cannot be understood if we adopt the narrow definition of consensus which insists on an aggregate of individuals sharing similar representations (Jovchelovitch, 1995; Parker, 1987; Potter & Litton, 1985). Instead we need to see individuals interconnected by a metasystem that accounts for both divergencies as well as similarities.

What we have here is the splitting of the social representation of Black in two. As such, the split reshuffles the content and organization of the central core. The racial characteristics of Black are confronted by new elements which give a cultural dimension to them. African American as an offspring of Black embodies the conflictual interplay of both constituent elements, race and culture, which can only coexist if one is suppressed. Of relevance here is the suggestion by Abric (1994a) that, when the central core of a representation contains different elements, as in the case with African American, some of those may lay dormant and become active only in certain situations.

To the extent that African American evolves into a new representation stressing cultural distinctions and the vision of America as a multicultural society, it does so by censoring race. In other words, the ideas and images evoked by African American require thought suppressions aimed at marginalizing race as the dominant issue defining black-white relations in America. But given its deep roots, the issue of race cannot be simply wished away. Research on thought suppression (Wegner, 1989; Wegner & Schneider, 1989; Wegner et al., 1987; Wegner et al., 1991; Wegner et al., 1990) has shown that the effort not to think of something that does not go away is likely to produce exactly the opposite result from what was originally intended, namely a latent obsession with the object to be suppressed. The obsession is latent because of a socially constructed and widely internalized consensus requiring continuous efforts at suppression. When it comes to the fore, it does so in a sudden outburst which may be termed a "rebound effect."

This explains perhaps why the current focus on a common ground between black Americans and white Americans is accompanied by recurrent explosions of racial tension, as with the Rodney King case and the Los Angeles riots or the Crown Heights confrontation in New York City, and by highly publicized media events centering on successful African American men (Clarence Thomas, Michael Jackson, O.J. Simpson). The obsessive nature of race as a social phenomenon, which has ripped this society apart, is so dominant that any attempt to bring about a more positive view of black Americans has to move away from it. This explains the conscious deemphasizing of race in favor of culture in the new social representation of black Americans as African Americans.

In sum, African American contains several elements in its central core. For one, the new denomination applies to a specific group which it redefines, in contradistinction to preexisting representations, as one of many groups in a multicultural society (Bernstein, 1994; Jaynes & Williams, 1989; Walzer, 1990). The emphasis is put here naturally on American as a second core element. The social representation of what it means to be an American, centered around a social-cultural context of individualism, evokes notions of self-esteem, social status, competence, personal security, happiness, wealth, and health (Bellah et al., 1985; Jones, 1989; Oyserman & Markus, 1995). A second core element is race, a well-embedded and reified construct in the American psyche (Myrdal, 1944; Terkel, 1992; West, 1994); despite its prominence, this element tends to get suppressed in the context of African American, much like Wegner (1989) demonstrated with the suppression of thoughts about a "white bear:" The suppression of race requires a sustained effort that often results in a rebound effect. Even when pushed into the background, race can never completely leave the structure of this representation, since African Americans remain, after all, black Americans.

The constellation of these central core elements is not yet stable and therefore subject to shifts. This instability is due to the relative newness of the underlying social representation. African American as a group denomination of black Americans only appeared in 1989. While it has become familiar since then, it is not yet objectified into a reified concept with a full existence of its own. Its existence is not yet detached from its articulation by African Americans, other black Americans, the media, or other agents of the American mainstream. In the absence of objectification the term's inner structure lacks a certain stability. At this stage African American plays a mostly symbolic role, crystallizing ideas and evoking images pertaining to the subgroup as a whole. It does not yet have complete independence from its source and therefore remains a representation in the making.

Chapter 4

The Emergence of African American as a Social Representation

The concept of African American has become part of our social life. It is indeed a major cultural phenomenon that formalizes behavior and orients communication. It does so through presuppositions that float in our heads (Moscovici, 1994). These presuppositions are based on certain assumptions which are articulated and expressed in our social interactions. To say "Carter is an African American" is to presuppose that Carter is an American, with all that this evokes. But it also implies that Carter is black. The sentence might, in synthesis, refer then to a person of African descent who has internalized the American ethos and, we all recognize, is included in this society.

Those presuppositions have facilitated the transformation of "African American" into a social phenomenon. Such transformation requires a complete infiltration of the name African American into people's everyday lives so as to concretize the name into a common reality. The images associated with African American are still being elaborated, yet the term is already being communicated in social exchanges. Here the media and other opinion makers play a crucial role. Those generators of public opinion, more than any other channel of communication, standardize these images with presuppositions that they themselves convey to their audiences. Thereby they facilitate the incorporation of the new name into everyday life.

These arguments point to the conclusion that African American is not just a new label for a group, but that it must be understood much more deeply as a new social representation still in the making. Framed in such a broader context, we can see how African American has acquired sufficient meaning for people in terms of reshaping their identity, directing attitudes about that identity, and eventually providing a figurative core for interactions between the different social actors. When the group is talked to or talked about, the name used defines and represents the group for those involved in the interaction. And this collective activity turns the name into a shared reality.

When studying such a social representation in the making, we can distinguish three processes at work (Philogène, 1994, 1995). The first one is the *anchoring*, which categorizes the new object within our preexisting mental systems, in this case through a new name, in order to render it familiar. The second process is the *objectification*, which assures the crystallization of the new object into a figurative core so as to allow the projection of images. At this point people can talk about the object, and through communication the object acquires meaning. This *naturalization* is the final process, concluding the transformation of the object into a shared social reality. In this chapter we shall look at these interrelated processes more closely, to understand how African American is gradually made into a new social representation capable of redefining black Americans.

Since the focus of this study is the elaboration of a new social reality, the question we face in particular concerns a social representation in the making. In the case of African American the key factor is related to the process of becoming familiar with the new object and giving it a name— that is, the anchoring process. On the other hand, the objectification of African American is incomplete, because it is an anticipatory social representation and as such lacks a stable structure to allow its full concretization into images. The new representation in the making, a novelty which at the point of its inception is quite abstract, must be anchored first before it can be objectified. This familiarization connects the term with preexisting mental categories, and it is only through this linkage that the new object becomes concretized.

Within this context, the relation between anchoring and objectification, we can observe an interesting epistomological difference in the presentation of both mechanisms among social psychologists working with the theory of social representation. The French school, from which this theoretical work emerged, positions objectification before anchoring. Within the Anglo-Saxon tradition these processes are presented in reverse. Such divergence in the elaboration of the theory reflects cultural specificities, different traditions relating to social psychology, and different social representations of the object of study and the experimenter's relationship to it. Yet the ordering sequence of an anticipatory representation is crucial for reasons that go beyond cultural differences in social representation theory. An anticipatory representation, which gives rise to a variety of conceptualizations that are not yet settled in individual minds, must be sufficiently familiarized before its reification is completed. That is why it has to become anchored before it can be objectified.

In the case of an anticipatory representation the intricate relation between the symbolic and the real is especially important. Not yet fully concretized into our social reality, the representation is kept alive through a collectively defined repertoire of symbolic references. It is for this reason that naturalization is a separate process. Social representation theory treats naturalization, which enables the images formed in the figurative nucleus to become real, as the second stage of the objectification process (Moscovici, 1976a, 1981, 1984). Yet in the case of African American, the new object has had to infiltrate communication despite the absence of a concrete figurative center. This could only be possible because the object itself consists, in large part, of projections. It represents an anticipation of what should be.

The object thus has a symbolic existence as an idea, yet still lacks the iconic quality of linking ideas to images so as to make the object real beyond the mental thought processes of individuals. In the absence of such objectification, the object in question is collectively articulated in a sort of "virtual space" kept alive by our public opinion makers. In that kind of situation the new denomination can become real only through a naturalization process which is distinct from its objectification.

THE SOCIO-GENESIS OF AFRICAN AMERICAN

According to Jodelet (1984), a representation always originates from a previous one, having altered in the process mental and social configurations. Jodelet emphasizes that the dynamic nature of a social representation, which is to be capable of continuous change, is rooted in its genesis—that is, in its linkage to preexisting representations. Consequently, the full understanding of a given representation necessarily requires us to start with those from which it was born (Moscovoci, 1984). It is, of course, precisely the creative quality of self-mutation and transformation which makes the concept of social representation so useful to the study of important phenomena in the modern world (Moscovici, 1988b). Contemporary society in particular is characterized by a high degree of fluidity and fast-paced change, and in the dynamic "global village" of today people are confronted with a much greater variety of representations.

An example of this accelerated pace is how rapidly African American has spread in public discourse and everyday conversation. But its proliferation, to the point that the term has become the official and exclusive name designation used by most public opinion makers, should not be mistaken for the term having already turned into a fully developed representation capable of existing in lieu of, or side by side with, Black. This takes much longer than a few years, and involves a gradual process of transforming the metasystem underlying what people think. That metasystem is not easily changed, given the stable and rooted nature of the central core of its underlying representations (Abric, 1994). The progressive stability of a social representation's central core will be an accurate indicator of the degree to which the representation has settled or is settling in the culture.

As already indicated in the previous chapter, African American is still a representation in the making, whose central core is not yet stabilized. African American originates from Black, and has the purpose of remaking the object associated with that term: Americans of African descent. The term is shaped therefore in contradistinction to Black, as an alternative representation of the same object. Yet it will only fully become such an alternative if it establishes its own stable central core in such a way that the object it refers to appears anew and thus different. The rapid propagation of the term is required for this to happen, since a representation can only be elaborated in the public sphere (Jovchelovitch, 1995; Wagner, 1994) as the product of a collective effort.

If we want to understand how African American becomes elaborated into a new reality that reshapes cognition and attitudes about black Americans, we need to look at preexisting representations through which the new term is filtered and integrated in the minds of people. In particular, two such representations pertaining to the new group designation need to be examined to understand this phenomenon in the making. To begin with, the social representation of African American takes its source directly from that of Black. The latter representation provides a context for the reinterpretation of black Americans as African Americans. Moreover, we will look at race, since this issue links the two denominations as the key mental category filtering each. Despite its downplaying of race-based differences, African American cannot eliminate the impact of race in its integration as a social representation.

When Black emerged as a new social representation out of the Civil Rights struggles in the late 1960s, replacing Negro, it was seen as an equivalent counterweight to White. At the beginning the term was especially favored by militants for precisely that reason (Carmichael & Hamilton, 1967; Wilkinson, 1990). The juxtaposition in extremis between Black and White served to form a mutual vision of homogeneity within each group and immutable differences between them (Tajfel, 1982; Turner, 1981). For African American to emerge as an alternative designation, it must be able to break down this rigid categorization by allowing for a degree of heterogeneity within the black American community and implying some common ground with other groups in the United States. Yet the long-held view of people of African descent as separate and distinct from the rest of American society, crystallized in the term

Black, is deeply entrenched. It is therefore quite possible, even probable, that many black and non-black Americans experience a dissonance today. On the one hand, they can have very positive attitudes about the new representation African American, yet remain wedded to the use of Black even if that is no longer their preferred term.

The persistence of Black in the minds of Americans, despite its negative connotations and the spread of a less antagonistic alternative presentation, is linked to race. Black is unequivocally a racial term, and the classification of people by their race is one of America's most persistent social practices. Following the abolition of slavery, racial inferiority was given a new and scientific justification. The biological paradigms that emerged in the late nineteenth century, most notably social Darwinism and eugenics, explained differences in physical, mental, and psychological abilities on the basis of race (Banton, 1977; Gossett, 1963; Kelves, 1985; Rose, 1968). These theories were transformed into common sense, providing society with clear definitions of race which were used to categorize and identify individuals in terms of racial groups. As a social practice, race-based differentiations have lasted longer than they would have, had they remained a scientific theory. African American tries to break the ubiquitous determinism associated with race by shifting the focus onto culture. Even though the new term moves us away from race, its attempt at disassociation cannot fully neutralize the issue. The reference to Africa is indeed to some extent a reminder of it. People's attitudes about race and racial categorization will strongly influence what they think of African Americans.

It is relevant to note that the new social representation emerged from within the black American community. A subgroup calling itself African American defined itself in distinction to Black on the basis of sociodemographic characteristics. According to a study by the Joint Center for Political and Economic Studies (1990), those referring to themselves as African Americans are predominantly young, male, educated, and from the urban centers of the Northeast and Midwest. Those characteristics have become the field of reference for the denomination, thereby providing a first filtering of its interpretation in the minds of individuals.

For other black Americans, this new social object is defined by projections. These projections can only be articulated through the dynamic distinctions between African American and Black. The most striking distinction relates to Black finding its direct opposite in the term White, while African American is defined in terms of a spectrum. Here, the dissonance of this group concerning its existence in the United States finds a novel expression. While its members are still excluded and marginalized from the rest of society, they nevertheless hold on to the American creed (Myrdal, 1944) and regard America as the cradle of liberty. After Congress passed the Ethnic Heritage Studies Program Act in 1974,

Blacks protested, along with other groups, the Anglocentric notion of America as "one people." The endorsement of African American by many leaders of the Black community has endowed the term with qualities that can reinvent a past to serve the future.

Yet it is only in the context of social exchange that African American takes on its full meaning, connecting individual mental processes to the social world. For non-blacks, the crystallization of the new social representation might result in conflicts between a preexisting system of mental categories and fundamental changes that have taken place in American society. The preexisting system consists, among other things, of deeply rooted feelings about Blacks as well as various beliefs and ideologies on race. These mental categories have been shaped over a long period of time and are therefore quite solidified. They may not adjust easily to changing values and conventions which create a new social reality. Hence it may be difficult for many non-black Americans to view Blacks as African Americans.

This tension notwithstanding, the adoption of African American does create a new social representation by allowing a sort of opening, termed by Moscovici (1984) a "fissure," through which the object can be redefined—not as a race apart, but as a culturally distinct group sharing values and attributes with the rest of America. Such an opening can only come about by reshaping the internal structure of the preexisting representations of the same object, the central core (Abric, 1984, 1989, 1994). Providing a stable and integrative structure, the central core cannot change unless the social representation changes. This is why the positivation of Black in the 1960s could not succeed. It did not alter the social representation of Black, centered on race. Let us now examine how African American might transform the social representation by removing race from the center of the structural core, creating a "fissure" that lets culture take its place.

THE ANCHORING PROCESS

Studying a social representation in the making offers us an opportunity to analyze the processes underlying the elaboration of a new reality. The introduction of African American in our ordinary language, mediatic communication, or symbolic exchanges makes clear and explicit such an elaboration. Within a decade this term has not only become the most acceptable one for non-blacks to use when referring to Americans of African descent, but it has also become the preferred self-designation for one out of three black Americans.

The social representation of an existing object can only be transformed if that object appears anew. For such a mental shift to occur, the contextual setting of the object has to have undergone some sort of qualitative change which permits a redefinition of the object in question. In the case of African American that change in context came when many Americans seemed ready to accept a group designation that deemphasized race in favor of culture and ethnicity. This created an opening for some black Americans to re-present themselves, and thus be redefined, with attributes establishing both their similarity to other Americans and their cultural distinctiveness. The subgroup calling itself African American was the agent that allowed the new term to become familiar.

Demographic Differentiation

Several surveys of black Americans, summarized in Table A.1 (see Appendix A), have confirmed the emergence and rapid spread of the term African American in the community. During the 1970s and 1980s the name was practically nonexistent. In June 1989, six months after its official introduction, a *New York Times* poll of 165 people showed 9 percent of the sample preferring "African American" over "Black," while 36 percent chose "Black" and 46 percent expressed indifference. Just three months later, in September 1989, a poll by ABC and the *Washington Post* asking 371 subjects the same question already showed 22 percent preferring African American, compared to 66 percent preferring Black and only 9 percent indifferent. A NBC/*Wall Street Journal* poll in July 1990, which gave its sample of 221 people the possibility to chose "some other term," had 25 percent preferring African American, 59 percent still chosing Black, and 8 percent using neither. More than a year later, in September 1991, the *Los Angeles Times* reported a 34 percent preference for African American in its poll, compared to 42 percent for Black and 18 percent preferring neither term. This sequence of surveys clearly illustrates the impressive impact of African American as a social representation in the making. Its rapidly and steadily growing use by black Americans just after its introduction has allowed the new denomination to be anchored on their own terms, based on the interpretations they give it when switching from Black.

A widely published survey (Joint Center for Political and Economic Studies, 1990) confirmed a particularly pronounced bias in favor of the new term among a subgroup which fits the profile of college students in the Northeast. In fact this survey identified sociodemographic characteristics associating the new term with a distinct subgroup. According to this nationwide survey, preferences for the denomination African American, as opposed to Black, seem to vary greatly with geographic location, age, gender, and education (see Table A.2 in Appendix A).

In the Northern part of the country 28 percent of black Americans preferred to be called African American, compared to 15 percent in the South. This geographic variation should be analyzed in light of the mas-

sive migration of black Americans from the South into the urban centers
of the Northeast and Midwest during the first half of this century, motivated by a search for greater economic opportunities in the North and
a belief in a relatively less institutionalized racism there. Concerning age,
28 percent among those 18 to 29 years preferred the new term, compared
to 19 percent for those 30 to 49 years old and 17 percent for those over
50 years. Its popularity among younger black Americans has been confirmed in the aforementioned 1989 ABC/*Washington Post* survey. In other
words, the term African American is most predominant among those
born after the Civil Rights struggles of the 1960s. The Joint Center for
Political and Economic Studies survey showed 28 percent of the men
preferring African American and only 15 percent of the women. This
gender gap may well be indicative of deeper differences in how race
relations have impacted on the two sexes.

Education, however, accounts for the largest difference. Among those
with a college education or beyond 29 percent chose African American,
compared to only 15 percent of those with a high school education or
less. It is no coincidence that education should emerge as the dominant
sociodemographic factor. Education is at the center of the American
ethos and consequently has always been a primary battleground in the
struggle for racial equality, from school desegregation and busing to the
"political correctness" movement. For black Americans reaching the college level (and this is still a small portion of the population), education
has opened access to new career opportunities and the possibility of
successful integration.

To interpret these demographic data is to classify an unfamiliar object.
This involves an ordering process which links the new term to people's
preexisting social categories. To the extent that a necessary degree of
coherence within an individual's mental organization is thereby maintained, the new denomination becomes anchored and familiar. When
African American emerged as a term of self-reference for certain black
Americans and not for others, it became inevitably associated with different social categories that people could already relate to, such as socioeconomic background, educational level, age, or gender.

The survey by the Joint Center for Political and Economic Studies confirmed the predominance of the term African American among younger,
urban black Americans with a college education. In adopting the new
denomination as a vehicle for group positivation, this subgroup seeks to
redefine itself, and in the process breaks down people's perception of
the group as a homogenous one. It is around the specific subgroup calling itself African Americans that the new social representation is anchored.

The conceptualization of the term is then, at least in part, based on the
projection of images resulting from the demographic profile of the sub-

group calling itself African American. It may be symptomatic for our time, when society seems to show extensive interest in this type of information, that demographic data are unambiguously taken as adequate descriptions with which to classify people. Through these data the notion of what constitutes an African American gets constructed in our mind, and its incorporation into preexisting categorizations makes the new term more familiar. This familiarization is propelled by communication, a process which leads to the formation of different attitudes and opinions about African Americans in contradistinction to those held about Blacks.

In Contradistinction to Black

Besides delineating and defining the African Americans, the aforementioned surveys also make clear that most black Americans still see themselves as Blacks; they thus decline to claim African American as an identity for themselves. This rejection is, however, a qualified one. Many Blacks still prefer non-black Americans to use the term African American when referring to them as a group. In this symbolic sense, as the official group designation, the new denomination serves one key purpose, namely to position all black Americans as integrated citizens of America. The denomination grants the group an ancestral cultural system that coexists harmoniously with its American cultural definition, as is the case with any other group of assimilated immigrants.

The duality of wanting to be included in the symbolic group denomination African American, while at the same time considering themselves Blacks, a term that implies separation and exclusion, shows that most black Americans continue to feel marginalized (Bell, 1992). The existence of the two group denominations in juxtaposition to each other is the second point of anchoring which enables this new social object to become part of our everyday thinking.

Even though Black became popularized with the end of segregation, it never changed the social representation of the group as a race apart from the rest of America. The rigidity implied by the dichotomization of society into Black and White Americans has always defined the interactions between these two groups. Their peaceful coexistence was attributed to segregation, which allowed for little contact between them. Yet Blacks in this country have also become Americans, albeit with a dual consciousness that attempts to reconcile their presence in America with their status as an excluded group. Given the continuing and widespread practice of de facto segregation in education, housing, and employment, it is no surprise that so many black Americans remain skeptical about progress toward integration (Bobo, 1987; Lawrence, 1987; Schuman & Hatchett, 1974; Schuman, Steeh, & Bobo, 1985) and consequently have a hard time shaking off their identity as Blacks. As Blacks they still signify deviation from accepted norms, and their representation accentuates a sense of marginalization as the "unmeltable immigrant."

At the same time, the emergence of African American represents a beacon of hope for Blacks, no matter how excluded they still feel from the rest of America. The term signals a break with past patterns inasmuch as it shifts attention away from the physical traits of a racially defined group to the cultural identity and shared experiences of people of African descent in America (Davis, 1991). Its widespread use by the media and in public discourse symbolizes their inclusion in a pluralistic society composed of many different peoples, each with their own institutions and cultural identity. To the extent that Blacks identify with this symbolic use of African American, they inherently project a different future for themselves in which race will have become much less important in America. As Davis (1991) states,

Some who encourage the use of the term "African American" hope its use will reduce the importance of race in American life and even help bring about a color-blind society. . . . Perhaps in time the American pattern of black-white relations will become less polarized, in which case African American would be a suitable designation to accompany that process. (p. 186)

Since African American sets the context for the equality and inclusion of a previously disenfranchised group, it has the prescriptive force to orient discussion towards a representation of that group as part of the ·American culture. This collective anticipation, which black and non-black Americans elaborate together, endows the new denomination with positive qualities. It comes to stand for everything that Black is not, and reflects what all black Americans aspire to be in this society. African American exists as a depository for all projections concerning an inclusive resolution of the racial dilemma which has divided this country for centuries.

THE OBJECTIFICATION PROCESS AND SOCIAL REGULATION

While settling in a structured context of preexisting internal hierarchies and mental categories, a new object must also undergo a sort of domestication (Moscovici, 1984). In this process individuals reproduce in their minds elements of the object in a figurative form, as a nucleus of images, making concrete what otherwise would remain an abstract notion. The images have their roots in previously formed representations and are shared by members of the community; thus they have a social character. Their elaboration provides the social context within which the attitudes and opinions of individuals are formed. That context is a normative one, and as such contains both explicit and implicit rules which govern the use of African American in public discourse. This process of objectification is central to the transformation of an "innocent" and unfamiliar label into a social representation. As a result, the term becomes part of a shared reality, so familiar and obvious that its nonexistence would be inconceivable.

As the unfamiliar object is evaluated and interpreted through preexisting systems of social representations, it turns into a new social representation that is assimilated by members of a community as an inextricable part of their social reality. This assimilation is never just a private exercise in the minds of individuals, but is imposed and reproduced by group pressure. Such social influence often takes the form of rules to guide communication and orient behavior. These rules may be implicit, as is the case when politicians and journalists decide to use African American in public discourse, or they may be explicit, as manifest in the propagation of the term as the only "politically correct" one for the group. In any case, the rules serve to create a normative context in which meanings are elaborated and validated.

For African American to become concrete and find its figurative form readily, some social structures are required to organize and regulate its usage in society (Doise, Clemence, & Lorenzi-Cioldi, 1993). The rules governing its use range from the fact of Civil Rights leaders formally adopting the term, and the emergence of a subgroup calling itself African American, to public opinion makers endorsing it as the socially accepted denomination for the entire group. All these rules facilitate mental accommodation to the term, by helping to turn it into an unquestionable reality with a crystallized social representation and by directing the images being formed in that normative context. The socially conditioned nature of the figurative nucleus resulting from objectification provides an institutional validation for what we think, and situates our thoughts in a consensual world.

The social regulation of the new term in intergroup exchange may engender in individuals a dichotomy between their private and public spheres. Individuals may use African American in conversation and charge that term with positive images, while maintaining in their own minds negative images of the group as a whole. In the absence of social constraints—that is, in private and semi-private settings—they may use any term and associate it with any images they please. Suppressing race in people's minds requires a lot of effort. Yet no matter what people think, they face an inescapable normative context, fuelled with presuppositions orienting thoughts and action. Private sentiments can never be completely insulated from the consensual world we share.

Objectification, as concisely defined by Jodelet (1993), structures the representation as a cognitive whole that maintains elements of the external world interconnected for the organization of the field of representation. The formation of such a structure, responsible for the creation of a figurative nucleus and the elaboration of social rules, is gradual. It takes a while to reach the point that the central core of an emerging representation gains a certain stability. This is especially so in the case of African American, which has to find its independence in contradistinction to an already made and well-established representation, that of Black. The objectification of the new term can only be completed when culture has effectively supplanted race at its central core. The new denomination has not yet reached this point. The formation of African American into a social representation is still in the middle of a gradual evolution. Once the new term is turned into something sufficiently familiar by virtue of anchoring mechanisms, its interpretations will eventually develop a stable figurative form, reintegrating the notion by means of images. This active process transforms the abstract concept into a concrete reality.

For African American to become as tangible as any other reality, it will have to secede from Black. Even though its objectification is incomplete, the term has already infiltrated our conversation and become part of our ordinary language. People do not yet perceive this new object figuratively, but they are nevertheless compelled to talk about it. During such exchanges we project positive images of this object. This projection and communication of images gradually forms and structures a figurative core. At this point the materialization of African American as a cultural production is confined to mostly symbolic expressions, referring to the entire group as an integral part of America.

Because African American is not yet fully objectified, it lacks the iconic qualities that give a social representation the normative force to shape individual minds. In the absence of such reification, the representation is still being made. What holds the representation, its anchoring, are presuppositions about the inclusion of the group in a multicultural America, presuppositions the term African American itself symbolizes. These presuppositions are collectively elaborated in the same direction, since everyone (i.e., African Americans, Blacks, and non-black Americans) has a vested interest in their successful propagation. All three groups project similar images of *what should be* and constantly validate them through public exchange. At this point thoughts get crystallized in a semi-real space, with the media and other opinion makers playing a crucial role.

In the case of an anticipatory social representation, one in which the underlying presuppositions crystallize around socially elaborated projections of an imagined future, the process of its making requires its constant elaboration. Such anticipatory representations do not naturally become part of our daily reality, because they are future-oriented *Vor-*

stellungen and in that capacity they have to transform the present rather than be a settled part of it. Driving collective thought towards a different, pluralistic, and democratic future for America, the presuppositions of such an anticipatory representation do not have to be real in the sense of being reified around a figurative core. They can to a certain degree remain abstractions, and in this way stay alive through a symbolic existence, allowing the object to be sufficiently represented in the minds of people for them to talk about it in a consensual manner.

In the case of African American this symbolic existence is propelled by the media, whose use of the term gives rise to quickly disseminated images which standardize its assimilation. This artificial image creation and symbolic existence is real in the limited sense that it redefines the object (black Americans) anew in a normatively prescribed public sphere. It is based on an implicit social consensus to replace race with culture, creating a sort of "virtual space" of projected inclusion and equality as an opening for change. Each group involved in its propagation has a vested interest in furthering this consensual vision of a multicultural America, be it to reconcile an otherwise conflictual dual consciousness, as a beacon of hope for a better future, or to relieve guilt and put a difficult past aside. This redefinition of the object in the public sphere applies to the group as a whole and is expressed in symbolic fashion through language—that is, by changing the official designation of the group and then building a normative context around the new term in public discourse.

At the same time individual members of the group may still be regarded as Blacks, as the entire group may be when thought about privately or talked about in semi-private settings. Hence African American is only semi-real, allowing one and the same object to be seen in diametrically opposed ways, depending on the context. Not fully objectified, African American is at best capable of suppressing race rather than pushing it out of the central core. In this semi-real, mostly symbolic existence African American needs to be constantly elaborated and its normative context continuously renewed. The public nature of these exchanges allows for the naturalization (Moscovici, 1981) of the term, and indeed this naturalization is a prerequisite for its eventual objectification. Here, in the case of an anticipatory representation which is not yet fully objectified, the naturalization process is separate from objectification, and is necessary to keep the emerging representation alive until it settles with a stable central core.

THE NATURALIZATION PROCESS

By giving an unfamiliar object a name and filling its figurative core with socially validated positive projections, the thoughts associated with

African American can, even without concrete images, be turned into presumed facts. For that to happen the name must be constantly communicated. Communication links the cognitive activities of individuals to their social conditions of expression. People talk about the new object and thereby give it specific meanings. As it is elaborated in social exchanges, the object becomes concretized in individual minds. The unbreakable link thus established between social context and cognitive phenomena allows the unfamiliar object to be integrated into our daily lives, and normalizes its existence as if it had always been present in our minds. It is during this phase of naturalization that the new social representation is turned into a reality capable of orienting thoughts and behavior; here the media as well as other public opinion makers take on a key role in directing attitudes, shaping opinions, and constructing stereotypes about the social object in question.

Social representation theory treats naturalization as part of the objectification process (Moscovici, 1976a, 1981). After all, an object has to have a figurative nucleus in order to be concrete enough for people to talk about it. In the case of African American, however, we face an exceptional situation where the naturalization is a separate process on its own. In essence just a name around which projections of a different future get crystallized, African American exists only as something that we imagine. When we use this term, we envision a re-presentation of black Americans as a culturally defined subgroup in a color-blind America.

Rooted in the world of anticipations, the term lacks a clearly identifiable, already existing object to which it can be attached, and which could provide it with the ready-made material for a figurative nucleus. The making of the term, an anticipatory representation, creates the object. Therefore the term, in order to crystallize into an object with a figurative nucleus, has to become part of our ordinary language. In other words, it has to be naturalized before it can be fully objectified.

Communication

In the case of African American, naturalization is a compensatory procedure that sustains the existence of a new representation, in its anticipatory forms, until the representation is fully established with a stable central core. That process is driven by how we communicate the term to each other. Communication helps create social representations by organizing the exchanges through which ideas take shape and acquire their significance. Under the influence of the media, in the course of daily conversations, or by means of other forms of communication we elaborate social representations. The cognitive content of our individual mental activities is shared with others, and these exchanges in turn impact greatly on our preexisting representations. That is to say, the communication process allows the emergence of social representations and is subsequently shaped by those. This is the essence of what transforms individual lives into a social experience.

Whether interindividual, institutional, or mediatic, communication is fundamental to the circulation of thoughts and the formation of social representations (Jodelet, 1989). To begin with, it enables individuals to collect information, which they use to construct their reality. The circulation of information allows a new object, such as a change in the denomination of a group, to emerge in the public eye as a social representation. Such information can come from diverse sources, and carries with it attitudes, opinions, and judgments about the defined object. Individuals process these attitudes, opinions, and judgments by communicating with each other. The amalgam of information pertaining to a particular object, and its circulation in exchanges between individuals, form common points of reference about that object. Individuals thereby create the consensual world that allows them to share images and ideas about their common reality. This interactive process may appear as a self-enclosed loop. Yet its motion is really more like a spiral, since the exchange between individuals expands ideas and transforms shared images about a particular social object.

Modulation of Images

To see how communication helps create a social representation of African American, three sources need to be examined: the group calling itself African American in contradistinction to Black, the rules and restrictions established around the usage of the denomination, and the ways the media and other opinion makers have accelerated the transformation of images associated with the new term into reality. These three channels of communication allow us to understand how the new denomination, only very recently introduced in ordinary language, has acquired meaning for a large portion of Americans so rapidly. Each one has provided information that has made individuals and groups think about the new denomination and communicate its representation.

The term African American may well be indicative of an emerging middle class among black Americans, thus expressing in its juxtaposition to Black a growing class differentiation within that community (Jaynes & Williams, 1989). The survey by the Joint Center for Political and Economic Studies (1990) has clearly identified a more pronounced preference for the new term among predominantly young, college-educated, and male group members residing in the urban centers of the Northeast and Midwest. The new term, with all of its multifaceted qualities, appears therefore to delineate class distinctions within the black American community and, once crystallized into a social representation, serves to accentuate the heterogeneity of the group.

Those calling themselves African American are important agents in the elaboration of images associated with the new term. The information they circulate about that term is closely tied to some of their specific characteristics. Qualities usually associated with that demographic profile, such as professional aspirations (Bradford, 1987), social mobility, and political engagement (Gurin, Hatchett, & Jackson, 1988), are accentuated or referred to during communication. In picking this name for themselves, African Americans have done two things. They have delineated, with their own specific characteristics, the process by which the new and unfamiliar term is anchored. And they have also directed its use in social exchange towards a more positive image of the group. It is no coincidence that the spread of the term has coincided with a dramatic expansion of the public space granted to members of that subgroup, whether in literature, art, academic curricula, politics, sports, the music scene, the world of fashion, television shows, or Hollywood.

The group presents itself in many ways as Afrocentric, although its imagery of Africa is often more dedicated to the revival of a glorious past than reflective of contemporary conditions. One can see symbolic expressions of this highly developed ethnic consciousness in heated debates over multicultural school curricula, the language of rap music, and the wearing of African cloth, hairstyles, or various insignia. While these expressions are rooted in ancient non-Western civilization, they are being reclaimed today as cultural specificities for a distinct group (Sanders Thompson, 1992, 1995). Yet at the same time we see the group presenting itself as an integral part of American society (Bradford, 1987; Hecht & Ribeau, 1991). This image is built on recognition of commonly shared values and ideals which are seen by everyone as quintessentially American, such as hard work, individualism, faith, or the search for well-being (Torrance, 1990).

The dual consciousness we observe here, one part African and one part American, has always defined the black American community (Baldwin, 1963; Du Bois, 1903). On the one hand, the group has fostered a vision of solidarity with all people of African descent, motivated by a commonly shared history of oppression. On the other hand, the group has been formed by American culture and has committed itself to a common destiny with the rest of this society. That duality developed into a dichotomy during the Civil Rights struggles of the 1960s, when Martin Luther King's "dream" of assimilation and Malcolm X's separatism presented themselves as two alternative roads to self-empowerment. The generations born out of that bipolar movement, today's African Americans, produce images of themselves that integrate both positions.

The name African American is an appropriately symbolic expression of such reintegration. Moreover, since other groups link their place of origin to "American" (as with the terms Irish American, Italian American, etc.), the choice of "African American" is consistent with the designations of everyone else (Banton, 1988; Walzer, 1990). The only difference is that Africa is not a country, reminding us that Americans of African descent were once slaves and therefore do not know where exactly they came from.

The second vector of communication propagating the images of African American is articulated in the rapport non-black Americans have with the new denomination. Within a very short period of time the term has become widely used in public discourse, and its rapid integration into ordinary language has allowed for a new social representation to crystallize. The use of African American has today become the most acceptable way to address or discuss members of the group in public exchanges. The social content of its use tends to be one of integration and equality. Accepting and conforming to these conversational norms shapes a view of African American that is embedded in the positive image implied by its creation (Davis, 1991; Oyserman & Markus, 1995).

When the term African American is used in conversation, its normative context orients the communication towards projections that are built around a common belief in the American Dream. Motivated by an optimistic view of integration, the images created in the process are polarized in a positive direction. This polarization is the result of a conflict between two sets of images targeted at the same object. The new representation may very well contradict previously held, and lingering, images of the group. Here we need to distinguish between images of the group in general and those specifically associated with the term African American. Since the images evoked by African American tend to be positive a priori, and the imposition of a rule for its usage affirms the collective consensus about this, the positive nature of those images may be reinforced in the course of an interaction.

The construction of social consensus and the transformation of representations it produces depend heavily on professional agents of communication, whose strategic position as public opinion makers allows them to define the main issues of our time. Today these agents are the mass media, in particular the producers of news, and politicians, supported by a large staff of pollsters, media analysts, and researchers. Both impact greatly on the construction of our consensual world. In this context it is worth noting that the new term African American made tremendous gains in the mass media in a very short period of time. A Computerized DataTimes search cited in Smith (1992) showed that in the second half of 1988, when the term was first considered among leaders of the black American community as a possible alternative to Black, it appeared in 24 articles of the *Washington Post* and 11 articles of the *Los*

Angeles Times. Over the following six months, right after its official introduction, those occurrences increased to 120 and 106 respectively. For the first half of 1991 the search found 288 *Post* articles and 612 *Times* articles mentioning African American.

As social instruments of communication, addressing large and anonymous audiences, both the mass media and politicians tend to standardize messages and homogenize the attitudes and opinions of an otherwise heterogenous population. They do this by endowing objects with an imagery that makes those attitudes and opinions real to the audience and accelerates their integration into everyday life. This capacity to project images leaves public opinion makers in a position to shape cognitive processes in individuals, their interaction in subgroups, and the social and cultural systems structuring our society.

By adopting the new denomination of the group and associating it with positive images (witness, for example, the Clarence Thomas confirmation hearings), both the media and the politicians have normalized the views held about African Americans. Their prototypical representation of that group is clearly much closer to the mainstream of America than is the representation of those shown and referred to as Blacks. The images associated with African American, reinforced by the term's nearly exclusive use in the ideological context of a multicultural society, accentuate common interests and shared values. Public opinion makers have the greatest impact when the new object is filtered in the minds of individuals through preexisting mental categories. Both the media and politicians intervene directly in the formation of attitudes and opinions about the object by providing a prepackaged figurative core for its assimilation in a virtual space that they themselves provide. In this way they have both played a crucial role in the remarkably rapid propagation and diffusion of African Americans as a new social representation for a group previously referred to as Blacks.

Chapter 5

Contextualizing the Study

What does it mean for this society, at the present moment of its evolution, to have created the notion and identity of African American in a polemical relationship to Black? The object of our investigation is the impact of a new group designation on the American culture. Unlike labels, the new name involves a collective effort to turn its object into a meaningful social creation, in other words to make it a reality. Empirical analyses have to aim at drawing out precisely this process of creation, whereby a name becomes a social representation of an object. Thus I will start with an onomastic approach (Dauzat, 1956), elucidating what the name African American has come to mean in relation to other names used to identify Americans of African descent and how this new social representation anchors itself in the culture. I shall then explore how ideas and attitudes generally associated with black Americans shift with the choice of the new name.

Since the focus of this study is on a cultural phenomenon evolving in front of our eyes, a large portion of my empirical material will try to capture the fluid and dynamic nature by which the phenomenon of African American is expressed in real-life events. Therefore, flexibility must be a primary requirement of the research design, which calls for a broadly conceived and multidimensional approach to the phenomenon. With this in mind, the study presented here tries to gain some familiarity with the name African American as an ongoing event that has become part of our daily reality in such a short period of time. I will sketch out the characteristics of an anticipatory representation by showing the extent to which the new name has impacted on the ways in which black as well as non-black Americans perceive and evaluate our social object, black Americans.

MEDIA ITEMS, PERSONAL DOCUMENTS, AND QUESTIONNAIRES

A good way to begin the interpretation of our phenomenon is to focus on a broad collection of documents that were not created for the purpose of the study. These materials include modern artifacts, newspaper articles, magazines, advertising, and literary productions. Some more personal documentation, in the form of 16 term papers written by students of Hofstra University on the difference between African American and Black, was also used and subjected to a content analysis (Bardin, 1989).

Such archival research has several advantages. First, these types of materials provide a rich source of data with which to look at the cultural change resulting from the switch in name. They make it possible to localize our phenomenon in the culture. When we think that prior to 1989 the name African American was not used, its presence in such a wide range of social productions today validates the existence of our phenomenon. A second advantage of the archival method is the unobtrusive nature of such materials, which alleviates the biases of demand characteristics as well as those of evaluative apprehensions often associated with a researcher's design of questionnaires (Rosenthal, 1985, 1991).

The other way in which data was collected for our empirical analysis is through questionnaires (see Appendices B and C). One set of questionnaires looks at the representational field concerning black Americans and maps a structure by which black Americans are evaluated. Most of the items on these questionnaires are directly taken from previous research. Such a meta-analytical approach allows me to match social psychological points of inquiry, already established in previous research on race and black Americans, with my theoretical framework applied to the phenomenon of African American. This has the advantage of putting my study into a temporal context in relation to other research on those subjects. A second set of questionnaires focuses on the study of names pertaining to Americans of African descent. These questionnaires show that names do matter when they are turned into social representations. They enable us to look at the instrumental as well as the evaluative dimensions of the new representation (Moliner, 1995).

After analyzing the results from each set of questionnaires separately (in Chapters 6 and 7 respectively), we go one step further and combine these two scales of measurement. The combination yields qualitatively different results, a synthesis which makes it possible to demonstrate how the choice of a new name impacts on our way of thinking about the object. The two scales of measurement combined here (in Chapter 8) are in fact interdependent, and were jointly designed to show that names, far from being used arbitrarily, represent reality as well as make it.

SAMPLE DESCRIPTION

The nature of the phenomenon would have called for a large sampling representative of the diversity in the American population and reflective of divergencies in regional trends, especially the North-South dimension. But because of time constraints and obvious limits in accessing such a broad population, the sample used here had to be more narrow. It derived from selected New York City–area educational settings (i.e., Berkeley Institute, the College of New Rochelle [Rosa Parks Campus], Hofstra University, Hunter College, the New School for Social Research, Pace University, and Queens College) which differ vastly in terms of the demographic characteristics of their students. The use of college students is justified, not least because it is precisely within this population that one is most likely to find those black Americans identifying themselves as African Americans. They are the subgroup most likely to have the opportunities for interaction with other subgroups of Americans. And this young population will also carry the use of the new denomination into the future.

Five hundred and four subjects participated in the study. This sample was subsequently stratified on the basis of a single criterion, namely race (e.g., black Americans and non-black Americans). However, participants were still asked to report their gender, age, income, educational level, political ideology, party affiliation (whether or not they are registered voters), and their overall living condition. While these demographic factors are not systematically analyzed in our investigation, they provide an overall description of the sample which could be useful in the interpretation of the data.

Tables 5.1 to 5.7 show the distributions of these sociodemographic characteristics. Gender was coded as female or male. Age was coded into four categories: between 18 and 29 years old, between 30 and 44 years old, between 45 and 59 years old, and 60 years or older. Living condition was coded as better today than four years ago, worse today than four years ago, or the same today as four years ago. Income was coded into five categories: $15,000 or less; between $15,000 and $30,000; between $30,000 and $50,000; between $50,000 and $75,000; and $75,000 or more. The voting status of our subjects was coded as registered voter or unregistered. Political ideology was coded as liberal, conservative, or moderate. Finally, political party was coded as Democrat, Republican, or Independent.

As reported in Table 5.1, over half of the black American subjects were female (59.4 percent) and less than a third were male (31.9 percent), with

Table 5.1
Gender Distribution of Sample by Race

	Race	
Gender	**Black**	**Non-black**
Female	59.4%	67.8%
Male	31.9%	26.6%

Table 5.2
Age Distribution of Sample by Race

	Race	
Age	**Black**	**Non-black**
18–29 years	59.4%	70.6%
30–44 years	24.6%	21.0%
45–59 years	5.8%	1.4%
60 years +	0.7%	0.7%

the remaining 10 percent unidentified. In the non-black American sample more than two-thirds were female (67.8 percent) while roughly a quarter were male (26.6 percent). It is worth noting that recent demographic shifts in the college population of the United States have resulted in more women attending college than men. Our sample, however, over-represents this trend.

The distribution by age in our samples (see Table 5.2) matches quite closely the typical college-student profile in this country, with black subjects on average somewhat older than the non-black sample.

Table 5.3 shows that the two samples tended to evaluate their individual overall living conditions in fairly similar fashion. In both samples slightly more than half of the subjects seemed to believe that their lives have improved from four years ago. About a quarter of the non-black subjects considered their living condition today to be pretty much the same as four years ago, with only one in five black subjects expressing that sentiment. Relatively few subjects in both samples thought their living condition was getting worse.

When I compared annual income for both samples (see Table 5.4), I found that there were more black subjects than non-black subjects with annual income below $50,000, and, conversely, more non-black subjects

Table 5.3
Living Conditions Distribution of Sample by Race

	Race	
Living Conditions	Black	Non-black
Better	55.8%	53.8%
Worse	15.9%	14.7%
Same	19.6%	24.5%

Table 5.4
Annual Income Distribution of Sample by Race

	Race	
Annual Income	Black	Non-black
< $15,000	13.8%	17.5%
$15,000–$30,000	27.5%	21.0%
$30,000–$50,000	24.6%	19.6%
$50,000–$75,000	15.9%	18.2%
> $75,000	2.9%	14.7%

than black subjects with an annual income above $50,000. However, there was a larger share of non-black subjects in the lowest income category than black subjects.

Tables 5.5 to 5.7 measure the political dimensions of our respondents. These tables illustrate the distributions of the subjects' voting status, their political ideology, and their political party affiliation. Our black sample was very similar to our non-black sample concerning voting status, with over two-thirds of the subjects in both samples claiming to be registered voters. More non-black subjects than black subjects seemed to adhere to the liberal ideology. However, black subjects seemed at the same time more inclined towards the Democrats than the non-black sample, a greater proportion of which sympathized with the Republicans.

The demographic information presented above shows us that our two samples are fairly similar, with an overrepresentation of 18- to 29-year-old females. While majorities of both groups of subjects were registered voters, our black subjects were likelier to be Democrats than were the non-black subjects.

Table 5.5
Voting Status Distribution of Sample by Race

	Race	
Registered Voters	**Black**	**Non-black**
Yes	66.7%	69.2%
No	23.9%	25.2%

Table 5.6
Political Ideology Distribution of Sample by Race

	Race	
Political Ideology	**Black**	**Non-black**
Liberal	23.9%	37.1%
Conservative	16.7%	13.3%
Moderate	21.0%	25.2%

Table 5.7
Political Party Distribution of Sample by Race

	Race	
Political Party	**Black**	**Non-black**
Democrat	55.8%	38.5%
Republican	4.3%	18.2%
Independent	9.4%	11.9%

FORMULATING HYPOTHESES

Before presenting our specific hypotheses concerning the differences between the social representations of African American and Black for both of our samples, let us first recall some key characteristics of this phenomenon for the American culture. The new name, which emerged less than a decade ago, has spread rapidly. Its use in the various contexts composing our public sphere has accelerated its diffusion and facilitated its anchoring. As a new social representation the denomination African

American reconceptualizes the object as something new. This phenomenon results from a cultural fissure that has allowed more permeability between groups by shifting the focus away from race onto a more cultural dimension.

Name Preference Questionnaires

Our study of names is based on a nominal scale and will be analyzed in terms of percentages. This particular measurement is consistent with our exploratory approach to the phenomenon and facilitates the understanding of African American in relation to Black and all other names previously used to refer to the object. It is obvious that some fundamental differences can be expected between our two samples.

Let us first consider the black American sample (see Tables B.3 and B.4 in Appendix B). We expect the percentage of subjects who use African American in reference to their own group to be higher than the one in four black Americans reported eight years ago in the aforementioned study by the Joint Center for Economic and Political Research (1990). Despite the progressive spread of African American, the term Black should still be the most widely used. In terms of preference the situation may already be reversed, with the gap between the two terms being much narrower than the gap in their actual use. Since the new term reflects an effort initiated by the group, we expect a larger percentage of people to prefer the term than to actually use it.

Our theoretical analysis of the term African American emphasized its role as a more positive representation of the group than Black, and for this reason we expect more subjects to view the new term as the most positive one for the group than to have this perception in the case of Black. This should be especially true when projected onto the outgroup, with the black subjects assessing the term African American as even more positive when used by non-black Americans than by themselves. Given the anticipatory nature of African American, we should see a similar distribution of name preferences concerning the term likely to be used most in the future. Moreover, the propagation of the new term by public opinion makers should result in subjects projecting African American to be the term used most in the future by the press, television, and political leaders.

In terms of negative evaluations of the names used for Americans of African descent, we have reason to expect two different juxtapositions. Those in our sample preferring Black should be most opposed to Negro, the term which it replaced during the 1960s as part of a broader social movement. On the other hand, those preferring African American might well be most negatively inclined toward the term "People of Color." The latter has in recent years emerged as an alternative designation for the growing non-white segment of an increasingly diverse population, which is no longer numerically dominated by those of European origin. While the term includes other groups, such as Latinos/Latinas, it competes directly with African American in its application to black Americans. Moreover, "People of Color" implies a polarizing distinction between white Americans and all non-white Americans, which the term African American seeks to overcome.

Turning now to our non-black subjects (see Tables C.2 and C.3 in Appendix C), Black should still be the most widely used term in that sample—by an even wider margin than in the first sample. Moving from use to preference, the gap between Black and African American should become considerably smaller. However, just as in the sample of black subjects, we foresee considerable agreement with African American as the most positive term. This assumption derives from our contention of a widespread consensus that the new designation projects the most positive images of the group. Similarly, we expect our non-black subjects to pick African American more often than any other denomination as the term of the future. Once again we should find a strong propensity to choose African American as the term to be used most widely by the press, television, and political leaders in the future.

Reflective of our central hypothesis that names do in fact matter, we also expect our non-black subjects to be impacted by the name they use for their own groups. As carriers of collectively elaborated meaning, the names White, American, Caucasian, or a national designation juxtaposed to American (e.g., German American, Korean American) are expected to influence the choice of name for Americans of African ancestry. More specifically, those calling themselves White or Caucasian may still be wedded to a racial view of the world and can therefore be expected to use and prefer Black. Conversely, those calling themselves American or using their national origin in conjunction with American (e.g., Italian American) stress culture and are therefore more likely to use and prefer African American when referring to Americans of African descent.

Evaluative Questionnaires

The questionnaires used here to evaluate social attitudes toward Americans of African descent are summated scales of the Likert type (see Tables B.1 and B.2 in Appendix B as well as Table C.1 in Appendix C). Items relevant to the social representation of the group were responded to via descriptors ranging from "strongly agree" to "strongly disagree." One of the advantages of such a scale is that it permits the expression of several degrees of agreement/disagreement. This questionnaire was designed based on a review of prior studies of attitudes toward black Americans in America (Campbell, 1971; Cross, 1980; Fairchild, 1985; Gordon, 1976; Hecht & Ribeau, 1987; Helms, 1990; Jackson & Gurin, 1987; Jaynes & Williams, 1989; Katz & Braly, 1933; Pettigrew & Meertens, 1995; Schuman & Hatchett, 1974). Items were classified into four categories: perception of racial discrimination, destiny of black Americans in America, separation of black Americans from America, and stereotypical images (both positive and negative) of black Americans. The item responses were then factor analyzed.

Since we believe that individuals' social attitudes are not formed in isolation but in relation to the opinions of others, each item was evaluated on three levels (i.e., the respondent's own opinion, mainstream opinion, and black Americans' opinion). In this regard we expect a fairly strong polarization effect in both samples, with respondents projecting more extreme attitudes onto their own group rather than presenting such opinions as their own. Non-black subjects should project onto mainstream attitudes, while black subjects can be expected to project onto the opinions of black Americans.

One of our key hypotheses in this study is the assumption that our two groups have a common ground, based on their shared space, language, and time. Therefore we expect to find scales of similar content and structure in the groups' respective opinions. This common ground should also be manifest in the projections of subjects onto either their own group or the other group. The nature of the common ground must reflect both the racially divided past and the hope for integration in the future, two forces struggling to shape the present. In connection with this fundamental dissonance experienced by black and non-black Americans alike, we should find a general sense of dual consciousness in the opinions of black subjects and a tendency towards the dissonance of Myrdal's Dilemma in our non-black sample.

For the black sample, the responses to the various items investigated can be expected to show greater divergence in terms of agreement or disagreement between their own opinion and what they project onto the mainstream than between their own opinion and what they project onto black Americans as a group. The black sample might think of the mainstream as having more negative opinions about black Americans than they project black Americans to have. However, at the same time, they are also more inclined to project the mainstream as evaluating more positively the state of race relations in America. In a similar vein, their projections onto black Americans will reflect a more negative appraisal of racial dynamic in this country, yet emphasize the positive qualities and self-sufficiency of black Americans.

Conversely, for the non-black sample the correspondence is in the other direction. These subjects are expected to show greater divergence between their own opinion and what they project onto black Americans than between their opinion and what they project onto the mainstream.

They can be assumed to project more negative evaluations of black Americans onto the mainstream than onto black Americans themselves. At the same time non-black respondents might very well project onto the mainstream the most positive attitudes towards the contemporary state of race relations in America, while attributing to black Americans greater dissatisfaction and disillusionment.

The Impact of Names on Group Evaluations

In the final part of our study we apply the choice of names to the evaluation of black Americans, identifying and analyzing any significant differences in attitudes about black American between those choosing African American and those opting for Black. For that purpose I decided to conduct an analysis of variance to understand how variations in the evaluation of black Americans result from the differences between the two social representations. In an effort to capture the distinction between African American and Black even more fully, the names used in the questionnaires to refer to black Americans become an additional independent variable, controlling for a context effect.

In this part of the research we expect black subjects to be less influenced in their evaluation of the object by the name they use to refer to their own group. However, the impact of the name is expected to change as we move into the realm of the anticipatory dimension of the new representation. For both samples we should find more significantly different responses to the evaluative scales when looking at the name that ought to be used rather than the name actually used. Furthermore, the choice of the most positive term and the choice of the term anticipated to be most used in the future are also expected to yield a large number of significant differences in the evaluation of our social object.

Chapter 6

What's in a Name?

In the linguistic construction of our culture, the act of naming is the starting point for the materialization and the articulation of our shared reality. In naming something we make it possible for that object to be represented and thus converted into communicable images (Moscovici, 1981). In the case of names that are made up, it is through consensus that association between the word and the social object becomes common. By giving the object in question a name, we first create a reference and endow it with significance, allowing the object in question to be described, characterized, and differentiated from other objects. Furthermore, the use of the name conventionalizes the object and in this way provides us with a structuring metasystem for interactions, so that the object may be anchored.

To the extent that names structure our reality and make it communicable, changing the name of an object marks the beginning of re-creating that reality. As with any other name substitution, changing one's group designation for another indicates significant changes in the social condition of the group, crystallized by the switch in name. These transformations, real or imagined, impact not only on the group claiming the new name, but also on the other social actors interacting with them. In fact, the underlying purpose of renaming a group is to change perceptions, cognitions, attitudes, and opinions about it by transforming its social representation.

Thus the names we choose for different groups are not innocent labels, but have deeper meanings and implications for those communicating them. With individuals claiming them as identities and others orienting their perceptions and attitudes accordingly, these group denominations are in effect social representations.

What's in a name, then? Everything, as we acknowledge that names are not merely words but concepts which suggest implications, values, history and consequences beyond the word or "mere" name itself. Words fit into a total symbolic and cultural system and can only be decoded within the context of that system. (Smitherman, 1977)

Indeed, the etymology of these denominations offers interesting and valuable insights for social psychological inquiries. Onomastic as well as anthroponymistic studies have recurrently sought to illustrate the richness of the information contained in names. For Dauzat (1956), a key proponent of the scientific study of names, it is only in relation to their particular history, within a specific culture, and in the various struggles over their transformations that names can be recognized as an important link between our psychological world and our social life. To the extent that their interpretation goes beyond quantifiable measurement, names can be integrated within our commonsense understanding of the world and understood as relevant for social psychology.

THE SIGNIFICANCE OF NAMES

The relevance of names and of the naming process remains a contentious issue in the social sciences. Some have asserted that names do not matter (Deloria, 1981; Du Bois, [1928] 1970; Gardiner, 1954; Rowan, 1989), following in the tradition of John Stuart Mill (1879), who claimed that names per se are "meaningless." As Du Bois noted already in 1928, in his much-discussed response to Roland Barton (who wrote a brief letter expressing his support of efforts within the black American community aimed at eradicating the term Negro):

Suppose now we could change name. Suppose we arose tomorrow morning and lo! instead of being "Negroes," all the world called us "Cheiropolidi"—Do you really think this would make a vast and momentous difference to you and to me? Would the Negro problem be suddenly and eternally settled? Would you be any less ashamed of being descended from a black man, or would your schoolmates feel any less superior to you? The feeling of inferiority is in you, not in any name. The name merely evokes what is already there . . . a Negro by any other name will be just as black and just as white; just as ashamed of himself and just as shamed by others, as today. It is not the name—it's the Thing that counts. (qtd in Bennett, 1970, pp. 379–380)

While one may reasonably assert, as Du Bois did, that names per se are objectively inconsequential in the sense that they do not themselves change the things they represent, they nonetheless become fueled with significance when used in the elaboration of our social reality. In fact, some social scientists have recognized that names do have symbolic and even direct consequences (Allen, 1990; Cross, 1980; Fairchild, 1985; Hecht & Ribeau, 1987; Jarrett, 1988; Jennings, 1965; Miller, 1937; Simpson & Yinger, 1972; Smith, 1992). According to Banton (1988), "to claim a new name could signify a recognition that the old identity was demeaned, a rejection of that identity, and the assumption of a new one" (p. 85).

Banton's argument is correct inasmuch as the denominations chosen symbolize how groups define themselves and/or are perceived by others. But what he and other social scientists have failed to capture fully is the central role of names in the collective elaboration of a commonly shared reality. Instead researchers too often take the elaboration of meaning as a given. In this positivistic conception the object in question is a priori nameable, because it is assumed to have underlying preconceived properties which can be categorized, represented, and communicated through an appropriate name. From this angle it is easy to see how and why we give specific names to certain things, but much more difficult to understand that society thinks beyond individual minds, and in the process certainly creates things for names.

While social scientists have had a hard time exploring the strategic significance of names, Chomsky (1975, p. 46) has given us some important insights concerning the complexity of names and naming. To begin with, a thing must meet certain conditions to be nameable. These in turn determine what the name does in the minds of individuals, and shape how its meaning is communicated. Chomsky elaborates:

Consider, for example, the category of names and the act of naming, which might be regarded as somehow primitive and isolable. A name, let us suppose, is associated with a thing by an original stipulation, and the association is then conveyed in some manner to others. Consider the original stipulation. The name is drawn from the system of language, and the thing is chosen in terms of the categories of "common-sense understanding." Thus two major faculties of mind, at least, place conditions on the stipulation. There are complex conditions—poorly understood, though illustrative examples are not hard to find—that an entity must satisfy to qualify as a "naturally nameable" thing: these conditions involve spatiotemporal contiguity, *Gestalt* qualities, functions within the space of human actions. . . . A collection of leaves on a tree, for example, is not a nameable thing, but it would fall within this category if a new art form of "leaf arrangement" were devised and some artist had composed the collection of leaves as a work of art. He could then stipulate that his creation was to be named "serenity." Thus it seems that there is an essential reference even to willful acts, in determining what is a nameable thing. (Chomsky, 1975, p. 44)

This quote points to a dialectical relation between things and the names we choose for them, captured in Chomsky's notion of "original stipulation." A thing might not be nameable a prior. It will only be capable of association with a name if it corresponds to our categories of "common-sense understanding." These, as illustrated in the example of the leaf arrangement, may involve "willful acts" of human creation, which the act of choosing a name completes. In other words, things might have to be created for a name, just as a name defines a thing. Once a thing has been determined as nameable, the name chosen for it assigns that thing to a defining structure of functions and properties, which our commonly shared factual beliefs (what Chomsky termed "common-sense expectations") automatically assume to exist whenever the name is used. The stipulation that a thing be given a specific name thus carries with it certain commonly shared presumptions about concepts and categories. Hence, the naming of a thing is neither a simple nor an arbitrary exercise, but one that requires a complex process of structuring and elaboration. As Chomsky noted,

Names are not associated with objects in some arbitrary manner. . . . Each name belongs to a linguistic category that enters in a determinate way into the system of grammar, and the objects named are placed in a cognitive structure of some complexity. These structures remain operative as names are "transferred" to new users. Noting that an entity is named such-and-such, the hearer brings to bear a system of linguistic structure to place the name, and a system of conceptual relations and conditions, along with factual beliefs, to place the thing named. To understand "naming," we would have to understand these systems and the faculties of mind through which they arise. (Chomsky, 1975, p. 46)

To name someone or something is to make a reference by which a causal or conventional relation is established between the object and the symbol; that is the name (Peirce, 1932; Quine, 1973). Indeed, in the act of naming we denote the class of all particular things to which the name applies. Names, and here we might include group designations as proper names, serve as identifying markers which by the application of a rule associates the object being named to a preordained class. Claude Levi-Strauss (1966) has referred to the naming process in this sense as an "enterprise of classification." In this exercise the name chosen makes reference to a meaningful system of commonly shared and understood characteristics that define a class of objects thus named.

The problem for linguists is the nature of proper names and their place in the system of the language. We are concernced with this problem, but also with another, for we are faced with a twofold paradox. We need to establish that proper names are an integral part of systems we have been treating as codes: as means of fixing significations by transposing them into terms of other significations. Would this be possible, if it were true, as logicians and some linguists have maintained, that proper names are, in Mill's phrase, "meaningless," lacking in signification? (p. 172)

Names thus are meaningful. But the meaning of a name, by which it connects to an object it represents, is not there a priori. That meaning has to be established by the act of naming a thing, has to be contextualized in a system of language, and has to be maintained by consistent use of that name. In other words, as part of our language, names have to be elaborated, and this elaboration of their meaning is a fundamentally social activity (Wittgenstein, 1958). This very point has been the central concern of a new theory of meaning, the so-called causal theory of reference, developed first by Saul Kripke (1972, 1980) and Hilary Putnam (1975, 1983). In this approach meaning is not a product of individual mental activity, but instead the result of collective creation. Putnam, emphasizing what he termed the "contribution of the environment" in the construction of "paradigms" through which we "fix reference" (i.e., give meaning) to names, made the point this way:

As I see it, "meanings aren't in the head"; the actual nature of the paradigms enters into fixing reference, and not just the concepts in our heads. Another important feature of both Kripke's theory and mine is that reference is determined *socially*. To determine whether or not something is really gold a native speaker may have to consult an expert, who knows the nature of gold better than the average person does. The chain of historic transmissions which preserve the reference of a proper name in the Kripke theory is another form of social cooperation in the fixing of reference. The idea that the extensions of our terms are fixed by collective practices and not by concepts in our individual heads is a sharp departure from the way meaning has been viewed ever since the seventeenth century. (p. 75)

That break with the traditional mentalist accounts of meaning and reference has led the theory's protagonists, Kripke and Putnam, to emphasize the importance of the origin and history of names in determining how they function and what they come to mean. This gets us back to Chomsky's point, cited earlier, about the need to understand the significance of "naming" an object. When we choose a name for an object, we place the name in a system of linguistic structure and place the thing so named in a system of conceptual relations and conditions, as well as factual beliefs.

For Kripke (1980) the naming process commences with an "initial baptism," in which the object is named or the reference of the name is fixed by description, and the name gets passed, as Kripke put it, "from link to link." In this "historic chain of transmission" (see Putnam's quote above) the reference fixed originally in the naming process is preserved and refined to the extent that it is commonly understood. As Chomsky stressed, the linguistic and cognitive structures associated with the name remain operative as it is transferred to new users. This does not mean that everyone using that name conceptualizes the object in precisely the same manner or endows its name with exactly the same descriptive interpretations. All that is required here is a critical mass of shared and collectively elaborated understandings as to what the name is supposed to mean and which object it refers to.

Any proper name, including a group designation such as African American, thus must be analyzed in its act of origination and through the history of its transmission. Only then can we comprehend to the fullest the elaboration of its meaning through the interaction of its users. For Wittgenstein (1958) this essentially social approach to meaning implied that things cannot have names except in a "language game," a term he applied to social contexts in which words are used in structured ways of interacting with the world. The meaning of a name thus lies entirely in how it is used in interactions. People are able to communicate what is on their minds because they share a language for describing what occurs outside their minds. They can therefore agree about the meaning of a word and maintain this agreement in their applications of it. While people sharing a vocabulary will have a tendency to preserve the agreed-upon meanings of words, the internalized rules governing their use can change over time. Wittgenstein (1958) argued strongly that nothing that is on your mind now predetermines how you will use the word in the future. When the meaning of a name changes, its reinterpretation will have to be verbally communicated between interacting agents until a new agreement emerges.

What this digression into the philosophy of language and mind seeks to clarify is how we mean what we mean by what we say. It should be clear by now that names are meaningful and therefore do matter a great deal. The establishment of meaning is not a product of the individual mind, but a process of social elaboration. A name is first endowed with meaning through its "initial baptism," an originating act which fixes its reference. Its meaning is preserved, elaborated, and possibly transformed in subsequent applications of the name, as a matter of interaction and interpretation, around a social consensus concerning the rules which govern its use. That consensus about the meaning of a name is possible not only because of the language we share, but also because of what Putnam (1983) called the "mental representations" we construct in our minds to understand the world "out there," and which we communicate to each other. In this sense it is useful to think of names as social representations, even as anticipatory social representations if we agree with Wittgenstein that what goes on in our minds now does not predetermine how we apply the name in the future. Since we do not rigidly adhere to the same representational system forever, we can project different meanings for a name. In the same vein we can also imagine how different names or different uses of the same name might recreate the object thus named.

THE "NAMING GAME" FOR AMERICANS OF AFRICAN ANCESTRY

We concluded in the last section that the meaning of a name is a matter of social elaboration. It depends on how the name is used in interactions between people and what kind of consensus underlies its interpretations. Thus, as Wittgenstein, Kripke, Putnam, and Chomsky have argued, we need to analyze both the name's origin and its subsequent transmission if we are to understand what the name comes to mean to everyone involved in its use. Regarding the name African American, it behooves us therefore to trace back the history of naming Americans of African descent, so as to provide a context for the origination of this latest effort at changing that group's designation.

Before returning to a discussion of African American, we should be aware that this effort at renaming a group of Americans is by no means unique. Public debates over naming processes in the United States have been particularly pronounced in recent years. During this past decade alone we have witnessed vigorous debates over the most suitable names for a variety of groups. One only has to recall the controversies over Hispanics preferring Latinos/Latinas or a nationality-specific term; Indians becoming Native Americans; Oriental being replaced by Asian American; or the more recent struggle over what to call Mexican Americans (referred to as the "battle of the name"). The accelerating pace of change in denominations is an interesting phenomenon of our times and seems especially evident in multiethnic societies struggling with the challenge of integration (Schlesinger, 1992; Walzer, 1990).

The sequence of different names used to identify Americans of African descent has consistently reflected attempts to change the perception of the group and, with this, affect more general developments in intergroup relations. The evolution in their denomination from "slave" to "Negro," "Colored," "Black," "Afro-American," "Person of Color," and finally "African American" was always fraught with controversy over presumed qualitative differences between those terms. The switch from Black to African American is only the latest manifestation of this continuous effort by Americans of African descent to find a label that will instill pride and self-esteem (Bennett, 1970; Miller, 1937; Smith, 1992; Williams, 1966).

Ever since the beginnings of slavery terms such as "African," "Negro," "Black," and "Colored" were all part of the standard vocabulary in America used to refer to people of African descent. After the Civil War, black Americans sought repeatedly to improve racial consciousness and regulate their status in a predominantly white society by changing their name. The first attempt came in the late nineteeth century, when influential group leaders argued in favor of Negro over Colored. Since then several other changes in the search for an "appropriate label" have taken place. While various rationalizations were used to justify the switches, the main reason for supplanting one name with another has been the need to improve the group's standing and redirect its relations with the rest of American society.

An important example of this process occurred when a large social movement emerged in the late 1950s and early 1960s with the intention to change prevailing race relations with a sustained attack on segregation. By the mid-1960s Malcolm X had challenged the integrationist spirit and the vision of a color-blind nation propagated by other Civil Rights leaders. His efforts reflected the concern of many black Americans by focusing on the need for racial self-awareness. Malcolm's rhetorical ability to turn the traditional juxtaposition of "White" and "Black" on its head, in order to create a sense of pride in Blackness, shifted the mood as well as the interest of the Civil Rights movement. "Black" became a positive concept associated with growth, enrichment, and self-esteem in the lives of black Americans. "Black Power," the title chosen by Stokely Carmichael and Charles Hamilton for their influential book that came to define the movement at the time (Carmichael & Hamilton, 1967), soon became a rallying cry of young militants. The rapid growth of the Black Panthers and of the "Black Is Beautiful" movement further crystallized the association of the term Black with racial self-pride among Americans of African descent. Black soon became the preferred denomination within the group, as an expression of unity in the struggle against racial intolerance in America. In addition, the term was also seen as the logical antonym to White (Allen, 1990; Wilkinson, 1990).

This concerted effort by the group to turn Black, a term inherently loaded with negative connotations, into a positive identification worked to the extent that many group members decided to adopt the denomination precisely in the context of an awakening racial consciousness. The effort also succeeded inasmuch as the term gained rapid acceptance in mainstream America, in lieu of Negro. However, once established as the primary group denomination, it lost much of its original political intent. In a way, the term was co-opted by non-black Americans in the early 1970s, when the Civil Rights movement petered out. At that point its negative connotations reemerged.

Given the deeply entrenched symbolism of white as good and black as bad (Williams, 1966; Williams, Tucker, & Dunham, 1971), it is not surprising that this earlier process of group positivation faltered with the end of the Civil Rights movement. Once mainstream America had adopted Black as the new group denomination, the term no longer possessed the positive attributes bestowed upon it by a social movement, and regained its essentially negative connotation. This "boomerang effect" clearly indicates that people's attitudes cannot be altered without changing the underlying representation of the object. And Black failed to do precisely that. Even in its positivation, as an expression of racial pride, it remained a racial term, referring to the group in question on the basis of skin color. Its connection with race can be seen most clearly in the fact that the term generalizes the group by invoking the most extreme possible color, in juxtaposition to an equally extreme White at the other end of the spectrum. This exaggerated contradistinction emphasizes difference and division. Failing to shift the central core of the group's traditional representation away from race, the term Black could never escape the troubled legacy of a racially divided country. For the same reason the term Afro-American, which gained widespread acceptance among academics (Thernstorm, 1980) and in certain influential circles within the black American community during the 1970s, never became widely used in the general population. Even though potentially a non-racial term, its prefix became associated with a hairstyle unique to black Americans and thus again with race.

The introduction of African American opened a new dimension in the reconceptualization of the group, emphasizing culture-based aspects rather than race. As Jesse Jackson aptly put it,

Just as we were called "colored," but were not that, and then "Negro," but were not that, to be called "black" is just as baseless. Just as you have Chinese Americans who have a sense of roots in China . . . or Europeans, as it were, every ethnic group in this country has a reference to some historical culture base. . . .

There are Armenian Americans and Jewish Americans and Arab Americans and Italian Americans. And with a degree of accepted and reasonable pride, they connect their heritage to their mother country and where they are now. . . . To be called African American has cultural integrity. (Smith, 1992, pp. 503, 507)

Hence the key purpose of this switch in denomination was to allow black Americans a sort of cultural identification with their ancestry in, and heritage from, the African continent ("Broad coalition seeks African American name," 1989; "From 'Black' to 'African American'?" 1989). The choice of African American as the vehicle was in this regard no coincidence. By combining African and American, the name chosen redefines the dual consciousness of black Americans in a new synthesis which makes explicit that they are inseperably part of America, while at the same time placing the unique specificities of the group in a cultural context. The reference to Africa is significant here for two reasons: it distinguishes the group from others in this nation of immigrants, and, by extension, it adds a unique dimension to that multicultural society. The notion of "African" in African American does not relate to contemporary Africa, but instead refers to a specific culture in contemporary America, with its own language, social expressions, and iconic symbols. The change from Black to African American, indicating a switch from race to culture, can in this way be seen as a conscious effort to widen perspectives on black Americans and project them onto a global context.

Moreover, as mentioned by Jackson, the new name had the added benefit of being consistent with the designations of everyone else, since other groups were already juxtaposing their cultural base to "America" (Banton, 1988). Having precisely the same semantic structure as other group designations (e.g., Italian American, Irish American), the new name also repositions the group in question on an equal footing with any other group of Americans. It is no longer defined in juxtaposition to White, but in relation to many other distinct groups.

Ethnic group designations linking the place of origin with America, such as Irish American, Japanese American, and, in fact, African American, were born out of an antinativist attempt to foster tolerance in an ethnic-pluralistic setting (Walzer, 1990). Their prevalence shows a long tradition of integration and ethnic pluralism concerning other groups. Becoming an American has not been bound to any particular national, linguistic, religious, or ethnic background. Notwithstanding severe episodic bigotry and discrimination other groups have experienced, the dominant cultural norm has been to regard American nationality as an addition to an ethnic consciousness (Kallen, 1924).

In contrast with other groups, Americans of African descent have been defined primarily on the basis of race. Compared to culture, race has always remained a more static concept, suggesting genetic and consequently innate and easily hierarchized differences between people (Dole, 1995; Yee et al., 1993; Yee et al., 1995). Perceptions and treatment of racially defined groups have tended to emphasize differences taken to reflect a more or less immutable condition. The long history of racial prejudice and discrimination in this country has crystallized race as a barrier (Omi & Winant, 1986), setting black Americans apart from the rest of society (Davis, 1991; Jaynes & Williams, 1989). This issue is so deeply entrenched in American society that is has taken on the qualities of an obsession (Terkel, 1992). Any attempt to change the perception of black Americans can therefore only succeed if it manages to deemphasize race. Redirecting the focus of attention away from race creates a vacuum which, if properly filled, might allow for greater inclusion and make people's interactions more permeative.

The term African American may very well achieve such a shift in focus towards culture and ethnicity, the very same criteria already applied in pluralistic fashion to other Americans. Yet at the same time, in contradistinction to the designation of any other group in America, the term African American references as the place of the group's origin a vast continent, not a country. This reminds us that people from Africa were brought to America against their will and under such conditions that in a matter of a just a few generations most of them had no idea where precisely in Africa they came from. Slavery, after all, is an issue that has shaped the history of this nation from its very beginnings and still provides a frame for the perception of black Americans.

For some, this reference to Africa and, by extension, slavery may make it impossible to disassociate the term from any racial connotation. To the extent, however, that overcoming the legacy of centuries of exclusion is widely understood to concern the entire nation, and the "African" in African American is seen as referring to a specific culture in contemporary America, the new term should be able to offer us a more flexible perspective on a group considered thus far a race apart. It is neither my goal nor within the purview of my study to speculate as to whether the future evolution of the term's meaning will or will not achieve this shift of focus away from race, especially in light of what Wittgenstein has said about not being able to judge the future use of a name on the basis of what people think about it now. All we can do here is to analyze what the name was meant to stand for at the time of its inception, and how it has evolved since then.

ORIGIN AND HISTORIC TRANSMISSION OF AFRICAN AMERICAN

African American is one of those proper names whose "initial baptism," to use Kripke's terminology, can be clearly identified. In December 1988, just one month after Bush's election victory and the end of Jesse Jackson's run for the presidency, a group of Civil Rights leaders met in New Orleans for a strategy session. At that reunion Ramona Edelin, then president of the National Urban League, proposed to introduce African American as the official group designation in lieu of Black. Her suggestion met with enthusiastic approval by the other participants and led to a 1989 campaign by the assembled leadership to establish a place for the term in the American vocabulary and confer official status upon the new group designation. Soon a sociodemographically distinct subgroup of black Americans began to call themselves African Americans, thus using the name to claim a new identity. The effort resonated among the nation's college students, where African American rapidly emerged as a central element of discourse in the "political correctness" movement. The term then spread from campuses to the media, whose rapid and widespread adoption introduced the term to mainstream America.

Such an explicit act of baptism, involving a concrete event and a promotional campaign is quite rare and thus deserves closer attention. As argued by Kay Deaux (1992, 1993), any study of social identification needs to understand why people choose to identify in the first place. In this context it is obviously significant that a group of Civil Rights leaders, many of them with their political roots in the Civil Rights movement, decided during a gathering in late 1988 to introduce African American as a new group designation and to launch a campaign in support of its use in lieu of Black. With the official endorsement of this new denomination, the leaders of the black American community decided to bestow upon their group a new self-identity and to make the rest of America see that group in a different light. By introducing the term at a crucial historical juncture, following the electoral campaigns of Jesse Jackson, who stressed the common destiny of Americans of all races, members of the black American community could turn a new self-designation into an instrument to break with past attitudes, opinions, and images. Their innovation also allowed them to define accommodation to the unfamiliar representation from their own perspective, with a strong deemphasis on race.

The campaign launched during 1989 in support of African American was successful. Within a couple of years the term had entered our everyday language, propagated by public opinion makers in the media and politics. When used in public discourse to refer to the group as a whole, the new term almost always implies inclusion, equality, and participation. It is symbolic, and as such it does express the transformation of America into a multicultural society. This linguistic process (that is, the use of African American in public discourse) is forward-looking, anticipating greater flexibility in intergroup relations and projecting images of a nation enriched by its ethnic diversity. When politicians, journalists, or talk-show hosts refer to African Americans as a group, they create images of a color-blind society in which race no longer plays a role in the justification of discriminatory treatment. The use of the term carries a normative context that regulates and orients exchange. The images being created here imply that African Americans are integrated and behave in compliance with the cultural standards of the mainstream.

The creation of African American as a vector of innovation had to have a concrete material existence to become part of our collective consciousness. It is no coincidence that the new group designation soon grew into the focus of a new self-identity claimed by some black Americans, who decided to call themselves African Americans (Deaux, 1994). That subgroup, mostly professional and young, identifies its self-interest and allegiance with a multicultural America. Its members anticipate the opportunity of participation in the mainstream while at the same time being acutely aware of the legacy of race as a barrier to equality. These African Americans have a significant impact on the remaking of intergroup relations, since they relate to both sides. They, more than anyone else, embody the group's dual consciousness of being part African and part American. Their new name evokes presuppositions of a different synthesis between their place of origin and their present culture, one that for the first time gives all of us hope of finally resolving the "American Dilemma" (Myrdal, 1944) by moving away from race as the dominant factor in relations between black and non-black Americans. As it becomes increasingly interpreted in association with this sociodemographically distinct group, the new name gradually gains meaning and imagery.

This process, whereby a denomination turns into a social representation, has a daily reality insofar as individual African Americans have in recent years come to occupy the public space as never before, and far beyond the traditional areas of music or sports. There are many noteworthy examples to illustrate this point. Take, for example, the popularity of Oprah Winfrey, who revolutionized network television with her talk show and is still the most watched in this arena despite some 70 imitators competing for viewers. More than 20 million people watch the *Oprah Winfrey Show* every day to see her discuss complex and relevant issues with her guests. The show has become the basic and most common source of information and opinions for millions of Americans (Squire, 1994). Ms. Winfrey is admired and cherished, not least because she appears so human. The more intimate details she reveals about herself (weight problems, previous substance abuse, etc.), the more people seem to believe in her. In 1989 she was voted the second most admired woman in the USA after Nancy Reagan.

Another good example is Colin Powell, who was chairman of the Joint Chiefs of Staff during the Reagan-Bush era. General Powell combines charisma and cool-headed pragmatism into a formidable projection of leadership qualities. He embodies the "Just World" view and so inspires confidence in the system. Despite his decision not to run for the president in 1996, his popularity is such that many still regard him as likely to be the first American of African descent in the White House. Both Oprah Winfrey and Colin Powell have crossed the invisible race barrier dividing this society, and in their public presentation as African Americans the question of their race no longer matters. They symbolize in the most complete fashion the tangible achievements of African Americans in their efforts to enter strategic positions in politics, business, the media, and the professions.

The diffusion of African American centers not only on specific people, but is also propelled by events that capture the nation's attention, such as the Clarence Thomas hearings in the fall of 1991. This spectacular confrontation between two African Americans—Anita Hill, a tenured law professor at the University of Oklahoma, and Clarence Thomas, a nominee to the United States Supreme Court—over allegations of sexual harassment was watched by millions. Those hearings crystallized the term African American, with both sides claiming it as their own and senators learning in a very public forum how to adjust their vocabulary accordingly (with an occasional slip into Afro-American, or, as in the case of Senator Kohl from Wisconsin, simply compressing the term into "African"). Yet the emergence of African American into a social representation cannot be a smooth and linear process. Since it essentially involves the reconceptualization of an already well-defined object, namely black Americans, it has to break with preexisting representations of that social object. It thus is created in contradistinction to Black, and sometimes the tensions inherent in this juxtaposition become all too visible.

One such moment came during the 1992 riots in Los Angeles. In the midst of this explosion of anger Rodney King, whose videotaped beating by several policemen had triggered the confrontation (an all-white jury found the police officers implicated in this act of violence not guilty), asked America a simple question: "Can We All Get Along?" This rhetorical question, by the man who epitomized the tense relationship between white police officers and young black American males, echoed throughout America. Posited at a moment of extreme intergroup conflict, the question touched on a central dissonance felt in the heart of so many Americans.

It was during this period that the term African American and the term Black were most sharply contrasted. In media coverage these two denominations came to reflect two different realities, one of integration and the other of division and separation. But even during such times of heightened racial conflict Americans cannot escape the challenge of coexistence. For any change to occur, however, race has to be pushed aside. As a dominant social representation that is well elaborated and internalized in the American culture, race provides the base for the emergence of African American as a new social representation. By shifting our attention away from the divisive practice of racial categorization and instead stressing culture, African American reconceptualizes and recreates a social object which until now had been seen as a race apart.

STUDY I: NAMING PREFERENCES

To measure the extent to which African American signals a transformation in the representation of black American, a study was conducted in the metropolitan area of New York City on the basis of questionnaires given to 282 college students and professionals. The questionnaires discussed in this section (see Appendices B and C) asked the subjects to rank six denominations for black Americans (i.e., African American, Afro-American, Black, Negro, Colored, and People of Color) on various

Table 6.1
Name You Use Most Frequently for Your Own Group

Name	Percentage
African American	33.8%
Afro-American	4.6%
Black	50.0%
Colored	2.3%
Negro	2.3%
People of Color	6.9%

Note: n = 130

levels. In that context several qualitative aspects of those names were analyzed.

The questionnaires were designed as a primary tool of investigation that looked at the broad-based conceptualization of the new term African American among Americans of different backgrounds. These questionnaires not only make it possible to compare Black and African American, but have the added advantage of relating the six denominations to one another. Such a matrix of comparisons shows not only a highly developed contradistinction between African American and Black, as could be expected, but also an interesting juxtaposition between African American and People of Color.

Black Americans

A total of 139 black Americans responded to this questionnaire. The questions were grouped into four subsets (see Tables B.3 and B.4 in Appendix B). The first subset sought to examine differences between the group denominations used and those that are preferred. The second category of questions looked at the group designations with the most positive images. A third set identified projections about the future use of the different names. These anticipations were studied in relation to their use by the general public as well as to their projected use by such public opinion makers as the media and politicians. Finally, subjects were asked to identify those terms they felt most negative about.

Tables 6.1, 6.2, and 6.3 show the extent to which the name Black is still the dominant denomination when referring to Americans of African descent. It is not only the name black Americans picked most often for themselves, but also the most frequently used by non-blacks to refer to black Americans. However, as indicated in Table 6.4, a much larger num-

Table 6.2
Name You Use Some of the Time for Your Own Group

Name	Percentage
African American	22.0%
Afro-American	16.5%
Black	38.6%
Colored	——
Negro	3.1%
People of Color	19.7%

Note: n = 127

Table 6.3
Name Outgroup Uses for Your Own Group

Name	Percentage
African American	14.6%
Afro-American	6.9%
Black	63.1%
Colored	6.9%
Negro	4.6%
People of Color	3.8%

Note: n = 130

Table 6.4
Name You Most Prefer for Your Group

Name	Percentage
African American	44.1%
Afro-American	10.2%
Black	30.7%
Colored	3.1%
Negro	——
People of Color	11.8%

Note: n = 127

Figure 6.1
Choice of Name, African American versus Black (black American sample)

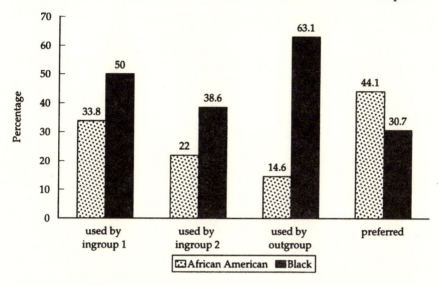

ber of black Americans prefer African American, implying a tension between practice and preference.

In order to illustrate the shifting juxtaposition between Black and African American as regards use and preference more clearly, we have summarized the sample results presented in Table 6.1 to 6.4 graphically and for just these two terms (see Figure 6.1). Half of the black American subjects in our study call themselves Black and one third call themselves African American. Yet nearly two thirds of the subjects still see themselves predominantly referred to as Black by members of other groups, compared to less than 15 percent claiming to be referred to as African American. The difference between those calling themselves African American and the percentage of those who say they are referred to as such may well indicate a disproportion between what these respondents claim to be and what others see them as. Concerning the term preferred, African American is already the choice of a plurality, with slightly less than a third still preferring Black.

The next set of questions (see Tables 6.5 and 6.6) asked subjects to make direct evaluations of the different names based on their ability to project positive images. Apart from the overwhelming two-thirds preference given to African American, it is worth noting that one out of ten considered Afro-American the most positive. This shows the resilience of a term targeted 20 years ago by a black American elite as a first substitution for Black.

Table 6.5
Name Projecting the Most Positive Images When Used by Ingroup (black
American sample)

Name	Percentage
African American	58.2%
Afro-American	9.0%
Black	17.2%
Colored	3.3%
Negro	3.3%
People of Color	9.0%

Note: n = 122

Table 6.6
Name Projecting the Most Positive Images When Used by Outgroup (black
American sample)

Name	Percentage
African American	64.7%
Afro-American	10.1%
Black	15.1%
Colored	3.4%
Negro	1.7%
People of Color	5.0%

Note: n = 119

African American was chosen by almost two-thirds of the sample as
the term projecting the most positive image when used by non-black
Americans, compared to only about one in seven still picking Black (see
also Figure 6.2). A similar pattern can be observed when the group is
asked to choose the term which projects the most positive image when
used by black Americans. More than half chose African American, while
Black was only picked by one in six subjects. The choice of African American as the most positive denomination to refer to Americans of African
ancestry accounts for the greatest consensus among our sample. This
convergence, which reflects a value judgment, indicates the degree to
which the new term has been endowed with meaning.

Tables 6.7 and 6.8 relate to the anticipated diffusion of the names in

Figure 6.2
Positive Projections, African American versus Black (black American sample)

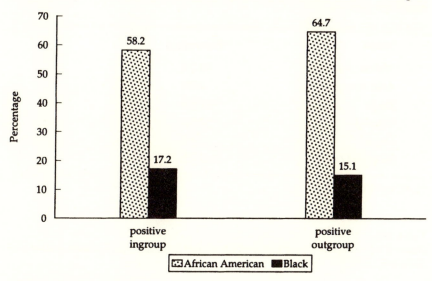

Table 6.7
Name That Will Be Used More in the Future (black American sample)

Name	Percentage
African American	55.0%
Afro-American	10.8%
Black	19.2%
Colored	3.3%
Negro	4.2%
People of Color	7.5%

Note: n = 120

the future. We measured which term black Americans expected to be used more in the future. This projection into the future was examined on two levels. First we analyzed their projections into the future in general, and then we looked at the name they thought the outgroup might use to refer to them in the future. As also illustrated by Figure 6.3, more than half of the population opted for African American as the name that will be used most in the future, while only roughly one in five chose Black. The difference between these two terms becomes even more pro-

Table 6.8
Name That Will Be Used More by Outgroup in the Future (black American sample)

Name	Percentage
African American	63.2%
Afro-American	9.4%
Black	17.0%
Colored	0.9%
Negro	0.9%
People of Color	8.5%

Note: n = 106

Figure 6.3
Future-Oriented Dimension, African American versus Black (black American sample)

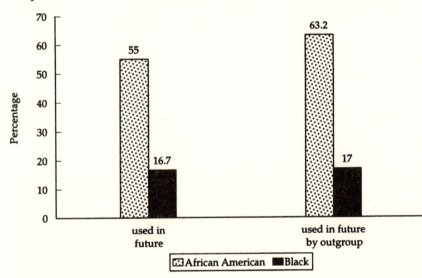

nounced in favor of African American when black subjects projected future use of those competing denominations by non-black Americans.

Since the diffusion of African American has been accelerated by the media and other public opinion sources, we looked next at projections of names that will be used in the future by different opinion makers. Once again African American is widely regarded as the denomination

Table 6.9
Name That Will Be Used by the Press in the Future (black American sample)

Name	Percentage
African American	59.1%
Afro-American	12.7%
Black	20.0%
Colored	1.8%
Negro	2.7%
People of Color	3.6%

Note: n = 110

Table 6.10
Name That Will Be Used by TV in the Future (black American sample)

Name	Percentage
African American	59.1%
Afro-American	16.4%
Black	15.5%
Colored	1.8%
Negro	1.8%
People of Color	5.5%

Note: n = 110

to be used most widely by a variety of public opinion makers in the future. The percentage reponses presented in Table 6.9, 6.10, and 6.11 demonstrate that African American seems to be favored over any other denomination by a large margin, especially in association with politicians. When comparing just African American and Black, as is done in Figure 6.4, the projections concerning their respective future use among public opinion makers closely mirror those applied to the public in general and the outgroup in particular (see Figure 6.3 for comparison).

Finally, we collected data about the negative dimensions of our denominations. As shown in Tables 6.12–6.15, the term Negro has been consistently chosen as the most disliked name, the term projecting the most negative images when used by members of the ingroup or the outgroup (i.e., non-blacks), and the name expected to be the least used in the future. The names Colored and People of Color are also consis-

Table 6.11
Name That Will Be Used by Political Figures in the Future (black American sample)

Name	Percentage
African American	64.0%
Afro-American	11.7%
Black	18.0%
Colored	0.9%
Negro	——
People of Color	5.4%

Note: n = 111

Figure 6.4
Future-Oriented Dimension for Opinion Makers, African American versus Black (black American sample)

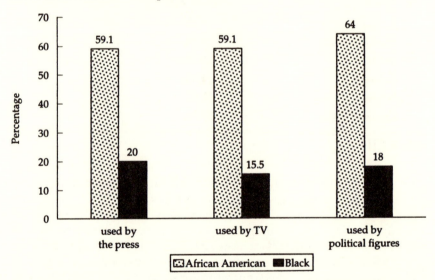

tently seen as having negative connotations. Both are conspicuous in the response profiles of all four questions. Noteworthy too is that one out of seven subjects expected Black to be the term most likely to be phased out in the future.

Figure 6.5 illustrates the negative dimensions people associate with different names, specifically Colored, Negro, and People of Color. These

Table 6.12
Name Most Disliked (black American sample)

Name	Percentage
African American	5.5%
Afro-American	4.7%
Black	5.5%
Colored	25.2%
Negro	37.8%
People of Color	21.3%

Note: n = 127

Table 6.13
Name Projecting the Most Negative Image When Used by Ingroup (black American sample)

Name	Percentage
African American	5.0%
Afro-American	5.9%
Black	6.7%
Colored	24.4%
Negro	37.8%
People of Color	20.2%

Note: n = 119

Table 6.14
Name Projecting the Most Negative Image When Used by Outgroup (black American sample)

Name	Percentage
African American	3.4%
Afro-American	3.4%
Black	12.8%
Colored	19.7%
Negro	35.9%
People of Color	24.8%

Note: n = 117

Table 6.15
Name That Will Be Used Least in the Future (black American sample)

Name	Percentage
African American	4.5%
Afro-American	6.3%
Black	14.4%
Colored	22.5%
Negro	28.8%
People of Color	23.4%

Note: n = 111

Figure 6.5
Negative Dimension of Names (black American sample)

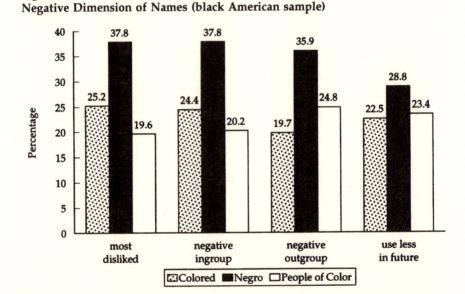

are the three names most disliked. They are also perceived as projecting the most negative images when referring to Americans of African descent, and as likely to be used less and less in the future. In Figure 6.6 the negative dimension of Black in comparison to African American is more closely examined. The results indicate that Black is perceived as more negative than African American when used by outgroup members (non-blacks) and that use of the name is expected to drop in the future, to a lower level even than Afro-American (see Table 6.15).

Figure 6.6
Negative Dimension of Names, African American versus Black (black American sample)

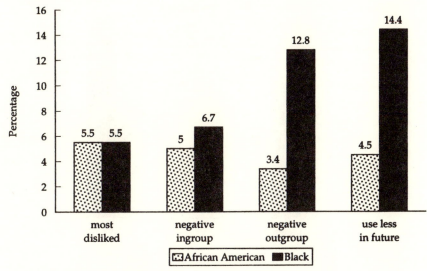

A deeper analysis of our results indicates that within our distribution there seems to be a connection between the most preferred term and those selected as projecting the most negative images. As shown in Figures 6.7 (a) to (d), those feeling most positively inclined toward African American also tended to feel most negatively about People of Color, while those wedded to the denomination Black were most opposed to Negro.

This difference concerning negative denominations is not coincidental, but a reflection of distinct historical circumstances in how the two name designations gained their positive meaning. For those calling themselves Black the obvious antipode is Negro, the term the Civil Rights movement successfully attacked and replaced with Black. On the other hand, those preferring African American are more inclined to dislike People of Color, which groups all non-white people, whether of African, Latin American, Asian, or Native American ancestry, together in contradistinction to those Americans of European ancestry. That juxtaposition, much like the one opposing Black and White, implies a race-based differentiation which the term African American seeks to overcome. Moreover, by putting all non-white Americans into one pool, the term People of Color denies black Americans the kind of cultural specificity implicit in African American.

Figure 6.7 (a)
Name Preferred Correlated with Most Disliked Term (black American sample)

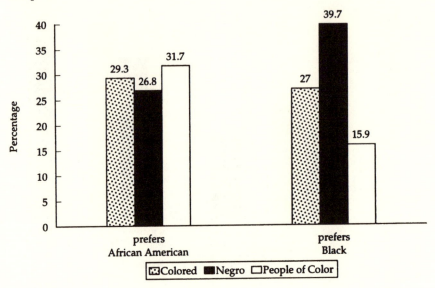

Figure 6.7 (b)
Name Preferred Correlated with Term Projecting the Most Negative Images When Used by Ingroup (black American sample)

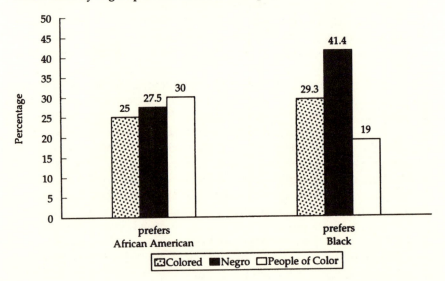

Figure 6.7 (c)
**Name Preferred Correlated with Term Projecting the Most Negative Images
When Used by Outgroup (black American sample)**

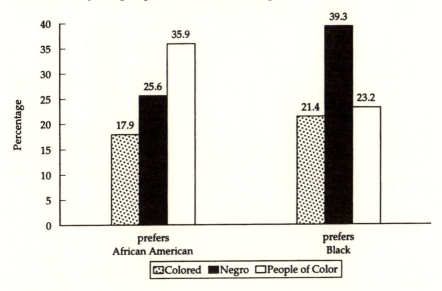

Figure 6.7 (d)
**Name Preferred Correlated with Term Expected to Be Used Least in the
Future (black American sample)**

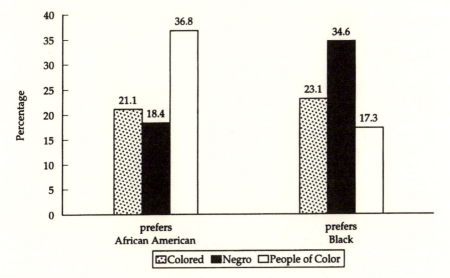

Table 6.16
Name You Use Most Frequently to Refer to People of African Descent (non-black American sample)

Name	Percentage
African American	19.1%
Afro-American	6.4%
Black	67.4%
Colored	2.8%
Negro	2.8%
People of Color	1.4%

Note: n = 141

Non-black Americans

A total of 143 non-black Americans participated in the study. The population was subdivided in half, with 56 percent of non-black Americans referring to themselves as either American, European, White, or Caucasian and 41.8 percent composed of Native Americans, Asian Americans, and Latino/Latinas. As was the case with the black American sample, the questions were grouped into four subsets (see Tables C.2 and C.3 in Appendix C). The first subset looked at the denominations non-black subjects currently used as well as those they preferred to refer to Americans of African ancestry. The second category dealt with the denominations subjects thought projected the most positive images. The next set looked at the names subjects expected to be used more in the future, especially projections concerning the use of terms by our public opinion makers. Finally, subjects identified the denominations seen as most negative.

Tables 6.16, 6.17, and 6.18 show that over two-thirds of the non-black Americans in the study most frequently use Black, and barely 20 percent use African American. There is, however, a gradual shift when the question is framed in terms of their preference. While four out of ten non-blacks preferred Black, nearly one-third indicated a preference for African American.

Worthy of attention in the tables presented above is the strong presence of the term Afro-American. Indeed this denomination, while being chosen by only 6.4 percent of the non-black subjects as the term most frequently used (and by 13.5 percent of those subjects as their second choice of denomination), is the term preferred by 20.4 percent of them. It appears that this term, which gained some acceptance in the late 1970s,

Table 6.17
Name You Use Some of the Time to Refer to People of African Descent (non-black American sample)

Name	Percentage
African American	34.9%
Afro-American	13.5%
Black	35.7%
Colored	5.6%
Negro	5.6%
People of Color	4.0%

Note: n = 126

Table 6.18
Name You Most Prefer to Refer to People of African Descent (non-black American sample)

Name	Percentage
African American	33.6%
Afro-American	20.4%
Black	40.1%
Colored	2.9%
Negro	0.7%
People of Color	2.2%

Note: n = 137

has a more persistent legacy among non-black Americans than among the black Americans, who reject the term because of its association with a hair style.

As the juxtaposition of Black and African American in Figure 6.8 shows, Black is far more frequently used and remains the most preferred term to refer to Americans of African descent. While the percentage of non-black subjects picking African American as a preferred name increases by 14.5 percent compared to the name they use, its percentage still remains lower than that for Black.

To take into account the diversity of our sample, especially based on the differences in the denomination picked to refer to one's own group, the sample was split into three different groups. We first looked at those

Figure 6.8
Choice of Name, African American versus Black (non-black American sample)

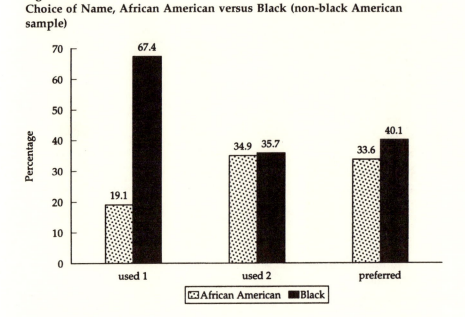

calling themselves American, then at those opting for the name White, and finally at a mixed group composed of Asian Americans, Latinos/Latinas, and Native Americans (i.e., non-black and non-white). Looking at this differentiation has allowed us to highlight the fact that those calling themselves White have a disproportionate preference for Black, while those identifying themselves as Americans, as well as the group of non-white subjects, prefer African American (see Figure 6.9).

Non-black Americans were asked about the term they thought projected the most positive images. As shown in Table 6.19, over three-quarters of them opted for African American. Among other terms chosen, it is interesting to notice that more than twice the number of subjects chose Afro-American as chose Black. The strong consensus in favor of African American is also illustrated in Figure 6.10, where that term emerges as the one evoking by far the most positive images.

In Figure 6.11 the data is examined in terms of the three different samples (i.e., American, White, non-white). The results indicate that those calling themselves White showed a stronger consensus concerning the positive nature of African American than either those calling themselves Americans or those belonging to another subgroup. Nearly nine out of ten Whites selected that denomination, compared to 77.3 percent for those calling themselves Americans and 70.4 percent for the non-whites. There seems to be a contradiction between the denomination our

Figure 6.9
Name Preference for Three Subgroups, African American versus Black

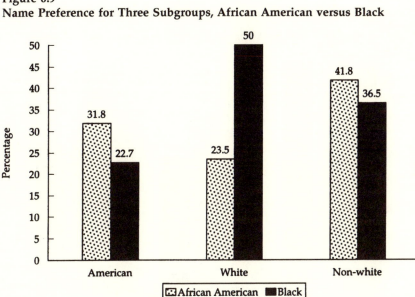

Table 6.19
Name Projecting the Most Positive Images (non-black American sample)

Name	Percentage
African American	76.9%
Afro-American	13.4%
Black	6.0%
Colored	——
Negro	0.7%
People of Color	3.0%

Note: n = 134

non-black subjects use or prefer the most and the name they over-
whelmingly perceive as projecting the most positive images. This contradiction is the driving force which maintains the dynamic nature of
the object.

The anticipated diffusion of the various denominations in the future
is summarized in Table 6.20. Two-thirds of the sample thought that African American will be used more in the future, compared to only one

Figure 6.10
Positive Projections, African American versus Black (non-black American sample)

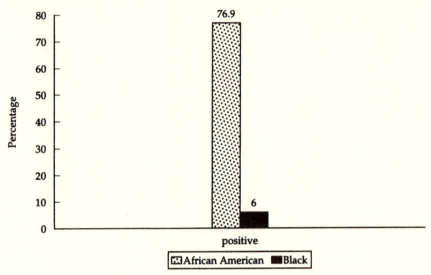

Figure 6.11
Positive Projections for Three Subgroups, African American versus Black

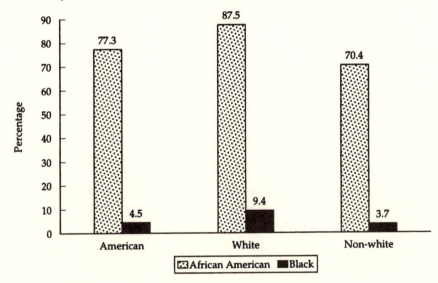

Table 6.20
Name That Will Be Used More in the Future (non-black American sample)

Name	Percentage
African American	66.4%
Afro-American	17.6%
Black	9.9%
Colored	——
Negro	1.5%
People of Color	4.6%

Note: n = 131

Figure 6.12
Future-Oriented Dimension, African American versus Black (non-black American sample)

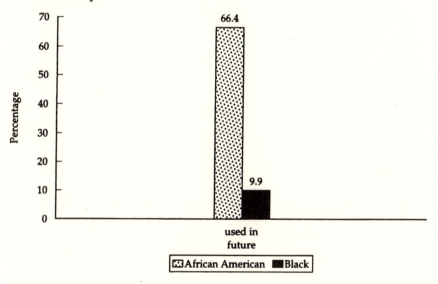

in ten subjects opting for Black. That future-oriented dimension of African American, combined with its positive meaning, show the anticipatory nature of the new term. In addition, we find once again confirmation of the persistence of Afro-American, while Colored is expected to disappear from circulation. We can see the disproportionate choice of African American over the denomination Black also in Figure 6.12.

Figure 6.13
Future-Oriented Dimension for Three Subgroups, African American versus Black

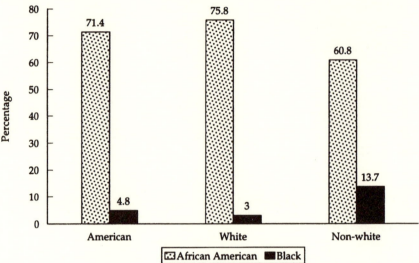

Once again, the names African American and Black are contrasted in terms of their future use, and the data are analyzed based on our three subgroups (see Figure 6.13). This graph shows that African American is widely projected as the term that will be used more in the future by all three subgroups in that sample. These results also indicate that those calling themselves White were the group likeliest to pick African American as the term to be used more in the future. Of equal interest is the fact that 13.7 percent of non-white subjects thought Black will still be used in the future.

Since the diffusion of the denominations in the future depends to a high degree on the different public opinion makers, I also asked the subjects what term they thought would be used the most by the press, television, and political figures in the future (see Tables 6.21 to 6.23). Notwithstanding the dominant presence of African American in those anticipations, we should note the consistent significance of Afro-American in the sample.

In Figure 6.14 we can see even more clearly how the term African American has already begun to replace Black in the anticipation of non-black subjects as the new official group designation used by those channels shaping public opinion the most—the press, television, and political figures. The expected predominance of African American as the denomination to be used in the future was especially pronounced with respect to politicians, with three out of four subjects picking that term.

Table 6.21
Name That Will Be Used by the Press in the Future (non-black American sample)

Name	Percentage
African American	61.0%
Afro-American	20.6%
Black	11.1%
Colored	——
Negro	2.4%
People of Color	4.0%

Note: n = 126

Table 6.22
Name That Will Be Used by TV in the Future (non-black American sample)

Name	Percentage
African American	62.7%
Afro-American	22.2%
Black	9.5%
Colored	——
Negro	3.2%
People of Color	2.4%

Note: n = 126

Table 6.23
Name That Will Be Used by Political Figures in the Future (non-black American sample)

Name	Percentage
African American	74.6%
Afro-American	15.1%
Black	5.6%
Colored	——
Negro	2.4%
People of Color	2.4%

Note: n = 126

Figure 6.14
Future-Oriented Dimension for Opinion Makers, African American versus Black (non-black American sample)

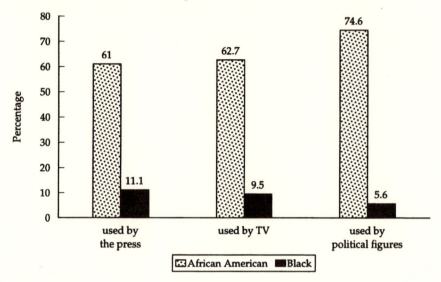

Table 6.24
Name Most Disliked to Refer to People of African Descent (non-black American sample)

Name	Percentage
African American	3.7%
Afro-American	5.1%
Black	7.4%
Colored	12.5%
Negro	50.7%
People of Color	20.6%

Note: n = 136

The data collected for the negative denominations were looked at in terms of the most disliked term, the one projecting the most negative images, and the name expected to be the least used in the future (see Tables 6.24 to 6.26). Half of the sample considered Negro to be the most disliked term as well as the one projecting the most negative image. A somewhat smaller percentage expected that term to fade out of conver-

Table 6.25
Name Projecting the Most Negative Image (non-black American sample)

Name	Percentage
African American	3.0%
Afro-American	3.0%
Black	5.3%
Colored	17.4%
Negro	49.2%
People of Color	22.0%

Note: n = 132

Table 6.26
Name That Will Be Least Used in the Future (non-black American sample)

Name	Percentage
African American	6.4%
Afro-American	2.4%
Black	4.8%
Colored	16.0%
Negro	37.6%
People of Color	32.8%

Note: n = 125

sation in the future. Negative sentiments were also consistently strong vis-à-vis People of Color and, to a somewhat lesser extent, Colored.

Figure 6.15 provides us with a clearer profile of the negative perception of Colored, Negro, and People of Color by focusing just on these three names.

Figure 6.16 examines the negative dimension of Black in comparison to African American. The results show that Black is more disliked than African American. It is also evaluated as projecting more negative images. However, more people in the sample expected African American to be used less in the future than Black.

Finally we looked at the negative dimension as related to the name subjects used to refer to their own group. In the distribution of those calling themselves American (Figure 6.17), half picked Negro as the most disliked term, while the majority thought People of Color was the term

Figure 6.15
Negative Dimension of Names (non-black American sample)

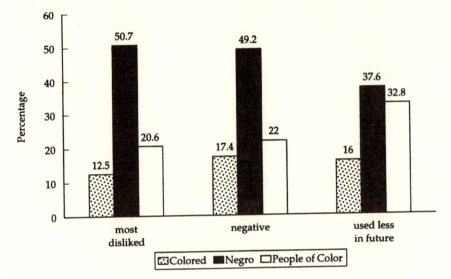

Figure 6.16
Negative Dimension of Names, African American versus Black (non-black American sample)

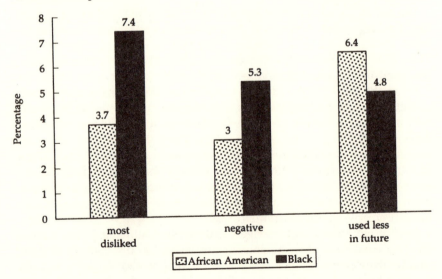

Figure 6.17
Negative Dimension of Name for Those Calling Themselves American

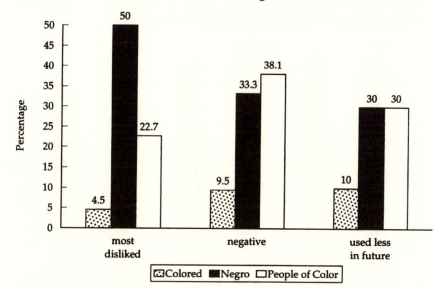

projecting the most negative images. Negro and People of Color were both in equal measure expected to be used less in the future.

In Figure 6.18 we show the negative dimension for those calling themselves White. For all questions, Negro was the term most commonly identified as negative.

We see in Figure 6.19 that the group of non-white subjects (e.g., Latinos/Latinas, Asian Americans, Native Americans) picked Negro as the most disliked term and the one projecting the most negative images. They, however, thought by a slim margin that People of Color would be less used in the future than Negro.

What this first study, which focuses on an onomastic analysis, indicates quite clearly is the tenuous and complex coexistence of Black and African American as competing denominations for Americans of African descent. In terms of current usage Black is still the dominant term used in everyday conversation; given the recent emergence of African American, this is no surprise. Nonetheless, already one in three black American prefers to be called African American. At the same time only one in five seems to be called that by non-black Americans, an estimate confirmed by the outgroup's own response. Non-black Americans still show a greater inclination towards Black than African American, even though the preference gap between those two terms is already significantly smaller than the usage gap. What is interesting in this regard is the differentiation between the various subcategories of the outgroup, with

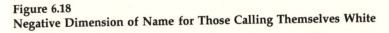
Figure 6.18
Negative Dimension of Name for Those Calling Themselves White

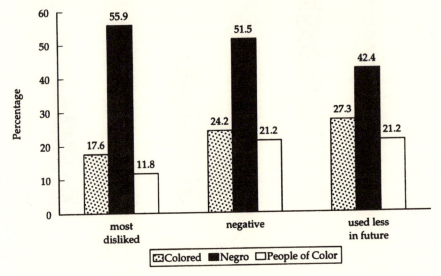

Figure 6.19
Negative Dimension of Name for Non-white Subjects (non-black American sample)

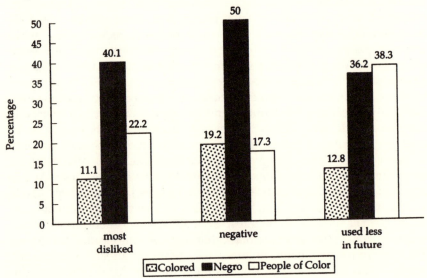

those calling themselves White significantly less inclined toward African American than those calling themselves American or those considering themselves non-white Americans. That difference is especially curious, since those calling themselves Whites have at the same time the most positive associations with the term African American.

The particular pattern of using Black while showing a greater preference and more positive attitude toward African American can be found throughout the entire sample. This kind of tension illustrates the emergence of a new social representation in competition with a well-established representation of the same object. Despite its novelty, the term African American is already anchored as an essentially positive representation of the group. Relative majorities of both black Americans and non-black Americans consider African American the term most likely to evoke positive images.

A second aspect of African American as a new representation still in the making is its orientation toward the future. Absolute majorities in both samples of our study believe that African American is going to be the dominant term in the future. This widespread consensus is obviously enforced by public opinion makers defining the rules of public discourse, a source of influence implicitly acknowledged (especially among the non-black Americans) by the even higher numbers picking African American as the term used more in the press, among television announcers, and by political leaders.

It is precisely the combination of positive and future-oriented qualities demonstrated in this study that characterizes African American as an anticipatory representation. Such a representation is by definition less concerned with what was or what is than with what will be or should be. It is a locus of projections and thus a vehicle for innovation—in this case, a collective effort to re-present a group hitherto excluded on the basis of race for possible integration on the basis of culture. Hence the new group designation can coexist with others (in particular, Black), even to the point of interchangeability, since these competing names evoke different, alternative, even complementary contexts of images and associations. This is why, for example, many people across the entire spectrum of the survey can think of African American as the most positive term and prefer it for that reason, yet at the same time still use Black more often than not in everyday conversation. The choice of name depends to a considerable extent on the precise context of references used for the object thus named, as is illustrated in the next chapter with the aid of content analysis.

Before moving on, however, there is room for one last remark about the study of name preferences presented in this section. An anticipatory representation still in the making, such as African American, does not yet possess a stable and well-settled central core which could give the name a reified existence apart from Black. Race, as crystallized in Black, coexists with ethnic culture and a multicultural version of the American Dream in that central core, and the constellation of these concepts shifts constantly. The term African American is consequently not yet objectified. In the absence of such objectification, the name exists as a social representation mostly in the realm of symbolic expressions, projecting integration with its positive dimensions. Racial integration is such a sensitive issue for most Americans, if not the most fundamental problem of this country, that it is difficult to uncover the varied, frequently contradictory feelings people have on this issue in direct questioning.

Onomastic investigations, such as the examination of name preferences conducted here, are an effective alternative with which to study an anticipatory representation that, contrary to a reified representation, lacks a stable central core. The results of our name-preference questionnaire, besides confirming the positive and future-oriented qualities of African American as an anticipatory representation, also give us a meaningful glimpse at the hidden history and conflicts behind the names used to identify Americans of African ancestry.

Chapter 7

Looking for the Topoi
of the American Culture

Our approach to social representations allows us to identify common grounds of our culture concerning the social object "black American." In looking at where our cultural realities converge, we can see how these points of convergence constrain our thoughts and actions. First we need to isolate those points of juncture in our culture concerning black Americans. It then becomes possible to analyze the ways by which those cultural connections nourish and are in turn nourished by social representations, such as African American or Black. Since these representations are collectively elaborated and commonly shared, they define the common ground of our culture.

In the American context race is obviously one such point of juncture. Like all the formative social representations defining a society, it is one that has been maintained fairly consistently throughout time. The issue of race, of course, is intimately tied to black Americans, the only group in this demographically complex multiethnic society whose social position has been persistently defined in every aspect on the basis of skin color, an exclusively racial category. As such it has been the determinant factor shaping the experience of that group as well as its relationships with the rest of society. But the impact of race extends much further, as Howard Winant (1994) reminds us:

Race provides a key cultural marker, a central signifier, in the reproduction and expression of identity, collectivity, language, and agency itself. Race generates an "inside" and an "outside" of society and mediates the unclear border between these zones; all social space, from the territory of the intrapsychic to that of the U.S. "national character," is fair game for racial dilemmas, doubts, fears, and desires. The conceptualization and representation of these sentiments, whether they are articulated in a track by Public Enemy or a television commercial for Jesse Helms, are framed in one or more racial projects. (p. 30)

When a diverse, multigroup society decides to single out a specific group as the only one to be defined exclusively in racial terms in order to justify its permanent exclusion, this society should expect to be completely shaped by this decision (Omi & Winant, 1986). Winant (1994) speaks in this context of "racial hegemony," both in the sense of an intergroup hierarchy of domination and in the sense of race as the determinant factor in the evolution of a society. As a "key cultural marker" race has therefore permeated every facet of American culture—its laws, its language, its political ideologies, and the basic context for social exchange within and between groups. The strategic position of race has been recognized by such astute observers of American society as de Tocqueville ([1869] 1966) and Myrdal (1944).

Ever since its inception as an independent republic in the late eighteenth century, this society has defined its mission as a unique experiment in human history founded on constitutionally guaranteed principles of equality for all. The flagrant denial of these principles in the case of one of its major groups is what Dyson (1995) has referred to as "American's national shame." The application of race as a justification for discriminatory and exclusionary practices aimed at a specific group, Americans of African descent, violates the most fundamental values of Americans. Both groups, black as well as non-black Americans, have struggled with this contradiction, and each period of societal transformation—the Civil War, Reconstruction, the mobilization against "Jim Crow" legislation led by an emerging black intelligentsia (W.E.B. Du Bois, Marcus Garvey, Mary Bethune, the anti-lynching crusaders formed by the NAACP), and the postwar Civil Rights movement—was to a major extent shaped by these struggles.

The issue of race has obviously evolved and over time found new symbolic expressions. Even though the most explicit mechanisms of race-based discrimination and exclusion have been removed in the aftermath of the Civil Rights movement 30 years ago, centuries of slavery and segregation have left their indelible marks on America. Their painful legacy lives on, and race continues to shape the social practices and debates in this country. It still maintains its grip over all Americans, as today's heated arguments about Affirmative Action, welfare, and crime—all social codes for race—illustrate.

The point of Study II presented here is to analyze the social representation of black Americans, to identify the points of convergence and divergence in the organization of the representational field concerning this social object in contemporary America. I gave the name "Evaluative

Questionnaire" to the inventory I set out to develop (see Appendices B and C). Its different items were either inspired by or directly taken from different studies of race in America (Campbell, 1971; Cross, 1980; Fairchild, 1985; Gordon, 1976; Hecht & Ribeau, 1987; Helms, 1990; Jackson & Gurin, 1987; Jaynes & Williams, 1989; Katz & Braly, 1933; Kleinpfenning & Hagendoorn, 1993; Lee, 1993; Pettigrew & Meertens, 1995; Plous & Williams, 1995; Schuman & Hatchett, 1974; Stephan et al., 1993). This inventory assessed the attitudes and opinions of black and non-black subjects about black Americans, and their perceptions of the relation this group has to the rest of America. Respondents were asked to indicate the extent to which they agree or disagree with each of the items. The questionnaires used the following response format: 7 = strongly agree; 6 = agree; 5 = somewhat agree; 4 = neutral/no opinion; 3 = somewhat disagree; 2 = disagree; and 1 = strongly disagree.

The opinions solicited from the subjects were not confined to "your opinion" (i.e., the personal opinion of the subject), but extended to the "opinion of mainstream America" (i.e., the subject's opinion of what most Americans think about the question) and the "opinion of the black community" (i.e., the subject's opinion about the views black Americans might hold on the question). The purpose of these response extensions was to examine how personal attitudes and opinions are formed in a broader social context of influence and thus come to depend to a considerable degree on what individuals believe the rest of society (or at least their own group) think about the question at hand. Moreover, certain attitudes and opinions, which might in the minds of subjects violate established norms and thus come to be suppressed or neutralized when expressing one's own opinion, might surface when projected onto others. I gave these opinion-scale questionnaires to 138 black Americans and 143 non-black Americans. The responses were then subjected to a principal-factors factor analysis using an orthogonal rotation (VARIMAX) for our two groups, to discover which variables in the set form coherent subsets. This type of analysis allows us to identify and interpret the common knowledge concerning the representation of black Americans.

FACTOR STRUCTURES FOR BLACK AMERICANS

This part of the study analyzes the responses of black American subjects on two questionnaires composed of 16 items and 18 items, respectively. The first questionnaire (see Table B.1 in Appendix B) measures attitudes concerning racial discrimination, the destiny of black Americans in America, their separation from the American culture, and different attributes used in the famous Checklist Technique of Katz & Braly (1933). Subjects were asked to answer on two levels: their own opinions and their perception of what mainstream America would think about the same issues. The second questionnaire (see Table B.2 in Appendix B), similar in format to the first one, combines questions measuring the attitudes of subjects concerning racial discrimination, the destiny of black Americans in America, their separation from the American culture, a sense of Afrocentrism, cross-categorization of race and gender, and responses to racism. This time subjects were asked to answer based on their own opinions and their perceptions of what the black American community would think concerning these issues.

Subjects' Own Opinions

The two questionnaires were combined and the item responses of black American subjects were factor analyzed. These items were examined on the basis of the subjects' own opinions. Eleven factors, all composed of variables with loadings of .30 and above, yielded eigenvalues greater than 1. From this extraction six factors were interpreted. On the basis of common theoretical dimensions that unify the group of variables loading on the factor, these were named *Negative Images, Cultural Exclusion, Separation, Positive Self-Image, Cultural Inclusion,* and *Cultural Participation.*

Table 7.1 shows the percentage of variance each factor accounted for, the mean responses of black American subjects on each item, their standard deviation, and their loading on factors. The six factors accounted for 50.3 percent of the total variance, but only two of them exceeded 10 percent. More specifically, they accounted for 15.7 percent, 12.2 percent, 7.8 percent, 5.8 percent, 5.2 percent, and 3.6 percent of the total variance individually. From a preliminary observation, the results seem to point out an interesting bipolarity in the factors. While the first three clusters (*Negative Images, Cultural Exclusion,* and *Separation*) are in fact related to the negative and alienating dimensions of segregation, the last three clusters (*Positive Self-Image, Cultural Inclusion,* and *Cultural Participation*) point to the positive and active role of black Americans in the American culture. The presence of this bipolarity, specifically in the data of black American subjects, appears to be the manifestation of black Americans' dual consciousness (Du Bois, [1903] 1965).

The first factor, *Negative Images,* is composed of attributes deriving from the Katz & Braly (1933) questionnaire. A high score on this factor is interpreted as an agreement with the association of these negative images to black Americans. The second factor, *Cultural Exclusion,* combines pessimism concerning the elimination of discrimination, a distrust of Whites, and a separate identification from the American society (Schuman & Hatchett, 1974). Scoring high on this factor is understood to indicate a sense of exclusion from society. The third factor, *Separation,* reflects a more conative dimension of the subject's opinions. A high score

Table 7.1
Evaluative Reactions of Black Americans (your opinion)

Factor (%)		M	SD	Loading
Factor 1: Negative Images (15.7%)				
black Americans are often rude		3.23	1.86	.79
black Americans are loud		3.91	2.03	.78
black Americans are talkative		4.14	1.95	.75
black Americans are quick-tempered		4.02	2.02	.73
black Americans neglect their family		2.67	1.84	.70
black Americans are lazy		2.59	1.89	.65
black Americans are arrogant		3.08	1.96	.64
	M:	3.38		
Factor 2: Cultural Exclusion (12.1%)				
discrimination will never end		4.59	2.29	.84
whites want black Americans kept down		4.39	2.33	.75
discrimination will never end in America		4.74	2.22	.73
there will be more discrimination in 20 years		4.38	1.97	.70
more important to be black American than American		4.67	2.13	.51
	M:	4.55		
Factor 3: Separation (7.8%)				
black American women should not date Whites		3.48	2.35	.77
black Americans should vote for black candidates		2.92	1.97	.65
black Americans should give kids African names		3.69	2.04	.59
black Americans should shop in black stores		4.86	2.05	.50
black/white Americans shouldn't organize on gender issue*		4.60	2.15	.47
	M:	3.63		
Factor 4: Positive Self-Image (5.8%)				
black Americans are proud of themselves		5.57	1.81	.80
black Americans are intelligent		6.16	1.41	.65
black Americans will no longer endure discrimination		5.33	1.98	.48
	M:	5.68		
Factor 5: Cultural Inclusion (5.2%)				
black Americans are beginning to have power in America		4.91	1.73	.71
black Americans want their share of the American Dream		6.30	1.53	.62
black Americans should teach kids the meaning of black		6.21	1.51	.48
	M:	5.80		
Factor 6: Cultural Participation (3.6%)				
black Americans are ambitious		5.73	1.59	.75
black Americans should try to succeed within mainstream		5.38	2.10	.52
there is less racial discrimination now		3.57	2.43	.45
	M:	4.89		

Notes: Factors are listed in order of percentage of variance.
* Item was adjusted to account for a (-) loading.

Table 7.2
Reliability Analysis of "Your Opinion" Scales for Black American Subjects

Factor	Alpha
Negative Images	.86
Cultural Exclusion	.79
Separation	.73
Positive Self-Image	.66
Cultural Inclusion	.48
Cultural Participation	.43

Note: Coefficient alphas are based on a sample of 138 black Americans.

expresses behavioral intentions towards dichotomizing the world of black Americans and that of white Americans (Bobo, 1987).

The other pole of black Americans' existence in this society is positive. The fourth factor on Table 7.1 is a combination of positive attributes and a clear awareness of discrimination in this country. This factor reflects the *Positive Self-Image* of the group (Gates, 1988; Levine, 1977; Poussaint, 1966). *Cultural Inclusion* is the fifth factor; it indicates a sense of inclusion along with the recognition of clear distinctions (Hale, 1980; King, 1964). A high score has been interpreted as an agreement with the gradual inclusion of black Americans in American culture. The last factor, *Cultural Participation*, extends the sense of cultural inclusion to an active state of cultural participation (Torrance, 1990). A high score on this factor is interpreted as a behavioral commitment to American society.

An analysis of the correlations between factors (see Table D.1 in Appendix D) reveals that the scales are not strongly intercorrelated. However, two factors had significant levels of correlation to other factors. *Cultural Exclusion* and *Separation* were correlated at almost .5 (p < .01). Their correlation makes theoretical sense, since a sense of cultural exclusion and a propensity towards separation are issues that arguably operate together. *Positive Self-Image* and *Cultural Inclusion* do not correlate quite as strongly at .37 (p < .01), but do match enough to indicate that they are not completely dissimilar. These factors must therefore be understood and interpreted in relation to one another.

Table 7.2 presents the internal consistency, or alpha coefficient, for each factor. The coefficients for the first, second and third factors are within the acceptable standard for scale (i.e., alpha > .70), which means that they have achieved a certain internal consistency and thus a satisfactory level of reliability.

Mainstream Opinion

The item responses of black Americans on the basis of their projections concerning mainstream American opinions ("mainstream" was not defined for the subjects) were analyzed in similar fashion. The two questionnaires (see Tables B.1 and B.2 in Appendix B) were combined and factor analyzed. Four factors, composed of items with loadings of .30 or above and yielding eigenvalues superior to 1, were extracted. With the help of our theoretical foundations, three clusters were retained and identified as *Negative Images, Cultural Integrity,* and *Belief in the "Just World."* Table 7.3 shows the mean responses for each item, their standard deviations, and the loading values on their respective factor.

These three factors alone accounted for 51.2 percent of the total variance, with factors 1, 2, and 3 accounting for 29.6 percent, 13.2 percent, and 8.4 percent of the total variance, respectively. In addition, from an analysis of their intercorrelations (see Table D.2 in Appendix D), a negative correlation was found between *Negative Images* and *Cultural Integrity*, $r = -.34$ ($p < .01$).

The first factor, *Negative Images*, is composed of attributes that stem in large part from the Katz & Braly (1933) stereotype questionnaire. Agreement with these negative images, in their association here to mainstream opinion about black Americans, corresponded to a high score. The second factor, a combination of positive images and a sense of autonomy, has been named *Cultural Integrity*. A high score on this factor suggests a strong sense of self-sufficiency ("African-American or Black," 1989; Hoskins, 1992). The third factor is called the *Belief in the "Just World"* (Lerner, 1980) as it combines the idea that black Americans should try to be successful in the mainstream culture and the principle that people get what they deserve (Furnham & Procter, 1989). A high score on this factor indicates a strong belief in such a "just world."

Internal consistencies were calculated for each factor on the basis of alpha coefficients (Table 7.4). Factors 1, 2, and 3 yield alpha coefficients of .83, .81, and .18, respectively. The coefficients for the first two factors show a satisfactory level of reliability. This is not the case for the last factor, the *Belief in the "Just World,"* which we therefore must reject as a scale.

Black Americans' Opinions

The item responses of black Americans on the basis of their projections concerning black Americans' opinions were factor analyzed. These items clustered into seven factors with loadings above .30 on their factor and eigenvalues above 1. Three of those, *Cultural Exclusion, Dual Consciousness,* and *Separation*, have been retained for further analysis. The results

Table 7.3
Evaluative Reactions for Black Americans (mainstream opinion)

Factor (%)		M	SD	Loading
Factor 1: Negative Images (29.6%)				
black Americans are quick-tempered		5.25	1.72	.82
black Americans are talkative		4.91	1.72	.81
black Americans are loud		5.19	1.86	.73
black Americans neglect their family		4.83	1.96	.66
black Americans are often rude		4.77	1.88	.61
black Americans are arrogant		4.73	1.89	.59
black Americans are lazy		4.88	2.00	.46
	M:	4.94		
Factor 2: Cultural Integrity (13.2%)				
black Americans should try to succeed outside mainstream		4.32	2.01	.73
black Americans are ambitious		3.57	2.01	.73
black Americans are proud of themselves		4.09	2.02	.72
black Americans are intelligent		3.84	2.08	.70
black Americans are suave		3.86	1.87	.67
black Americans are responsible towards their community		3.20	1.89	.60
	M:	3.81		
Factor 3: Belief in the "Just World" (8.4%)				
there is less racial discrimination now		3.96	2.12	.77
black Americans should try to succeed within mainstream		4.77	2.10	.38
	M:	4.37		

Note: Factors are listed in order of percentage of variance.

of an intercorrelation analysis (see Table D.3 of Appendix D) demonstrate that these factors are for the most part independent from one another. The means, standard deviations, and loading of these items on the factors are presented in Table 7.5. Factors 1, 2, and 3 accounted for 20 percent, 11.6 percent, and 9.4 percent of the total variance, respectively.

Cultural Exclusion is the first factor, combining a pessimistic view of discrimination in this country, mistrust of white Americans, and the need for autonomy. A high score on this factor reflects a sense of exclusion from American culture. The second factor addresses Du Bois's dual con-

Table 7.4
Reliability Analysis of "Mainstream Opinion" Scales for Black American
Subjects

Factor	Alpha
Negative Images	.83
Cultural Integrity	.81
Belief in the "Just World"	.18

Note: Coefficient alphas are based on a sample of 138 black Americans.

Table 7.5
Evaluative Reactions for Black Americans (black Americans' opinion)

Factor (%)		M	SD	Loading
Factor 1: Cultural Exclusion (20.0%)				
whites want black Americans kept down		4.43	2.50	.89
discrimination will never end in America		4.61	2.33	.84
more important to be black American than American		4.32	2.28	.72
there will be more discrimination in 20 years		4.09	2.13	.71
	M:	4.36		
Factor 2: Dual Consciousness (11.6%)				
black Americans should teach kids an African language		4.46	2.02	.71
black Americans should shop in black stores		4.98	2.01	.67
black Americans should teach kids the meaning of black		5.78	1.85	.61
black Americans want their share of the American Dream		5.91	1.76	.58
	M:	5.28		
Factor 3: Separation (9.4%)				
black Americans should give kids African names		4.25	1.74	.76
black American women should not date Whites		4.88	2.22	.71
black Americans should vote for black candidates		4.41	2.16	.64
	M:	4.51		

Note: Factors are listed in order of percentage of variance.

Table 7.6
Reliability Analysis of "Black Americans' Opinion" Scales for Black American Subjects

Factor	Alpha
Cultural Exclusion	.82
Dual Consciousness	.66
Separation	.61

Note: Coefficient alphas are based on a sample of 138 black Americans.

sciousness of being divided into two selves, one stressing roots in Africa and the other paying allegiance to America. This scale has been named *Dual Consciousness*. A high score on this factor reflects a strong awareness of this dualistic existence. *Separation* is the third factor, and corresponds to the behavioral intention of separating from the American culture. A high score expresses a desire for such separation.

As indicated in Table 7.6, factors 1, 2, and 3 yield alpha coefficients of .82, .66, and .61 respectively. The coefficient for *Cultural Exclusion* is within the acceptable standard for scale, and so boasts a satisfactory level of reliability. While not qualifying as scales, the factors *Dual Consciousness* and *Separation* had alpha coefficients high enough to merit close monitoring in our analyses.

FACTOR STRUCTURES FOR NON-BLACK AMERICANS

We will now look at the responses of non-black American subjects. A questionnaire, which solicited three dimensions of responses from the subjects (i.e., their own opinions, their perceptions of what mainstream America thought about the same issues, and their projections of what black Americans would think concerning these issues), was distributed to our sample (see Table C.1 in Appendix C).

The inventory of questions, very similar to the one presented to the black American subjects, consisted of 23 items. Those items measure attitudes related to racial discrimination, the destiny of black Americans in America, black Americans' separation from the American culture, different attributes derived from the Katz & Braly (1933) questionnaire, cross-categorization of race and gender, and responses to racism.

Subjects' Own Opinions

A first factor analysis was conducted on the basis of the subjects' own opinions, using an orthogonal rotation. Eight factors with eigenvalues greater than 1 were extracted, and all the factors were retained for further analysis. The loading of each item on its corresponding factor was above .30. These clusters were named, respectively, *Negative Images, Image of Black American Women, Integration of Black American Women, Assimilation, Permanence of Discrimination, Cultural Inclusion, Separation,* and *Coping with Discrimination.* The composition of these factors is presented in Table 7.7 below in terms of the mean responses of non-black American subjects for the various items, their standard deviations, and their loadings on factors.

Together these eight factors explained 64.3 percent of the total variance, with factors 1, 2, 3, 4, 5, 6, 7, and 8 accounting for 19.4 percent, 10.2 percent, 7.7 percent, 6.2 percent, 5.9 percent, 5.3 percent, 5.1 percent, and 4.5 percent of the total variance, respectively. The *Negative Images* factor was responsible for by far the largest percentage of the variation.

The first factor, *Negative Images,* combines items derived in large measure from the Katz and Braly (1933) questionnaire. A high score on this factor confirms the prevalence of largely negative images associated with black Americans. The second and third factors reveal a cross-categorial approach to black Americans, based on a differentiation by gender. *Image of Black American Women* (factor 2) clusters two general—and in this context, strongly positive—attributes (i.e., intelligence and ambition) with a question implying that black American women deserve better than what they got (Lerner, 1973). This gender-biased contextualization of positive attitudes is repeated in *Integration of Black American Women* (factor 3), which points to the interrelation underlying this cross-category perspective (Garvey, 1925).

The fourth factor presented in Table 7.7, *Assimilation,* refers to the positive, assimilationist vision of King. A high score on this factor corresponds to a belief in the destiny of black Americans in America (Gordon, 1964). *Permanence of Discrimination,* the fifth factor, is a prospective measure of discrimination. A high score on this factor reflects a belief in the permanence of discrimination in the American culture (Feagin & Feagin, 1986). The sixth factor expresses a culturally inclusive view of black Americans, and thus has been named *Cultural Inclusion.* The feeling that black Americans should make it on their own by taking care of their own community is the seventh factor. This factor has been named *Separation,* and a high score reflects such a separatist view. The last factor, *Coping with Discrimination,* relates to *Permanence of Discrimination* (factor 5); it was measured by combining the pessimistic idea of the permanence of discrimination with a possible means to deal with it by endorsing America's "Protestant work ethic."

The intercorrelations among the factors confirm that the factors are nearly independent from one another (see Table E.1 in Appendix E). However, three factors had significant correlations with each other. *Image*

Table 7.7
Evaluative Reactions for Non-black Americans (your opinion)

Factor	M	SD	Loading
Factor 1: Negative Images (19.4%)			
black Americans are often rude	4.13	1.90	.83
black Americans are loud	4.40	1.80	.82
black Americans are quick-tempered	4.44	1.66	.75
black Americans are lazy	3.43	1.75	.68
black Americans are talkative	4.48	1.43	.67
black Americans are arrogant	3.79	1.67	.66
black Americans neglect their family	3.48	1.73	.62
M:	4.02		
Factor 2: Image of Black American Women (10.2%)			
black Americans are ambitious	4.78	1.51	.77
gender discrimination and black American women	4.97	1.60	.63
black Americans are intelligent	5.34	1.27	.57
M:	5.03		
Factor 3: Integration of Black American Women (7.7%)			
black Americans are beginning to have power in America	5.34	1.38	.73
black Americans are not suave*	3.75	1.34	.58
black/white Am. should organize on gender issue	5.67	1.53	.44
M:	5.03		
Factor 4: Assimilation (6.2%)			
black Americans should try to succeed in mainstream	5.73	1.40	.76
relevance of King versus Malcolm X today	5.30	1.65	.58
M:	5.51		
Factor 5: Permanence of Discrimination (5.9%)			
discrimination will never end in America	4.35	1.91	.65
there is more discrimination now*	3.76	2.00	.64
M:	4.06		
Factor 6: Cultural Inclusion (5.3%)			
black Americans are proud of themselves	4.97	1.50	.87
black Americans want their share of the American Dream	6.15	1.20	.46
M:	5.56		
Factor 7: Separation (5.1%)			
black Americans should try to succeed outside mainstream	4.61	1.80	.78
black Am. are responsible towards their community	4.42	1.75	.55
M:	4.51		
Factor 8: Coping with Discrimination (4.5%)			
there will be less discrimination 20 years from now*	3.85	1.87	.75
best way to handle discrimination is to work hard	4.32	2.00	.63
M:	4.08		

Notes: Factors are listed in order of percentage of variance.
* Item was adjusted to account for a (-) loading.

Table 7.8
Reliability Analysis of "Your Opinion" Scales for Non-black American Subjects

Factor	Alpha
Negative Images	.86
Image of Black American Women	.54
Integration of Black African Women	.41
Assimilation	.37
Permanence of Discimination	.21
Cultural Inclusion	.32
Separation	.34
Coping with Discrimination	.20

Note: Coefficient alphas are based on a sample of 143 black Americans.

of Black American Women correlated with *Cultural Inclusion* at .30 (p < .01) and with *Separation* at .28 (p < .01). This paradox is reproduced in the correlation of .24 (p < .01) between those last two factors.

As illustrated in Table 7.8, calculations of internal consistency for the different factors yielded alpha coefficients of .86, .54, .41, .37, .21, .32, .34, and .20, respectively. The coefficient for *Negative Images* is within the acceptable standard for scale. The lack of reliability on the other factors is in part due to the significant diversity and heterogeneity of the sample.

Mainstream Opinion

The item responses of non-black Americans were then factor analyzed on the basis of the subjects' projections concerning mainstream America's opinions ("mainstream" was not defined). Eight factors were extracted with items loading at .30 or above and yielding eigenvalues greater than 1. Six of those have been retained for further analysis. On the basis of our theory these factors were identified as *Negative Images-1, Negative Images-2, Separation-1, Separation-2, Civil Rights Legacy*, and *Myrdal's Dilemma*. Table 7.9 shows the means of the items, their standard deviations and their loading values. Factors 1, 2, 3, 4, 5, and 6 accounted for 17.2 percent, 11.0 percent, 7.9 percent, 6.0 percent, 5.5 percent, and 4.7 percent of the total variance, respectively.

The clusters *Negative Images-1* and *Negative Images-2* are composed of attributes mostly derived from the Katz & Braly (1933) racial stereotype questionnaire. Their projected differentiation here into two separate factors can be interpreted along the nature-culture distinction. The items of

Table 7.9
Evaluative Reactions for Non-black Americans (mainstream opinion)

Factor		M	SD	Loading
Factor 1: Negative Images–1 (17.2%)				
black Americans are talkative		4.71	1.56	.83
black Americans are loud		5.02	1.79	.70
black Americans are quick-tempered		4.94	1.62	.69
black Americans are often rude		4.81	1.69	.63
	M:	4.87		
Factor 2: Negative Images–2 (11.0%)				
black Americans are lazy		4.59	1.77	.80
black Americans are arrogant		4.51	.81	.74
black Americans neglect their family		4.48	1.83	.68
	M:	4.53		
Factor 3: Separation–1 (7.9%)				
black Americans are intelligent		4.01	1.71	.74
black Americans are ambitious		3.69	1.69	.69
black Americans should try to succeed outside mainstream		4.33	1.74	.38
	M:	4.01		
Factor 4: Separation–2 (6.0%)				
black Americans are proud of themselves		4.48	1.75	.69
black Americans are responsible towards their community		3.59	1.92	.63
there is more racial discrimination now*		3.97	2.02	.55
black Americans shouldn't try to succeed within mainstream*		5.50	1.67	.51
	M:	4.38		
Factor 5: Civil Rights Legacy (5.5%)				
black Americans are beginning to have power in America		5.08	1.58	.77
best way to handle discrimination is to work hard		4.94	1.78	.70
relevance of King versus Malcolm X today		5.13	1.76	.44
	M:	5.05		
Factor 6: Myrdal's Dilemma (4.7%)				
there will be more discrimination in 20 years		4.04	2.00	.82
black Americans want their share of the American Dream		5.43	1.75	.46
	M:	4.74		

Notes: Factors are listed in order of percentage of variance.
* Item was adjusted to account for a (-) loading.

Table 7.10
Reliability Analysis of "Mainstream Opinion" Scales for Non-black American Subjects

Factor	Alpha
Negative Images–1	.80
Negative Images–2	.78
Separation–1	.56
Separation–2	.47
Civil Rights Legacy	.48
Myrdal's Dilemma	.25

Note: Coefficient alphas are based on a sample of 143 non-black Americans.

Negative Images-1 (i.e., rude, loud, talkative, and quick-tempered) are characterizations of a more recent origin, essentially emerging with the Black Panthers in the 1960s and associated today with "hip hop" (Dyson, 1993). In contrast, *Negative Images-2* (lazy, arrogant, and neglect their family) encapsulates long-held views about the irresponsibility of black Americans which have ever since the beginning of slavery been used to justify the racial ideologies of this country (Hacker, 1995; Kluegel & Smith, 1986).

Separation-1 and *Separation-2* correspond to the idea expressed in the formula "separate but equal." The factors suggest very similar outlooks on separation. *Separation-1* (i.e., intelligent, ambitious, and trying to succeed outside mainstream) expresses a sense of self-sufficiency tied to positive attributes which allow for a clear dissociation from the mainstream culture. *Separation-2* (i.e., proud, responsible, more discrimination now, and should not try to succeed within mainstream) derives from a sense of the impossibility of eliminating discrimination; the separation referred to is thus separation by default (Bobo, 1987). The fifth factor, *Civil Rights Legacy*, assesses the positive impact of the Civil Rights movement. Scoring high on this factor means viewing the sixties movement as successful in advancing integration (Carson, 1986). The last factor expresses a dissonance between the treatment of black Americans in this country and the American creed, and has been named *Myrdal's Dilemma* (Huggins, 1971; Myrdal, 1944).

Table 7.10 illustrates the internal consistency for each factor on the basis of their alpha coefficients. Factors 1, 2, 3, 4, 5, and 6 yield alpha coefficients of .80, .78, .56, .47, .48, and .25, respectively. Only two of these factors can be generalized beyond this sample. The alpha coefficients for *Negative Images-1* (alpha = .80) and *Negative Images-2* (alpha =

.78) are within the acceptable standard for scale, insuring a satisfactory level of reliability.

Calculations of how those factors correlate (see Table E.2 in Appendix E) show, not surprisingly, the strongest connection ($r = .55$, $p < .01$) between *Negative Images-1* (factor 1) and *Negative Images-2* (factor 2). Similarly, *Separation-1* and *Separation-2* (factors 3 and 4) correlate at $r = .26$ ($p < .01$). *Negative Images-2* correlates negatively with *Separation-1* at $r = -.29$ ($p < .01$). Finally, *Civil Rights Legacy* (factor 5) correlates with the two *Negative Images* scales at $r = .24$ ($p < 01$) and $r = .22$ ($p < 01$), respectively.

Black Americans' Opinions

Finally, we examined the item responses of non-black Americans on the basis of their projections concerning black Americans' opinions, factor analyzing their responses. These items loaded at .30 or above on their respective factors. Seven factors were extracted (eigenvalues > 1), and five of those were retained on theoretical grounds. These factors are *Negative Images, Cultural Inclusion, Welfare, Declining Significance of Race*, and *Sustaining Integration*. In addition, there are five significant correlations between the factors.

Table 7.11 shows the five factors accounting for 49.9 percent of the total variance. *Negative Images* is composed of stereotypical images derived from the Katz & Braly (1933) questionnaire. A high score on this factor means agreement with these negative images and their associations with black Americans. The second factor, *Cultural Inclusion*, combines positive attributes that point to the possibility of assimilation. *Welfare* (factor 3) deals with negative projections that are typically used to characterize a population dependent on welfare. Factor 4, the *Declining Significance of Race*, points to the success of the Civil Rights movement by anticipating a color-blind society (Williams, 1988). The last factor is concerned with the perseverance of black Americans in efforts at integration, despite a pessimistic view of discrimination. This factor has been named *Sustaining Integration*.

Internal consistency was calculated for the each factor (see Table 7.12). Factors 1, 2, 3, 4, and 5 yielded alpha coefficients of .74, .71, .73, .50, and .38, respectively. *Negative Images, Cultural Inclusion*, and *Welfare* (factors 1, 2 and 3) were found to be within the acceptable standard for scale, which means that their internal consistency rises to a satisfactory level of reliability. The correlations between those factors were also calculated (see Table E.3 in Appendix E). The strongest correlation ($r = .50$, $p < .01$) exists between *Negative Images* (factor 1) and *Welfare* (factor 3). That same factor also correlates negatively with *Cultural Inclusion* (factor 2) at $r = -.30$ ($p < .01$). Similarly, *Cultural Inclusion* (factor 2) and *Welfare*

Table 7.11
Evaluative Reactions for Non-black Americans (black Americans' opinion)

Factor		M	SD	Loading
Factor 1: Negative Images (19.7%)				
black Americans are loud		3.40	1.84	.79
black Americans are quick-tempered		3.66	1.76	.75
black Americans are talkative		4.13	1.59	.73
black Americans are arrogant		3.13	1.78	.55
	M:	3.58		
Factor 2: Cultural Inclusion (9.6%)				
black Americans want their share of the American Dream		6.21	1.38	.72
black Americans are responsible towards their community		5.23	1.73	.68
black Americans are intelligent		5.36	1.75	.66
black Americans are proud of themselves		5.21	1.94	.63
gender discrimination and black American women		5.26	1.76	.44
	M:	5.45		
Factor 3: Welfare (7.6%)				
black Americans are lazy		2.52	1.57	.73
best way to handle discrimination is to work hard		3.51	1.96	.68
black Americans are often rude		2.98	1.72	.62
black Americans neglect their family		2.85	1.65	.59
	M:	2.97		
Factor 4: Declining Significance of race (6.9%)				
relevance of King versus Malcolm X today		3.83	1.81	.65
there is less racial discrimination now		3.08	2.42	.64
black Americans are beginning to have power in America		4.58	1.93	.60
black/white Americans should organize on gender issue		4.48	1.93	.58
	M:	3.99		
Factor 5: Perseverance in Integration (6.1%)				
discrimination will never end in America		4.12	2.42	.69
black Americans should try to succeed within mainstream		5.24	1.79	.61
black Americans are ambitious		5.14	1.64	.44
	M:	4.83		

Note: Factors are listed in order of percentage of variance.

Table 7.12
Reliability Analysis of "Black Americans' Opinion" Scales for Non-black
American Subjects

Factor	Alpha
Negative Images	.74
Cultural Inclusion	.71
Welfare	.73
Declining Significance of Race	.50
Sustaining Integration	.38

Note: Coefficient alphas are based on a sample of 143 non-black Americans.

(factor 3) correlate at $r = -.32$ ($p < .01$). These two factors also correlate, albeit in opposite directions, with *Sustaining Integration* (factor 5), at $r = .24$ ($p < .01$) and $r = -.27$ ($p < 01$) respectively.

THE "CULTURAL MARKERS"

Factor analyses of the kind conducted in the previous sections of this chapter allow us to understand the representational field concerning the social object in question, in this case Americans of African descent. Having identified different attitudinal clusters of our two samples, we are left with a rich inventory to assess black Americans as a central social object in the topography of the American culture. Six sets of scales were developed from the factor analyses, with each scale focusing on relatively distinct aspects relating to our social object. The structures as well as the contents of these scales allow us to study the points where the attitudes of our groups converge and where they diverge from one another.

These scales have located central core elements which, in my opinion, have shaped and continue to shape America as a society primarily operating on a racial paradigm. That racially filtered world view, well incorporated into everyday existence, has been an immutable constant in this culture (Bell, 1992; Du Bois, [1903] 1965; Dyson, 1993; Hacker, 1992; Kovel, 1984; Baldwin & Mead, 1971; Myrdal, 1944; Terkel, 1992; West, 1994). Our factor analyses make it quite obvious that our subjects look at black Americans from a racial perspective, thereby confirming that such an issue is a "cultural marker" in American society. In addition, our analyses indicate that the issue of race is organized around negative characterizations.

Indeed, the uniformly strong presence of a *Negative Images* scale at all levels of the analysis points to an interesting cultural convergence. At

Table 7.13

Comparison of *Negative Images* Scales on "Your Opinion" Level for Black and Non-black Subjects

Black Americans (Your Opinion)		Non-black Americans (Your Opinion)	
Factor 1: Negative Images (15.7%)	M	Factor 1: Negative Images (19.4%)	M
black Americans are often rude	3.23	black Americans are often rude	4.13
black Americans are loud	3.91	black Americans are loud	4.40
black Americans are talkative	4.14	black Americans are quick-tempered	4.44
black Americans are quick-tempered	4.02	black Americans are lazy	3.43
black Americans neglect their family	2.67	black Americans are talkative	4.48
black Americans are lazy	2.59	black Americans are arrogant	3.79
black Americans are arrogant	3.08	black Americans neglect their family	3.48
X:	3.38	X:	4.02

Notes: Midpoint for mean value is at 4.
X denotes the average mean value of each column.

the level of the subjects' own opinion the scales from both the black American and the non-black American responses are composed of exactly the same items. Notwithstanding some important differences, *Negative Images* scales have also been found to dominate other levels of the analysis (e.g., mainstream opinion for both samples), giving this "cultural marker" even more credence and establishing its response items as key central core elements. Such convergence warrants closer examination.

Table 7.13 shows the two versions of the *Negative Images* scale, composed of precisely the same seven items. On both "your opinion" questionnaires this factor carried the greatest weight. For black Americans, the scale accounted for 15.7 percent of the total variance in subjects' answers, while for non-black Americans it accounted for nearly 20 percent. In addition, this scale had, for both of our samples, the strongest alpha coefficient (alpha = .86).

It is also clear from the means obtained for the items comprising the factor that black Americans had a general inclination towards disagreeing with the scale (M = 3.38), while non-black Americans were basically neutral with a slight tendency in the direction of an agreement with the scale (M = 4.02). Figure 7.1 presents some of those differences graphically, illustrating in this fashion a striking pattern.

The parallelism of the two curves in Figure 7.1 is remarkable. The most

Figure 7.1
Relative Mean Responses of *Negative Images* Scales on "Your Opinion"
Level for Black and Non-black Subjects, with Midpoint at 0

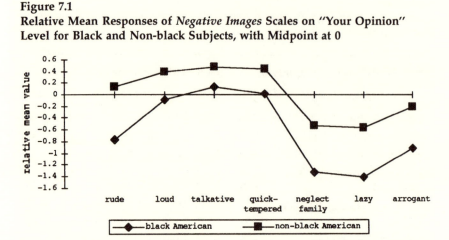

interesting aspect of this concordance is the fact that these *Negative Images* scales resulted from two separate factor analyses. One such analysis derived from the black American sample, and the other from the non-black sample. As mentioned above, both scales accounted for the largest percentage of variance. In each case the first two items to load on their respective factors were "rude" and "loud." While the curves in Figure 7.1 were based on the pattern of answers for black Americans, they are similar to those of non-black subjects, who, however, tended in the aggregate to agree more with these depictions.

At the level of what subjects projected onto the mainstream, the *Negative Images* scale proved again the factor that accounted for the highest variances. Table 7.14 presents the two versions of the scale resulting from our factor analyses. Again, the same seven items are found for those scales in both samples.

The first scale in the non-black sample is composed of characteristics of the group which relate to group interactions (i.e., talkative, loud, quick-tempered, and often rude). These interactional characterizations appear to comprise a "nature" dimension, and black subjects themselves were more inclined to agree with them. The second factor comprises items (e.g., arrogant, lazy, neglectful of their families) which project the group as irresponsible. These items are characteristics of a "nurture" dimension. We see that the mean value for *Negative Images-1* is higher than the mean value of *Negative Images-2*. While our subjects projected that the mainstream would to some extent agree with these particular images in their association to black Americans, our black American subjects projected stronger agreement with these images than did our non-black American sample (see Figure 7.2).

The means found here are generally higher than the "your opinion"

Table 7.14

Comparison of *Negative Images* Scales on "Mainstream Opinion" Level for Black and Non-black Subjects

Black Subjects (Mainstream Opinion)		**Non-black Subjects (Mainstream Opinion)**	
Factor 1: Negative Images (29.6%)	**M**	Factor 1: Negative Images–1 (17.2%)	**M**
black Americans are quick-tempered	5.25	black Americans are often rude	4.71
black Americans are talkative	4.91	black Americans are loud	5.02
black Americans are loud	5.19	black Americans are quick-tempered	4.94
black Americans neglect their family	4.83	black Americans are talkative	4.81
black Americans are often rude	4.77	X: 4.87	
black Americans are arrogant	4.73		
black Americans are lazy	4.88		
X: 4.94			
		Factor 2: Negative Images–2 (11.0%)	
		black Americans are lazy	4.59
		black Americans are arrogant	4.51
		black Americans neglect their family	4.48
		X: 4.53	

Note: Midpoint for mean value is at 4.

means depicted in Figure 7.1. In the case of black subjects this is not surprising, since they obviously will project that mainstream opinion holds more negative images about them as a group than they hold themselves. In the case of our non-black sample this difference implies that these subjects were more extreme in their opinions when those judgments reflected the norms of their group. What we witness here is in fact a manifestation of group polarization (McCauley & Segal, 1987; Moscovici & Zavalloni, 1968; Paicheler, 1976) which results from normative influences.

The presence of a group-polarization effect in this context, manifest in the divergence between "your opinion" and "mainstream opinion," may be best explained by the idea that the subjects, hesitant to admit the strength of their own negative feelings about black Americans, downplay

Figure 7.2
Mean Responses of *Negative Images* Scales on "Mainstream Opinion" Level for Black and Non-black Subjects, with Midpoint at 0

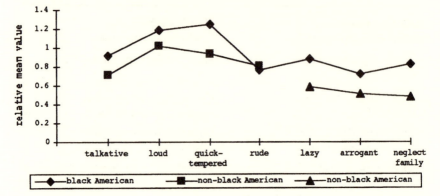

them when explicitly applied to themselves and project them instead onto the mainstream as generally held images. The black Americans in our sample by and large rejected these characterizations, as indicated (in Figure 7.1) by consistently giving us means far below the neutral 4 for each of the three items, even though they show themselves (in Figure 7.2) quite conscious of its presence in the minds of non-black Americans (the "mainstream").

When we analyzed the projections subjects made concerning the opinions of the black American population, we obtained a scale, for the non-black subjects, composed of four items also found in the other *Negative Images* scales. Those characterizations of "loud," "quick-tempered," "talkative," and "arrogant" also appeared in the four other variants of that factor, at the levels of the subjects' own opinions and their projections onto mainstream opinion, for both black and non-black Americans.

Table 7.15 shows the mean values of non-black subjects for each item. Note that black American subjects in our survey were not asked to project onto the black American population the particular items composing the scale. With the exception of the item "talkative," non-black subjects tend to believe that black Americans would disagree with these negative images and their association with Americans of African descent.

The cultural markers of a society are precisely those elements presumed stable and fixed in a culture. Here we have identified such a point of convergence in the American culture. The presence of these *Negative Images* scales at all levels of our different factor analyses shows the extent to which these items are central to the social representation of black Americans, even though the mean responses indicate sometimes agreements and sometimes disagreements with these depictions. Table 7.16 is

Table 7.15
Comparison of *Negative Images* Scales on Black Americans' Opinion Level for Black and Non-black Subjects

Black Americans (black Americans' opinion)	Non-black Americans (black Americans' opinion)	
	Factor 1: Negative Images (19.7%)	M
	black Americans are loud	3.40
not applicable	black Americans are quick-tempered	3.66
	black Americans are talkative	4.13
	black Americans are arrogant	3.13
	X:	3.58

Note: Midpoint for mean value is at 4.

a cumulative table which shows the means of the seven items for both samples on each level of analysis. This table shows that the items composing the scale—"rude," "loud," "talkative," "quick-tempered," "neglect their family," "lazy," and "arrogant"—are all images of black Americans with remarkably deep roots.

It seems at this point useful to divide the seven items into two separate image clusters. This division, in fact, replicates the separation of the *Negative Images* scale into two distinct subscales evoked by non-black American subjects projecting mainstream opinions about black Americans (see Figure 7.2). The items "rude," "loud," "talkative," and "quick-tempered" are all interactional characterizations and denote a boisterous side, a "wild" (distinctly non-Anglo) spirit, among black Americans. The items "neglecting their family," "lazy," and "arrogant," on the other hand, all project an image of irresponsibility. We find this very same duality in negative imagery, albeit in different manifestations corresponding to the specific period in question, throughout history.

In 1738 the Swedish naturalist Linnaeus divided the human species into four categories, each allegedly endowed with its own distinct characteristics. The category "Afer" (i.e., African) Linnaeus described as "cunning, slow, negligent, ruled by caprice" (qtd. in Dunn & Dobzhansky, 1952, p. 189). "Cunning" carries the negative sense of being sly or skilled at deception, implying someone not to be trusted and as such not dissimilar to today's characterization of "arrogant." The references to "negligent" and "ruled by caprice" clearly imply irresponsibility. Additionally, the attribute "slow" may be linked to this irresponsible-lazy dimension as well. Thomas Jefferson (1781), who drew up the Declara-

Table 7.16
Comparison of *Negative Images* Scales for Black and Non-black Subjects

Negative Images	BY	BM	NY	NM	NB
black Americans are often rude	3.23	4.77	4.13	4.81	—
black Americans are loud	3.91	5.19	4.40	5.02	3.40
black Americans are talkative	4.14	4.91	4.48	4.71	4.13
black Americans are quick-tempered	4.02	5.25	4.44	4.94	3.66
black Americans neglect their family	2.67	4.83	3.48	4.48	—
black Americans are lazy	2.59	4.88	3.43	4.59	—
black Americans are arrogant	3.08	4.73	3.79	4.51	3.13

Notes: Midpoint for mean value is at 4.
BY = Black Americans/Your Opinion. BM = Black Americans/Mainstream Opinion. NY = Non-black Americans/Your Opinion. NM = Non-black Americans/Mainstream Opinion. NB = Non-black Americans/Black Americans' Opinion.

tion of Independence of the United States, described "the other race" as "in reason inferior to whites," as incapable of creating art because "in imagination they are dull, tasteless, and anomalous," and as "ugly," "stupid," and "shallow" (see Collier, 1990). The Founding Fathers of America, like Jefferson, could reconcile their moral dictum of "equality for all" with slavery, because they obviously considered Americans of African descent as innately inferior. Slavery created its own negative imagery of black Americans, aimed at justifying such an extreme social practice as owning humans as property. That imagery centered on an implied wildness (which had to be tamed) in the nature of blacks, coupled with the assumption that blacks were incapable of taking care of themselves and thus had to be looked after by others.

This latter notion has outlived slavery. Bache (1895) made the point, repeated later by a number of other psychologists around World War I (see Harris, 1990), that black Americans are less intelligent because their mental development stops in adolescence, thus anchoring a mainstream view of them as childlike and morally deficient, an attitude that seems to continue to date with the public discussions on welfare issues. Bache also asserted that black Americans were "inferior" and "quicker in movement," and that they resembled automatons. Ferguson (1916) reproduced the prevailing duality of negative imagery vis-à-vis black Americans perhaps most clearly by characterizing the group in terms of "strong and changing emotions, an improvident character and a tendency to immoral conduct," which he saw "all rooted in uncontrolled impulse" and produced by "a deficient development of the more purely intellectual capacity." His characterization of the group combined the following traits: moral deficiency, "instability of character," "deficient ambition," volatility, "lack of foresight," "lack of persistence," and "stronger emotions" (pp. 123–124).

The famous study of group attributes by Katz and Braly (1933) identified the items "superstitious," "lazy," "happy-go-lucky," "ignorant," "musical," "ostentatious," "very religious," "stupid," "physically dirty," "naive," "slovenly," and "unreliable" as the ones most widely applied to black Americans. The adjective-checklist procedure introduced by Katz and Braly, which reproduced the deeply rooted imagery of emotionality, intellectual inferiority, and irresponsibility, was repeated in 1951, 1969, and 1982 to show constancies as well as changes in attributions (Dovidio & Gaertner, 1986; Gilbert, 1951; Karlins, Coffman, & Walters, 1969). Some of those characterizations remained important throughout (e.g., musical, very religious) or declined but retained considerable significance (e.g., lazy, happy-go-lucky). Others disappeared over time (e.g., stupid, physically dirty). New characterizations of the group, such as "pleasure-loving," "sensitive," "aggressive," "materialistic," "loyal to family," "arrogant," "ambitious," and "tradition loving" arose in their place.

Even though my questionnaire incorporated only some of the Katz and Braly attributes to make space for a greater range of items more applicable to our times, several components of our *Negative Images* scale, specifically "lazy," "arrogant," and "talkative," confirmed the findings of the original 1933 study or one of its follow-up studies. Three other items of our scale—"rude," "loud," and "quick-tempered"—all have close substitutes in the Katz & Braly checklist, such as "ostentatious" or "aggressive." The only deviation is our item "neglect their family" which seems to contradict directly "loyal to family," the most important attribute in the 1982 follow-up study. The difference here may reflect the fact that the 1982 study occurred before today's mainstream concerns with crime and welfare surfaced and transformed popular notions about black American family life.

The components of the *Negative Images* scale are displayed on Figure 7.3 for all the different conditions. We can observe that the lines follow a very similar pattern. The strongest agreement with this scale came from black Americans in their projections of mainstream opinion. The non-black subjects also projected a strong agreement with these depictions on the part of the mainstream, while the lowest agreement with the scale came from their projections onto black Americans. On average, concerning subjects' own opinions, black Americans scored lower than non-black Americans. In other words, they disagreed more with the scale.

When the items are compared based on the dual cluster found in the

Figure 7.3
**Mean Responses of *Negative Images* Scales on All Levels of Analysis for
Black and Non-black Subjects, with Midpoint at 0**

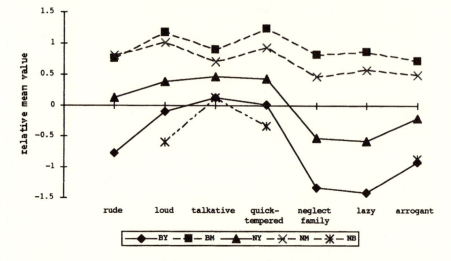

projections non-black subjects made of mainstream opinion, we see that
for that sample the boisterous attributes are by and large accepted, while
black Americans are neutral to them (excepting "rude," with which they
disagree). Concerning the irresponsibility cluster, both samples disagreed; black Americans disagreed more. The only item for which there
was agreement on all levels of the analysis is "talkative." This consensus
could imply that talkativeness is not necessarily seen as negative. There
is a generally appreciated oratorical tradition in the black American community which may be reflected in this characterization.

INTERPRETING THE RESULTS

Apart from the strong consensus around a *Negative Images* scale, the
factor analysis also revealed interesting convergences among black
American subjects concerning two distinct, yet interrelated, scales. One
is *Cultural Exclusion* (see Table 7.17), which reflects a rather pessimistic
attitude as to the intentions of whites vis-à-vis black Americans, and with
regard to the prospects of discrimination in the future. These negative
feelings produce an obvious counterreaction which emphasizes the distinctiveness of black Americans and the need to rely on one's own group,
rather than viewing oneself as an integral part of the broader (i.e., American) society. The other scale, *Separation* (see Table 7.18), follows up on
this point by clustering items that describe behavioral intentions towards
self-reliance, group solidarity, and separatism. Our subjects seem less

Table 7.17
Comparison of *Cultural Exclusion* Scales for Black Subjects on "Your Opinion" and "Black Americans' Opinion" Levels

Black Americans (Your Opinion)		Black Americans (Black Americans' Opinion)	
Factor 2: Cultural Exclusion (12.1%)	M	Factor 1: Cultural Exclusion (20.0%)	M
discrimination will never end	4.59	whites want blacks kept down	4.43
whites want blacks kept down	4.39	discrimination will never end	4.61
discrimination will never end	4.74	more important to be black than American	4.32
more discrimination in 20 years	4.38	more discrimination in 20 years	4.09
more important to be black than American	4.67	X:	4.36
X:	4.55		

Note: Midpoint for mean value is at 4.

Table 7.18
Comparison of *Separation* Scales for Black Subjects on "Your Opinion" and "Black Americans' Opinion" Levels

Black Americans (Your Opinion)		Black Americans (Black Americans' Opinion)	
Factor 3: Separation (7.8%)	M	Factor 3: Separation (9.4%)	M
black American women should not date whites	3.48	black Americans should give kids African names	4.25
black Americans should vote for black candidates	2.92	black American women should not date whites	4.88
black Americans should give kids African names	3.69	black Americans should shop in black stores	4.98
black Americans should shop in black stores	4.86	X:	4.70
black/white Americans should not organize on gender issue	4.60		
X:	3.63		

Note: Midpoint for mean value is at 4.

Figure 7.4
Comparison of Mean Responses of *Cultural Exclusion* Scales for Black Subjects on "Your Opinion" and "Black Americans' Opinion" Levels, with Midpoint at 0

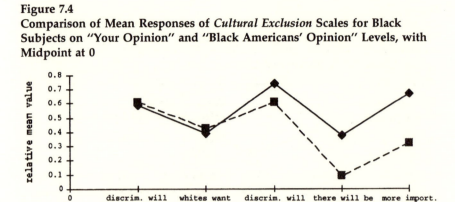

separatist on their own than they project their group to be, which may again support a group-polarization effect.

The two scales account for a fairly large percentage of the variance in responses, and their alpha reliability ranges from .61 to .82. They also strongly correlate with each other at $r = .5$, $p < .01$, which makes sense theoretically.

In Figures 7.4 and 7.5 the *Cultural Exclusion* and *Separation* scales are graphically presented on the basis of mean values for each item. Those items, which were present in the "your opinion" variant but missing when subjects projected group opinion, were superimposed on the latter variant of the scale. This technique of superimposition makes it possible to project factors onto different levels of analysis by clustering them so as to reproduce the original structure of the factor. The aggregate mean value of the factor is calculated by averaging the mean values for all relevant items as obtained on the projected level of analysis.

According to this technique the *Cultural Exclusion* scales exhibit a strongly similar and parallel shape, with all items agreed on in both versions. However, as we can see in Figure 7.5, there is greater divergence between the two *Separation* scale variants. Our black subjects have less separatist feelings than they project onto their group at large. In other words, they consider themselves more moderate than their reference group when it comes to acting out those separatist feelings through concrete behavior.

The *Cultural Integrity* scale, which concerns black subjects' projection of mainstream opinion, was another strong scale, accounting for 13.2 percent of the variance and having an alpha of .81. This factor combines

Figure 7.5

Comparison of Mean Responses of *Separation* Scales for Black Subjects on "Your Opinion" and "Black Americans' Opinion" Levels, with Midpoint at 0

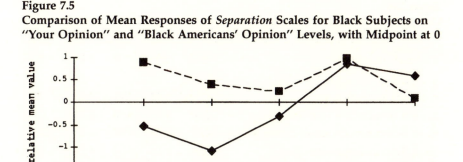

positive attributes of black Americans with measures of their cohesion as a community. We have superimposed the items composing this scale onto other levels of the analysis (see Table 7.19 and Figure 7.6). Black subjects (BY) obviously are in strong agreement with these items, a fact appreciated by non-black subjects (NB). The latter group seems willing to accept the basic premise of cultural integrity among black Americans (NY). As a matter of fact, Figure 7.6 illustrates clearly the almost perfectly parallel response pattern of both groups concerning their own opinion. Also noteworthy here is that both groups project a much less favorable mainstream opinion (BM and NM).

The samples also share ideas on items relating to *Cultural Inclusion*, albeit not at the level of a reliable scale. This factor, which combines the notion of black Americans wanting their share of the American Dream with positive group attributes such as pride, shows up in the opinions of black subjects (see "your opinion," factor 5) as well as non-black subjects (see "your opinion," factor 6). Among black subjects the notion of pursuing the American Dream also shapes their projection of a *Dual Consciousness* in their group (see "black Americans' opinion," factor 2). Such a conflicted sense of being both African and American is confirmed in turn by the positive correlations of *Cultural Inclusion* with *Separation* ($r = .5$, $p < .01$) and with *Positive Self-Image* ($r = .37$, $p < .01$).

A similar pattern can be observed among non-black subjects, for whom the notion of black Americans pursuing the American Dream forms the central item in the projection of *Myrdal's Dilemma* onto the mainstream (see non-black subjects' projection of "mainstream opinion," factor 6). The most complete *Cultural Inclusion* factor can be found among non-black subjects' projection onto black Americans' opinion where five items

Table 7.19
Comparison of *Cultural Integrity* Scale for Black and Non-black Subjects

Cultural Integrity	BM	BY	NY	NM	NB
black Americans should try to succeed outside mainstream	4.32	5.98	4.61	4.33	4.74
black Americans are ambitious	3.57	5.73	4.78	3.69	5.14
black Americans are proud of themselves	4.09	5.57	4.97	4.48	5.21
black Americans are intelligent	3.84	6.16	5.34	4.01	5.36
black Americans are suave	3.86	4.58	3.75	3.61	4.52
black Americans are responsible towards their community	3.20	4.72	4.42	3.59	5.23

Note: Midpoint for mean value is at 4.

Figure 7.6
Mean Responses of *Cultural Integrity* Scale for Black and Non-black
Subjects, with Midpoint at 0

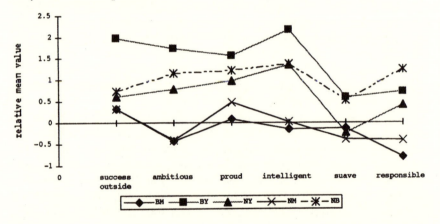

are clustered almost into a reliable scale (see factor 2, with an alpha
reliability of .71). In Table 7.20 I have projected this factor onto four other
levels of analysis by stringing together the relevant mean values for each
item on that particular level of analysis.

In Figure 7.7, the graph shows once again a clearly similar (i.e., parallel) pattern for the different levels of analysis. The only exception is
the black subjects' disagreement with gender discrimination as a problem
for black American women, which may imply a broader rejection on
their part of the implied preference extended to the female members of

Table 7.20
Comparison of *Cultural Inclusion* Scale for Black and Non-black Subjects

Cultural Inclusion	NB	NY	NM	BY
black Americans want their share of the American Dream	6.21	6.15	5.43	6.30
black Americans are responsible towards their community	5.23	4.42	3.59	4.72
black Americans are intelligent	5.36	5.34	4.01	6.16
black Americans are proud of themselves	5.21	4.97	4.48	5.57
gender discrimination is a problem for black American women	5.26	4.97	4.34	3.51

Note: Midpoint for mean value is at 4.

Figure 7.7
Mean Responses of *Cultural Inclusion* Scale for Black and Non-black Subjects, with Midpoint at 0

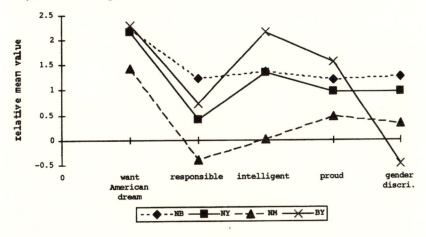

the group. That non-black subjects in fact tend to make this gender based distinction vis-à-vis black Americans seems confirmed by factors 2 and 3 ("your opinion") relating to positive images and integration of black American women.

An important factor of scale quality that non-black subjects projected onto black Americans is *Welfare*, which combines rudeness with two negative attributes used to characterize welfare recipients. One is that they are lazy, because they expect to get paid without work. The other is that they neglect their families, with poverty and welfare dependency linked to single mothers, fatherless children, and teenage pregnancy. Those negative images are then linked to the notion that the victims of discrimination should stop complaining and instead work their way out of their difficulties—in other words, adopt positive, all-American values that are precisely opposite to a "welfare mentality." Non-black subjects did not openly admit this cluster of opinions as their own; they did not even want to project it onto the mainstream. Yet they are obviously thinking about it and doing so in association with race (see *Welfare's* positive correlation with *Negative Images*, and its negative one with *Cultural Inclusion*, in non-black projections of black Americans' opinions).

Given the overlap in factor items between the *Negative Images* and *Welfare* scales, it is quite possible that the *Welfare* scale presents a convenient channel for repressed racial prejudice and thus serves as a code, a vehicle for substituting socially censored attitudes with those that are permitted. Since it serves as a proxy, it makes sense to express its presence in this mediated fashion as something that the other group, against whom it is directed, would surely reject (Kovel, 1984; Lawrence, 1987). It may also be that the indirect expression of the *Welfare* scale is due to the fact that this issue, in its association with the black American community, is primarily a product of public opinion makers, in particular politicians and the media. Non-black subjects may have assimilated this construct of a proxy for race while not yet admitting it as their own opinion. To elucidate this point I have superimposed the scale onto the other levels of our analysis (see Table 7.21).

The graphic presentation of these results (see Figure 7.8) shows remarkably parallel sequences of relative mean values between the two groups in their different projections of opinions. The only deviation from this consensual pattern arises from the underestimation by non-black subjects of the degree to which black subjects actually agree with the quintessentially American middle-class value of hard work as the solution to adversity.

This *Welfare* scale obviously has a certain political relevance in contemporary America, where both political parties have committed themselves to a radical overhaul of the nation's welfare programs as a result of the highly partisan and often acrimonious debate following the Republican takeover of Congress in 1994. It is in this context interesting to see that the issue of welfare emerges in our sample only indirectly, namely as something that the non-black subjects projected black Americans would reject.

When considering the results of these multilevel factor analyses in their entirety, we see a very interesting pattern in the distribution of factors. It is quite obvious that both groups in the sample, black subjects and non-black subjects, show a profound ambivalence in their attitudes

Table 7.21
Comparison on Welfare Scale for Black and Non-black Subjects

Welfare	NB	NY	NM	BY
black Americans are lazy	2.52	3.43	4.59	2.59
best way to handle discrimination is to work hard	3.51	4.32	4.94	4.39
black Americans are often rude	2.98	4.13	4.81	3.23
black Americans neglect their family	2.85	3.48	4.48	2.67

Note: Midpoint for mean value is at 4.

Figure 7.8
Mean Responses of *Welfare* Scale for Black and Non-black Subjects, with Midpoint at 0

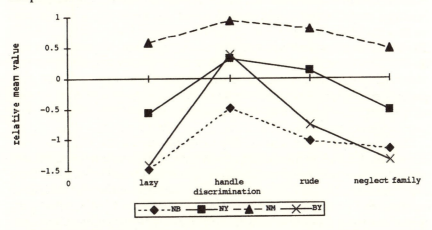

and opinions towards black Americans. On the one hand, that group remains strongly defined by race-based characterizations and thus continues to be viewed primarily in terms of marginalization. Yet at the same time we see already the beginnings of a redefinition of that same group as a culturally distinct, yet equivalent, subgroup of Americans, sharing the American Dream with the rest of society.

The prevalence of race in the American culture can be seen in the consistently strong presence of *Negative Images* on all levels of our factor analysis. The seven items composing that scale are cultural markers that organize everyone's thinking about black Americans around a racial paradigm. They comprise what Joyner (1989) called a "deep structure," helping to generate our specific cultural patterns. Black Americans, the ingroup in our study, respond to this negative depiction of their group with a sense of alienation from the American culture (the *Cultural Exclusion* and *Separation* scales). At the same time they are developing a *Positive Self-Image* which reinforces a sense of belonging to the American culture (the *Cultural Inclusion* and *Cultural Participation* factors). Shaped by the negative experience of their group in this country, our black subjects project this dialectic response onto their own group as a *Dual Consciousness* factor, in juxtaposition to *Cultural Exclusion* and *Separation*. Their projection of a *Cultural Integrity* scale onto the mainstream implies that, in their minds, non-black Americans deny them this positive sense of group autonomy.

Non-black subjects had strong *Negative Images* scales throughout. Yet their attitudes and opinions about black Americans have a potentially more complex structure, as indicated by the presence of various factors of sub-scale strength. They obviously feel less negatively about black American women (see the *Image of Black American Women* and *Integration of Black American Women* factors). It is also clear from looking at the *Assimilation* and *Cultural Inclusion* factors that our non-black subjects have internalized Martin Luther King's integrationist message, expressing a consistent approval of black Americans wanting to pursue the American Dream. At the same time they sense that discrimination persists and can only be changed slowly through patience and hard work (see the *Permanence of Discrimination* and *Coping with Discrimination* factors). In the face of that reality non-black subjects accept aspirations by black Americans to develop separately as a group (see their *Separation* factor).

This acceptance of separate group development appears more refined in non-black subjects' projections onto their own group (i.e., an unspecified "mainstream") where both the *Separation-1* and *Separation-2* factors imply a sense that black Americans can take care of themselves. Here, on this level of analysis, we see again the legacy of the Civil Rights movement towards gradual integration and equality (the *Civil Rights Legacy* factor). This duality of opinions towards separation and integration shows up in the *Myrdal's Dilemma* factor. The same ambivalence appears in non-black subjects' projections of what black Americans think. The great weight and high means of the *Cultural Inclusion* scale indicate that non-black Americans are very conscious of integrationist aspirations among black Americans. Correspondingly, they assume that black Americans would strongly reject *Welfare* scale characterizations as a proxy for race-based negative images. They conclude their projections of black American opinion with two essentially optimistic clusters of items. One indicates the *Declining Significance of Race*, even though its split structure of means reflects some uncertainty. The other is the *Perseverance of Integration* factor, a clear counterweight to the *Welfare* scale.

In conclusion, it seems obvious from our multileveled factor analysis that both groups look at their intergroup relation with a great deal of ambivalence and nuance. While race remains the dominant prism through which the status quo is defined, there are indications of greater willingness on both sides to consider the possibilities of integration and equality based on a consensual vision of what it means to be an American. These may be first signs that we as a society are beginning to move away from race and to see our societal conditions from the point of view of culture, in the context of a multicultural society.

Chapter 8

The Polemic of Names
in Group Evaluation

It is evident from the study of name preferences in Chapter 6 that the term African American has been endowed with a positive and future-oriented significance by a good number of Americans. Such a consensus, widely shared by black and non-black subjects, does not necessarily mean that everyone thinks and acts alike. Consensus, not to be confused with shared beliefs, allows for differences in attitudes and opinions between various social groups (Doise, 1986, 1989, 1992). These divergencies notwithstanding, different groups within the same space and at the same time experience the social world based on a common ground, as part of the culture they share. Whether they agree or disagree with a certain phenomenon, they bring to their judgments the same organizing principles, derived from a shared culture and language. This context is the consensus (Moscovici & Doise, 1992). In the case of African American the consensus is defined by both the positive and the future orientation attributed to the new name, as well as by its persistent linkage to the name Black.

Even though the new group designation seems to have succeeded as a vehicle for new thoughts and attitudes about Americans of African descent, the group remains strongly defined by what has until now dominated its social representation, its definition on the basis of race. As illustrated in Chapter 7, the overwhelming evidence of a *Negative Images* scale in both our samples, as a strong cultural marker, points to a defining common ground on the basis of which we still structure the social representation of Americans of African descent. This cultural marker is embodied in the social representation Black.

For non-black subjects the denomination Black is a racial category

(Banton, 1988; Hacker, 1992; Omi & Winant, 1986; Smith 1992; Terkel, 1992) and remains endowed with negative meanings (Davis, 1991). For black subjects, on the other hand, that same representation is obviously more complex since it concerns themselves. As demonstrated by Kenneth Clark (Clark, 1965; Clark & Clark, 1947), many Americans of African descent develop from an early age problems with their self-esteem; these problems are caused by constant exposure to racial prejudice in American society (Proshansky & Newton, 1968). At the same time they have always countered this imposition of negative evaluations with a strongly positive image of their own group, a response clearly evident in the "Black Is Beautiful" slogan of the late 1960s.

Given the underlying consensus expressed by the overwhelming presence of a *Negative Images* scale in both samples, it is clear that the denomination African American, far from being untouched by Black, actually originates from that previous representation (Jodelet, 1984). Even though the new denomination aims to separate itself from its predecessor, it still is mediated by the content of that race-based categorization of the group. This is precisely why African American remains an anticipatory representation, pointing with its positive and future-oriented connotations to how the object may eventually be redefined. Often it is only through its connection to preexisting representations that a new representation can be fully understood (Moscovici, 1984).

The example of the Citroën 2CV ("Deux Chevaux") illustrates this point quite clearly: a long-established representation of transportation, namely the horse carriage, continues to live on in a new representation of transportation, a car. Even today we measure the power of a car's engine in terms of horsepower. In the same vein, the presence of the *Negative Images* scale in both samples pertaining to Americans of African descent shows how the old representation still reverbarates in our minds.

Such an omnipresent organizing principle has to be understood as part of the central core of the representation. Its consistent presence throughout American society's brief history seems to support our argument (Bell, 1992; Myrdal, 1944; Omi & Winant, 1986; Winant, 1994). Moreover, for the black subjects, our analysis revealed two additional scales which completed the structure of the representation. These scales, *Cultural Exclusion* and *Separation*, are present in the opinions of black subjects as well as in their projections onto the group of black Americans at large. For the non-black subjects it is the *Separation* scale, evident in their own opinion and in their projections onto the mainstream, that completes the structure.

The present chapter differs from what we have discussed so far. The idea here is to integrate the measurements of our two studies and create from this integration a multilevel assessment for African American as a cultural phenomenon. My hypothesis is that obvious response differences between subjects concerning the aforementioned scales, as well as any other factors revealed by Study II, when linked to the choice of name, can be taken as an indication of change in the conceptualization of our social object. Such a dynamic of change and innovation demonstrates a split in the social representation of black Americans.

The differences between the two denominations (African American and Black) as independent variables should also be reflected at the various levels of our scale measurements, which are our dependent measures. In addition, this type of multileveled assessment allows us to contrast how black Americans and non-black Americans think about, perceive, and relate to black Americans. In this context the judgments of our subjects are examined not in isolation, but as they relate to the evaluations concerning the social object they project onto their own group and onto the "other" group.

The approach presented in this chapter allows us to clarify the dualistic relationship of African American and Black. It is clear that each name finds its meaning in contradistinction to the other. The predominantly negative definition of Black endows African American with a positive meaning, and vice versa. Such a polarity between the two names, while confirming the existence of two different representations of black Americans, also reveals that the shift in denomination, as a cultural phenomenon, expresses a transformation in the conceptualization of the object. After first presenting everyday examples to illustrate the relationship between these two names, we will examine the cultural markers found in our previous chapter, which define and redefine the object.

ANCHORING MECHANISMS: THE DYNAMICS OF TWO NAMES

Judging from its widespread use in public discourse and everyday conversations, African American is already anchored as a new social representation. The choice of this specific name is itself a major part of the anchoring process, which aims above all at familiarizing the new object. In fact, since the object in question is not a complete novelty but rather a reconceptualization of what already exists, we need to understand the elaboration of this new representation as much as the one from which it has emerged (Jodelet, 1984). Consequently, it is the dynamic relationship between the two social representations, also reflected in the struggles over the use of a specific name, that is of interest.

We can observe the duality of our two competing representations in "real life" examples from contemporary America—in advertising, academia, political discourse, the arts, literature, etc. A selection of everyday examples drawn from a variety of sources, besides confirming the relevance of names as social representations of the group, will also accentuate the link between Black, the previous representation, and African American, the new representation still in the making. That linkage sets African American in direct contradistinction to Black, as a vehicle for progress towards integration and as a vector for projections of a different, more inclusive future.

As part of this transformation African American also becomes a symbolic expression for redefining the group as a cohesive, culturally autonomous entity that coexists with other groups in a multicultural society. Each of the examples presented here illustrates this innovative quality of the new name. It is clear from these illustrations that African American is a positive name which redirects the social object away from the tenacious issue of race. The examples, illustrative of commonsense thinking, express the consensual nature of meaning given to African American across group lines. African American takes its root from Black, and attempts to redefine the latter.

The first example, an ad appearing in the *New York Times,* is presented in Exhibit 8.1. It illustrates quite concisely the historic sequencing of names given to black Americans, and relates each shift in name to progress in education, as a measure of integration.

On November 13, 1993, President Clinton, addressing 5,000 black ministers, delivered a speech from the same church pulpit in Memphis, Tennessee, from which Dr. Martin Luther King, Jr., spoke the night before he was assassinated 30 years ago. The speech is reproduced in Exhibit 8.2. In this speech President Clinton called on black church leaders to help fight what he characterized as a spiritual crisis in the black American community, and the violence this crisis has produced. His speech, noteworthy for its frankness and emotion, is also interesting for the purposes of our study insofar as it highlights the differentiation of the black American community and, at one point in the speech, expresses this juxtaposition clearly by switching from "Black" to "African American."

Our third illustration (Exhibit 8.3) is a memo sent by Arnold Rampersad, Director of the Program in Afro-American Studies at Princeton University, to Amy Gutmann at the Office of the Dean of the Faculty on August 24, 1995, concerning a proposed name change for the program.

In his latest book, mystery writer Ed McBain gives us two interesting examples of how ordinary Americans are forced to cope with the term African American even when they reject that group designation. In the first excerpt (Exhibit 8.4) McBain has a black private investigator explain why he cannot identify with that term, because he feels like an American who had lost all ties to Africa.

In the second excerpt (Exhibit 8.5) McBain presents a white man who, while complaining about a black man stealing away his girlfriend, moves

Exhibit 8.1
United Negro College Fund Advertisement in the *New York Times* April 16, 1995

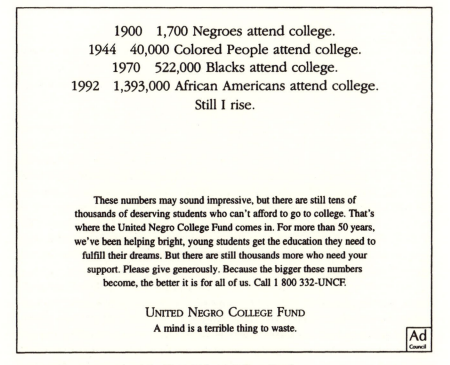

1900   1,700 Negroes attend college.
1944   40,000 Colored People attend college.
1970   522,000 Blacks attend college.
1992   1,393,000 African Americans attend college.
Still I rise.

These numbers may sound impressive, but there are still tens of thousands of deserving students who can't afford to go to college. That's where the United Negro College Fund comes in. For more than 50 years, we've been helping bright, young students get the education they need to fulfill their dreams. But there are still thousands more who need your support. Please give generously. Because the bigger these numbers become, the better it is for all of us. Call 1 800 332-UNCF.

UNITED NEGRO COLLEGE FUND
A mind is a terrible thing to waste.

Reprinted by permission of the United Negro College Fund.

in his anger from "nigger" to "black man" before acknowledging the competitor grudgingly as an "African American."

The contradistinction of Black and African American as two competing social representations of the same object is also evident in day-to-day conversation and the production of imagery. I have enclosed below (Exhibit 8.6) the content analysis of essays by 16 non-black college students on the question, "What distinguishes Black and African American?" to demonstrate that juxtaposition explicitly.

As an anticipatory representation still being made, the new name African American derives its meaning from its contradistinction to Black, a well-established and reified representation. This dynamic, characterizing the extent to which the two names are interrelated, can be illustrated by reexamining the response distributions for the name preference study (Study I) first presented in Chapter 6. Table 8.1 shows the percentage distributions of responses for the black American sample.

Exhibit 8.2
Excerpt from a Speech by President Clinton, November 13, 1993, in Memphis, Tennessee

PRESIDENT CLINTON: I tell you unless we do something about crime and violence and drugs that is ravaging the community, we will not be able to repair this country. (applause) If Martin Luther King, who said, "Like Moses I am on the mountain top and I can see the promised land but I'm not going to be able to get there with you, but we will get there," if he were to reappear by my side today and give us a report card on the last 25 years, what would he say? He'd say, "You did a good job," he would say, "voting and electing people who formerly were not electable because of the color of their skin. You have more political power, and that is good. You did a good job," he would say, "letting people who have the ability to do so live wherever they want to live, go wherever they want to go in this great country. You did a good job," he would say, "elevating people of color into the ranks of the United States armed forces to the very top, or into the very top of our government. You did a very good job," he would say. He would say, "You did a good job creating a black middle class of people who really are doing well, and the middle class is growing more among African-Americans than among non-African-Americans. You did a good job. You did a good job in opening opportunity." But he would say, "I did not live and die to see the American family destroyed. (applause) "I did not live and die to see thirteen-year-old boys get automatic weapons and gun down nine-year-olds just for the kick of it." (applause) "I did not live and die to see young people destroy their own lives with drugs and then build fortunes, destroying the lives of others. That is not what I came here to do." (applause) "I fought for freedom," he would say, "but not for the freedom of people to kill each other with reckless abandon, not for the freedom of children to have children and the fathers of children to walk away from them and abandon them as if they don't amount to anything." (applause) "I fought for people to have the right to work but not to have whole communities of people abandoned. This is not what I lived and died for." My fellow Americans, he would say, "I fought to stop white people from being so filled with hate that they would wreak violence on black people. I did not fight for the right of black people to murder other black people with reckless abandon." (applause) The other day I was in California at a town meeting, and a handsome young man stood up and said, "Mr. President, my brother and I, we don't belong to gangs, we don't have guns, we don't do drugs. We want to go to school. We want to be professionals. We want to work hard. We want to do well. We want to have families, and we changed our school because the school we were in was so dangerous, so when we showed up to the new school to register, my brother and I were standing in line, and somebody ran into the school and started shooting a gun, and my brother was shot down right in front of me at the safer school." The freedom to do that kind of thing is not what Martin Luther King lived and died for. (applause)

Exhibit 8.3
Memo by Arnold Rampersad, Director of Princeton University's Program in Afro-American Studies, Proposing a Name Change for His Program

August 24, 1995

To: Amy Gutmann, Office of the Dean of the Faculty

From: Arnold Rampersad, Director

Re: Name change for AAS

At a meeting of the Interdepartmental Committee some months ago, there was unanimous agreement that the name of the program should be changed to "Program in African-American Studies."

Although no one on the committee considers this question the most urgent we could be addressing at this time, there is agreement that such a change would be good for the program. Over the centuries, as you know, the formal naming of Americans of African descent has often been controversial. Terms such as "Negro" and "Colored" have fallen into disrepute, although the NAACP preserves the latter. "Aframerican," once favored by some, is heard no more. There was a long and sometimes bitter dispute over the need to capitalize "Negro."

"Black" was once thought to be insulting, then became fashionable in some quarters, and still is much in use although it is a questionable way to identify many persons of African descent. And so on. "Afro-American" gained a measure of prominence in the 1960s, but many people have found the term "Afro" curious and thus somewhat diminishing.

The virtual consensus now seems to be (following a bold public endorsement from Rev. Jesse Jackson some years ago) that "African-American" is a term of dignity and also of sufficient clarity and precision to make it preferable to all other terms. I agree with this position.

I trust that this request for such a modest change of name will not spark a hot debate at the former College of New Jersey.

Reprinted by permission of Arnold Rampersad and Princeton University.

African American is used by a third of the sample, but less than 15 percent report being referred to as such by non-black Americans. Already nearly one in two picked African American as the most preferred name for themselves. Fifty-eight percent considered the term to be the most positive when used by the ingroup, while nearly two-thirds thought of it as the most positive when used by the outgroup. Finally, more than half anticipated the term to be used more in the future. The terms Afro-American and People of Color are each preferred by at least 10 percent of the sample and still maintain a consistent presence in public discourse.

The non-black American subjects in our second sample were asked similar questions. The percentage distributions of their answers are summarized in Table 8.2.

Over two-thirds used the term Black. Only one out of five non-black

Exhibit 8.4
First Excerpt from Ed McBain (1994), *There Was a Little Girl*

"Who did this?" she asked.
Frank shook his head.

It all kept passing in the dark like a parade, all the circuses blaring, the elephants and clowns, the wild-animal acts and high-wire artists, the flyers and the girls in their sequined tights and tops. All the girls Matthew had ever kissed or never kissed, passing in the dark while voices whispered we've got a bleeder and the band played brass and gold. He'd never met a circus he'd liked, even when he was a kid, he'd always hated circuses, always.

"So what was he doing here?" Warren asked.
"I guess he was waiting for somebody," the bartender said, and shrugged.
He was black, like Warren. But in this neighborhood, you didn't get involved in police business. Warren had identified himself only as a friend of the victim. The bartender was wary nonetheless, brother or not. This section of the city was called Newtown, exclusively black until recent years when an Asian population had begun moving in, causing a somewhat volatile mix in a neighborhood already seething with racial unrest. Warren wondered when the hell it would ever end.
He was not a black man who chose to call himself African-American. He had been born in this country, as had his mother and his father and his grandparents, and if that didn't make him one-hundred-percent American, then he didn't know what did. One of his liberated slave ancestors who'd been carried here in chains from the Ivory Coast might have reasonably called himself *African*-American—which was what he'd been, after all—but the label simply did not apply to Warren, and he wasn't having any of it, thanks. Nor did he believe, the way some black people did, that *every* black act was justified,

Exhibit 8.5
Second Excerpt from Ed McBain (1994), *There Was a Little Girl*

140   ED McBAIN

nigger is still a nigger. I was the only one befriended Andy.
So he pays me back by stealing her away from me."

Bloom was listening harder and harder.

"Nobody'd have anything to do with her anymore. This
was five or six years ago, and here's a white girl starting up
with a *black* man? In the *South*? Who's fifteen, twenty years
older than she is? He used to work on a construction crew
for a housing development my company was putting up, that's
how they met. They call themselves African-Americans now,
I wish they'd make up their fuckin minds. A blonde, you
should see her. She's still blond, but I think she's partners
with Revlon now."

Five years ago, Bloom was thinking. Maria Torrance woul-
d've been seventeen, about the same age as young Jeannie
Lawson.

"And you say she wanted to run off with the circus?" he
asked.

"Yeah. Crazy idea. Well, she was crazy altogether, am I
right? Starting up with Andy?"

"Which came first?" Bloom asked. "Starting up with Andy,
or wanting to run off with the circus?"

"Andy. All the kids at Calusa High were ready to run *both*
of 'em out of town on a rail, you know. Cut off Andy's balls,
tar and feather 'em both, run 'em both out of town. She called
me one night, told me she was going to run away with the
circus. She said she could become an elephant girl, ride around
the ring on an elephant's back. I asked her where she'd got
such a crazy idea, she told me she'd talked to the owner, he
said she had good legs, with practice he could make her a
good elephant girl."

"Which circus?" Bloom asked.

"Ringling, I guess. Why?"

"Are you sure?"

Exhibit 8.6
Content Analysis of the Distinction between "African American" and "Black" (essays by non-black college students)

African American	Black
Sounds more professional.	Sounds less professional.
I think of an educated person with a degree, a good job, and a family.	I think of a less educated person, lower paying job, and limited family values.
Better sense of heritage.	
Well educated.	Trouble maker, uneducated, loud, and violent.
A business person.	
Higher level of education.	Not highly educated.
Individuals understand their rights and opportunities.	Shows less respect.
	Low self-image.
Gives more dignity and respect, while positively building the self-image.	Not an important part of society.
Reminds people that they are an essential part of this society.	
Creates a greater sense of importance and acceptance in this society.	
Can help forge closer race relations.	
Sounds nicer.	Not degrading when used by African Americans.
Most people do not look into its meaning.	May be offensive for some, since not all dark-skinned people come from Africa.
	Black is not as evil as it is presented to be.
More educated and successful.	Criminal.
Improves mental images.	Lower-class citizen.
Not criminally involved.	No definite opinion about Black.
In terms of races, it causes more understanding in relations.	
Creates a more positive view.	
In general more effective.	
Has more positive images.	Do not feel other groups recognize the legitimacy of African American as a culture.
Synonym for Black.	
Insinuates a national difference rather than a racial difference.	Whites see majority of Blacks as uneducated welfare recipients.
This terminology is temporary due to so much racism.	The ghetto.

Exhibit 8.6 (continued)

African American	Black
It is dependent upon the white society's acceptance or rejection.	
The term will survive in the political arena, where addressing people properly should be a duty.	
Racists see it as a depraved effort to identify with a culture to which black Americans have no right.	
The positive effects associated with the term will be temporary, it will soon have a negative connotation, and a new word will take its place.	No negative meaning at all.
Reflects pride in heritage and in this country.	Implies negative stereotypes.
A positive move.	
Positive.	A designation given by Whites.
Defines ethnic background.	
Identifies one's culture, although no one goes around saying they are Italian American, etc.	Insulting term.
The most gentle term to use for Americans of African descent.	Not necessarily derogatory.
Distinguished individual.	Lower class.
Well dressed and respected.	Whites use it to refer to Blacks as an inferior group.
Denotes higher class.	Always poor.
May help stimulate a sense of equality between people of different backgrounds.	Living in the poorest section of town.
	Involves troubles.
Because of prejudices in society it will not have a long-lasting impact.	
It is not a question of label, but also an issue that goes along with the identity of the group.	
A positive step.	
A key to success.	
A choice.	

Exhibit 8.6 (continued)

African American	Black
Intelligent.	Little education.
Independent.	Involved in crime.
Driven.	Low social standing.
American.	
More positive.	Bad images.
Does not have any bad images associated with it.	
Well-educated person.	
It may become permanent, because it is chosen by the group.	

Table 8.1
Choice of Name (African American versus Black) for Black American
Sample

Name	used by ingroup	used by outgroup	preferred	positive/ ingroup	positive/ outgroup	used in future
African American	33.8	14.6	44.1	58.2	64.7	55.0
Afro-American	4.6	6.9	10.2	9.0	10.1	10.8
Black	50.0	63.1	30.7	17.2	15.1	19.2
Colored	2.3	6.9	3.1	3.3	3.4	3.3
Negro	2.3	4.6	—	3.3	1.7	4.2
People of Color	6.9	3.8	11.8	9.0	5.0	7.5

subjects used African American, slightly more than the proportion of
black subjects in our first sample who reported having the term applied
to them by non-black Americans. Yet their evaluation of the new term
was much more favorable than indicated by its limited usage. When
subjects were asked to indicate their preference, already one-third of the
sample chose African American and 40 percent chose Black. Over three-
quarters of the subjects thought that the new denomination projected the
most positive images, whereas only 6 percent picked Black. Two thirds
of the sample thought that African American will be used more in the
future, compared to 10 percent who opted for Black. The name Afro-
American is, even more than in the black sample, preferred by a significant percentage of the subjects (i.e., 20 percent).

Figure 8.1 shows the respective reponse distributions of African Amer-

Table 8.2
Choice of Name (African American versus Black) for Non-black American Sample

Name	used	preferred	positive	used in future
African American	19.1	33.6	76.9	66.4
Afro-American	6.4	20.4	13.4	17.6
Black	67.4	40.1	6.0	9.9
Colored	2.8	2.9	—	—
Negro	2.8	0.7	0.7	1.5
People of Color	1.4	2.2	3.0	4.6

Figure 8.1
Choice of Name (African American versus Black) for Black American Sample

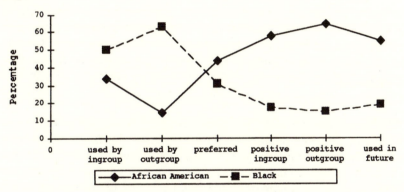

ican and Black, across the different levels, to be exact mirror images of each other. While African American is only used by one out of three black Americans, and is projected to be used even less by non-black Americans, its overall evaluation is much more favorable. The switch from Black to African American seems to occur at the level of the preferred term. But the tendential convergence of the two terms concerning their future use (also observed among non-black subjects in Figure 8.2 below) indicates a degree of uncertainty about the continuing evolution of the name.

In Figure 8.2 we compared the percentage distribution of the two dominant terms, Black and African American, for the non-black sample. Once again, as was the case in our first sample, the curves appear as mirror images of one another. For the non-black subjects, the switch from Black

Figure 8.2
Choice of Name (African American versus Black) for Non-black American Sample

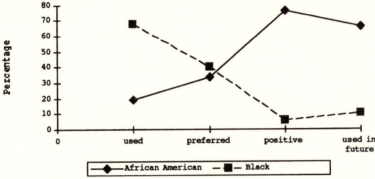

to African American occurs when subjects are asked to select the most positive terms.

This study of name preferences shows quite clearly the tenuous and complex coexistence of Black and African American as competing denominations to refer to Americans of African descent. It is precisely this tension, found in both of our samples, that indicates the extent to which the two terms exist in mutual contradistinction. Given the recent emergence of African American, it is obvious from these findings that the new term, a representation still in the making, derives its meaning primarily in opposition to that of Black, a stable representation.

That consensus around a positive and future-oriented significance, regardless of whether people use the term or not, leads to an important conclusion. Individual attitudes and opinions develop in a social context and are thus fundamentally shaped by what others think. Such a conclusion is not so evident from the point of view of mainstream social psychology, which, as Farr (1996) reminds us has individualized the concept of attitude ever since Allport (1935) and thereby reduced it to a stimulus-response phenomenon designed to explain why people respond differently to objectively similar situations (Jaspars & Fraser, 1984). Mainstream studies of attitudes and opinions (Pratkanis and Greenwall, 1989; Roberts, 1985; Rokeach, 1960) have often emphasized structure over content, a focus that has led to a bias in favor of verifying and validating the methods of measurement rather than discovering new phenomena (Moscovici, 1963).

We need to return to an earlier tradition of analyzing the cultural and social dimensions of attitudes on the basis of representations that are shared by individuals composing a community (Thomas & Znaniecki, 1918–20). Such an approach emphasizes that people, rather than forming attitudes in isolation from each other, elaborate judgments about an object in relation to what others think about that same object. When considering the social context underlying the formation of individual attitudes and opinions, we need to look at social representations as providing the consensus-forming organizing principles for the attitudes and opinions of groups.

THE EFFECTS OF NAMES AND DIFFERENCES IN ATTITUDES

Changes concerning race are as important as the underlying issue itself, since they indicate broader transformations going on in a society. After all, slavery ended in a civil war; its successor, segregation, was overcome a century later by an unprecedented wave of social agitation across the entire nation. Each time, America had to undergo major convulsions to rid itself of anachronistic paradigms of racial hegemony, and in both instances that struggle reorganized the common ground from which people derived their meaning as Americans. If race has defined America like no other issue, it stands to reason that any change in its status will inevitably reverberate through the many facets of society. This is precisely what we face today with the emergence of African American as a new group designation in lieu of Black. This new social representation marks the first time a group, until now defined on the basis of race alone, is being redefined on the basis of culture (and thus in correspondence with America's idealistic self-definition as a multicultural society of equals).

Race and the American creed—central topoi of American culture in the Aristotelean sense of common ground—thus compete with each other today in novel ways. The society-transforming dynamics of their interaction center not least on the coexistence of African American and Black as competing social representations of the same object, Americans of African descent. The purpose of the analysis presented here is to see how the switch in names, which in fact amounts to a change in the social representation of the object, impacts on our way of thinking about black Americans. If it is true that African American redefines the object in a way that deemphasizes race, we ought to see that the choice of this name produces significantly different perceptions and evaluations of black Americans.

The denominations African American and Black are compared as independent variables in terms of differences in the mean values of the factors resulting from the Evaluative Questionnaire introduced in Chapter 7 (see also Appendices B and C). These response differences based on name will be examined via a two-dimensional approach to social representation, emphasizing both its instrumental and its evaluative nature (Abric, 1994; Moliner, 1995). Specifically, those differences are projected onto which name is used, which name ought to be used, which name is best to use, and which name will be used. In addition, we controlled for a "context effect" by giving half the subjects in each sample a questionnaire referring to Americans of African descent only as Blacks, white the other half received a questionnaire using African American when referring to the group. The particular approach described here enables us to identify differences in the scale value as a result of the denomination chosen by the subject. Based on our theoretical understanding of African American as an anticipatory representation favoring culture over race, we would expect those who choose African American to have mean values that reflect a more positive and inclusive evaluation of the object than would those choosing Black.

Although African American is a recent denomination and still a social representation in the making, it seems to have already had a discernible effect on the various scales used to assess the social representation of black Americans. Summaries of statistically significant F values for black subjects and non-black subjects for the three levels of analysis—"your opinion," "mainstream opinion," and "black Americans' opinion"—are included in Appendices F and G. From these summaries it is clear that the choice of name has had a broader impact on black subjects than non-black subjects, yielding more significant differences on a wider range of scales for the former group both on the level of their own opinions and in terms of their projections onto their own group.

The disproportionality in the amount of significant mean differences between our two samples implies that African American, as a new representation, is more clearly differentiated from Black for the black Americans than for the non-black Americans. This particular conclusion has, as we shall see, important implications for the objectification of such a social representation in the making. Beyond that first basic distinction between the two samples, a more detailed look at the findings also suggests some interesting differentiations in the evaluation of black Americans based on the denomination chosen in both groups.

The first set of data examined whether the name used to refer to Americans of African descent had an impact on subjects' evaluations of black Americans. Focusing on the main effects, we summarized (in Table 8.3) the response means and F ratios for those evaluative measures that yielded significant differences between African American and Black. Consistent with our main hypothesis, the data revealed, for both samples, some significant differences between the two names as regards the subjects' evaluations of black Americans.

In the case of our black American sample, subjects were asked to evaluate the different scales based on the name they used for themselves and the name the outgroup used to refer to them. Interestingly enough, when

Table 8.3
Mean Scores of the Name Used with Respect to Various Scales, and Results of One-Way Analyses of Variance

	Name Used		F
	African American	Black	
Black sample			
Ingroup			
Cultural Inclusion[1]	5.85	6.21	4.60*
Dual Consciousness[2]	5.44	5.75	6.46**
Outgroup			
Negative Images[1]	2.51	3.34	4.60*
Non-black sample			
Images of Black Women[1]	5.56	5.03	4.22*

Notes: 1 is for the "your opinion" scales; 2 is for the "mainstream opinion" scales.
* p < .05; ** p < .01.

looking at the name they use, the first significant difference concerned the *Cultural Inclusion* scale (F [1,78] = 4.60, P < .03). Subjects agreed in their own opinion more with this scale when the name used was Black rather than African American. For the *Dual Consciousness* scale (from the projection onto black Americans' opinion), subjects also agreed more with the scale when the name used was Black than when it was African American (F [1,59] = 6.46, P < .01). Similarly, when focusing on the name the outgroup uses to refer to them, a significant difference could be observed with regard to the evaluation of the *Negative Images* scale (F [1,67] = 4.60, p < .03). The only significant difference to emerge from the analyses of the name used by non-black subjects concerned the evaluation of the *Images of Black Women* scale (in their own opinion), where those using the denomination Black agreed less with this scale than those using African American.

The next analysis of data examined whether preferences in terms of the name that ought to be used impacted on subjects' evaluations of black Americans. The results are summarized in Table 8.4, which shows the mean values and the F ratios for the scales. These point to some significant differences between African American and Black.

The data indicate that both samples evaluated the scales differently when opting for African American over Black as the name that ought to be used. Black American subjects in favor of African American, when presenting their own opinion, were significantly less inclined to agree with the *Negative Images* scale (F [1,70] = 7.95, P < .006) and the *Cultural Participation* scale (F [1,70] = 5.54, P < .02). On the other hand, the same

Table 8.4
Mean Scores of the Name that Ought to Be Used with Respect to Various Scales, and Results of One-Way Analyses of Variance

	Name That Ought to Be Used		F
	African American	Black	
Black Sample			
Negative Images[1]	3.00	3.81	7.95***
Cultural Participation[1]	4.84	5.33	5.54**
Dual Consciousness[3]	5.82	5.17	8.70***
Non-black Sample			
Negative Images[1]	3.70	4.28	4.26*
Images of Black Women[1]	5.52	4.60	13.56***
Permanence of Discrimination[1]	3.91	4.71	6.36*
Myrdal's Dilemma[2]	4.46	5.23	4.97*

Notes: 1 is for the "your opinion" scales; 2 is for the "mainstream opinion" scales;
    3 is for the "black Americans' opinion" scales.
* $p < .05$; ** $p < .01$; *** $p < .001$.

subjects projected stronger agreement with the items composing the *Dual Consciousness* factor onto their group than those still wedded to Black (*F* [1,46] = 8.70, *P* < .005).

Non-black subjects who thought that African American ought to be used showed a similar pattern of agreeing less with the *Negative Images* scale (*F* [1,68] = 4.26, *P* < .04). That same group also revealed a much more positive attitude toward the *Images of Black Women* factor (*F* [1,74] = 13.56, *P* < .000) and seemed less pessimistic about the *Permanence of Discrimination* (*F* [1,74] = 6.36, *P* < .01) than those non-black subjects who thought that Black ought to be used. Those non-black subjects inclined towards African American also projected lesser agreement with the *Myrdal's Dilemma* factor (*F* [1,84] = 4.97, *P* < .02).

The next table (Table 8.5) presents the statistically relevant differences in mean values and their *F* ratios pertaining to the subjects' choice of the name that is best to use.

As is obvious from the results presented here, the differences between those opting for African American and those choosing Black are more extensive and more complex than those found in the two earlier levels of analysis (name used, name that ought to be used), especially within our sample of black Americans.

With respect to the black sample, those subjects opting for African American as the best name to use by the ingroup were much less inclined

Table 8.5
Mean Scores of the Name That Is Best to Use with Respect to Various Scales, and Results of One-Way Analyses of Variance

	Name That Is Best to Use		F
	African American	Black	
Black Sample			
Ingroup			
Negative Images[1]	3.15	4.40	9.27**
Separation[3]	4.96	3.91	4.56*
Outgroup			
Separation[1]	3.98	3.10	5.05*
Positive Self-Image[1]	5.96	5.04	7.51**
Cultural Inclusion[1]	6.10	5.67	5.09*
Cultural Exclusion[3]	4.82	3.98	4.04*
Dual Consciousness[3]	5.84	4.80	16.94***
Separation	5.07	3.92	9.02**
Non-black Sample			
Images of Black Women[1]	5.17	4.00	5.59**
Permanence of Discrimination[1]	4.29	5.60	4.29*
Negative images–2[2]	4.66	5.93	4.08*
Declining Significance of Race[3]	3.82	5.15	5.53**

Notes: 1 is for the "your opinion" scales; 2 is for the "mainstream opinion" scales;
    3 is for the "black Americans' opinion" scales.
* $p < .05$; ** $p < .01$; *** $p < .001$.

to agree with the *Negative Images* scale (F [1,65] = 9.27, $P < .003$). At the same time, those subjects projected more agreement onto their own group with regard to the *Separation* scale (F [1,52] = 4.56, $P < .03$) than did those picking Black as the best name for the ingroup. When the choice of best name applied to the outgroup, those black subjects picking African American seemed more inclined to agree with the *Separation* scale (F [1,85] = 5.05, $P < .02$), with the *Positive Self-Image* factor (F [1,88] = 7.51, $P < .007$), and with the *Cultural Inclusion* factor (F [1,78] = 5.09, $P < .02$). They also projected much stronger agreement onto their group than did those opting for Black when it came to the issues of *Cultural Exclusion* (F [1,60] = 4.04, $P < .04$), *Dual Consciousness* (F [1,67] = 16.94, $P < .000$), and *Separation* (F [1,76] = 9.02, $P < .004$). The response differences concerning the last two factors are especially pronounced.

Table 8.6
Mean Scores of "the Name That Will Be Used in the Future" with Respect
to Various Scales, and Results of One-Way Analyses of Variance

	Name That Will Be Used		F
	African American	Black	
Black Sample			
Separation[1]	4.13	2.97	8.84**
Cultural Inclusion[1]	6.19	5.73	6.80**
Negative Images[2]	5.30	4.56	4.34*
Dual Consciousness[3]	5.84	5.01	15.25***
Separation[3]	4.99	4.02	5.36**
Non-black Sample			
Images of Black Women[1]	5.18	4.26	7.18**
Cultural Inclusion[1]	5.81	5.15	6.89**
Negative Images[3]	3.41	4.34	4.46*

Notes: 1 is for the "your opinion" scales; 2 is for the "mainstream opinion" scales;
    3 is for the "black Americans' opinion" scales.
* p <. 05; ** p < .01; *** p < .001.

Regarding the non-black subjects, those picking African American as
the best name to use had much more positive *Images of Black Women* (F
[1,75] = 5.59, P < .02) than those chosing Black. On the other hand, the
latter group seemed to believe more strongly in the *Permanence of Discrimination* (F [1,76] = 4.29, P < .04) than those picking African American
as the best name. Subjects opting for Black also projected stronger agreement with the *Negative Images-2* scale onto the mainstream (F [1,75] =
4.08, P < .04), while at the same time projecting even stronger agreement
with the *Declining Significance of Race* factor (F [1,75] = 5.53, P < .02)
onto black Americans.

Table 8.6 summarizes differences in mean values and the F ratios for
the relevant factors with regard to the name that will be used most in
the future. Our black subjects opting for African American were more
inclined to agree with the *Separation* scale (F [1,59] = 8.84, P < .005) and
with the *Cultural Inclusion* scale (F [1,69] = 6.80, P < .01). In addition,
they projected stronger agreement with the *Negative Images* scale (F [1,53]
= 4.34, P < .04) onto the mainstream than did those in the sample opting
for Black. Finally, those subjects seeing African American as the group
designation of the future also projected stronger agreement with the *Dual
Consciousness* factor (F [1,59] = 15.25, P < .000) and the *Separation* factor

(F [1,54] = 5.36, p < .02) onto their own group than did those in the sample who foresaw the retention of Black.

In the non-black sample *Images of Black Women* emerged once again as a key area of difference, with those believing in the future of African American indicating significantly stronger agreement than those choosing Black (F [1,76] = 7.18, P < .009). Those expecting African American to be dominant in the future also agreed more strongly with the *Cultural Inclusion* factor (F [1,83] = 6.89, P < .01). Finally, the future orientation towards African American also seemed to have an impact on projections about black American attitudes toward the *Negative Images* scale, with those picking the new group designation more inclined to believe that black Americans disagree with its items (F [1,85] = 4.46, P < .03).

These analyses indicate that both our samples evaluated black Americans differently when the representation of the object was African American than when it was Black. Moreover, it seems evident from our results that black subjects had already incorporated African American more strongly into their thinking than the non-black subjects. Differentiations between African American and Black were generally more pronounced and covered a wider range of scales in the first sample than in the second. While black subjects opting for Black were not necessarily inclined to agree with the race-dominated categorization of the group, those choosing African American clearly agreed more with the notion of *Cultural Inclusion*. At the same time the latter subgroup, those black subjects identifying with African American, also revealed a more developed sense of group autonomy as captured in the items composing the *Cultural Exclusion* and *Separation* scales. This more pronounced duality of attitudes is also present in their consistently stronger projection of agreement onto their group concerning the *Dual Consciousness* factor. Those differences emerged less on the level of the name used than on the other levels of analysis that projected African American into the future or into a normative context, thus confirming the quality of the new name as an anticipatory representation.

With respect to non-black subjects it is obvious that the inclusive reference of African American is differentiated on the basis of gender, with a greater willingness to accept female members of that group consistently crystallized in the response differences concerning the *Images of Black Women* scale. Apart from this gender-differentiated attitude, non-black subjects favoring African American show less acceptance of the *Negative Images* scale. They also appear more optimistic about the future, as reflected in lower *Permanence of Discrimination* and higher *Declining Significance of Race* statistics than their counterparts still wedded to Black. That difference is also reflected in how the two subgroups view *Myrdal's Dilemma*.

These results are consistent with our theoretical analysis of African

American as an anticipatory representation that aims to transform the object from a racially categorized to a culturally defined group, coexisting on an equal footing with others in a multicultural society. Yet it is also clear that this transformation effort has advanced more within the black American community than in the mainstream, and this difference in progress deserves closer attention.

Chapter 9

Conclusion

The interaction between these alternative group designations, as two social representations defining the same object, has provided anchoring
points for a possible reconceptualization of the object. Old conceptions
associated with Black and new projections carried by African American
clash to the extent that they embody different visions of America, one
based on racial differentiation and the other striving for a truly American
culture shared by all. The interdependent coexistence of these two different visions concerning the relative position of black Americans has
bred a dynamic fueled by conflicts and motivated by the search for a
resolution to the dissonance underlying those conflicts.

Festinger (1957), who gave us the theory of dissonance in the first
place, referred to Myrdal's Dilemma (the conflict between the American
creed and racial discrimination) as an important example that illustrates
the possibility of continuous dissonance. The role of African American
in this context has to be understood as an attempt to resolve the dilemma
by creating for the social object a more positive representation. As a
collective effort to shift America from a racially antagonized society to a
multicultural society in which diversity becomes a national quality, this
new social representation places itself at the center of a profound cultural
debate.

THE INTERPLAY OF RACE AND CULTURE

Given the historic weight of race, the shift in vision projected by the
emergence of African American is neither smooth nor straightforward.
There is much resistance to change. The climate today is not very hos-

pitable to a renewed effort at integration. Uncertainty about the future has been heightened by two decades of eroding living standards for the majority of Americans, a trend that has only recently begun to change for the better. In recent years the political tide has shifted to a New Right able to capture the anger and confusion of an embattled middle class. The evolving multiculturalism, imposed on America not least by the changing demographic realities of its population, puts the existing power structure under stress. So the processes of transformation at hand are rife with conflict. As always during periods of tumultous change in this society, the focus of tensions is on Black America.

Yet at the same time there is a basic consensus, driven by shared visions of America as a unique experiment in democracy, about the need for peaceful coexistence and a common culture. If that basic consensus, carried by African American, is to give Americans sufficient cohesion as "one nation, one people" and reverse long traditions of prejudice and strife, it has to be able to overcome race in favor of culture. In this endeavour it is not enough simply to suppress race, because such suppression leads to tensions that tend to be externalized in sudden outbursts. These rebound effects (Wegner et al., 1991) have been observed numerous times in recent resurgences of race as an openly admitted national problem and obsession. Because the issue of race is so deeply entrenched in the social psyche of America, we cannot simply wish it away. Therefore, to the extent that African American challenges the precarious stability reached by the post–Civil Rights decades of race suppression, its appeal to multiculturalism and the recognition of a common culture also generates conditions for tension, in which the centrality of race comes suddenly to the fore as an inextricable part of the culture.

These tensions have had many forms of expression in recent years. The Clarence Thomas confirmation hearings, the Los Angeles riots that followed the acquittal of three police officers in the beating of Rodney King, and the O.J. Simpson trial and the polarizing reactions to its verdict were overt expressions of race in relation to culture. Of similar intensity, yet more covert, are manifestations of those very tensions in the mounting attacks aimed at integrationist efforts, such as Affirmative Action policies and the "political correctness" movement. These efforts in particular seem to have fostered an angry reaction among many white male Americans, whose revolt has turned into the principal force behind the rise of right-wing populism (Walczak, 1995).

In reaction, black Americans have begun to put renewed emphasis on separatism. This isolationist response, an expression of anger and disillusionment, started with the revival of Malcolm X's memory (in the context of Spike Lee's film biography and new evidence surrounding his assassination). It has played a significant part in the jubilant reaction of many black Americans to the O.J. Simpson trial, which they felt "sent a message" to a judicial system widely seen as racially biased. The strength of nationalism within the black community could be seen most sharply in the "Million Man March" on Washington in October 1995, which catapulted the controversial leader of the Nation of Islam, Rev. Louis Farrakhan, to national attention. Thirty years after the historic Civil Rights legislation race still remains a remarkably contentious issue dividing America. Joel Kovel's observation is quite to the point:

The most difficult, because unpleasant, fact that we must face is that for all its malevolence, racism served a stabilizing function in American culture for many generations. Indeed it was a source of gratification to whites. It defined a social universe, absorbed aggression, and facilitated a sense of virtue in white America—a trait which contributed to America's material success. Racism was an integral part of a stable and productive cultural order. Because of the incompatibility of this old order with advanced industrial life, with our ideals, and with the will of black people, we must try to eradicate racism and to move away from its delusions. But this change of direction brings in its wake instability, and a set of anxieties and counterresponses which threaten the advances our culture has made. (Kovel, 1984, p. 4)

Since race and its manifestations have served a "stabilizing function" in the culture, any effort to eradicate racism can only succeed if the very concept of race as a social representation is somehow uprooted and replaced with a new central organizing principle of potentially equal force. As James Jones suggests,

culture, not color, is the better way to approach matters of race in this society. The color approach emphasizes differences that are clear and undeniable. However, the important differences (those associated with culture and character) are not addressed by the focus on skin color. Thus, when we talk about blacks, for example, or whites, what are we saying? Perhaps little more than that skin color has been the organizing principle or schema for much of race relations in the United States for over three centuries.

The cultural approach, by contrast, emphasizes the content of experience and its historical antecedents as a basis for coming together, sharing cultures, and recognizing the contributions different cultural groups make to our national culture. In this view, culture represents a way of bringing people and groups together, of both acknowledging boundaries (of ethnicity and culture) and transcending them by embedding them in the broader cultural context. (Jones, 1986, p. 311)

The recognition of a shared culture is captured by the presence of "American" in the new denomination. African American is supposed to remake the object in a way that downplays race. Yet, because race is so central to the definition of this culture, the impact of race is felt through the polemic raised by the sheer emergence of the new group denomination. This new social representation, originating from the previous one (Black), cannot have the same straightforward integrationist effect as Italian American or Irish American. In its complex relationship to Black, it must somehow manage to transform the social representation of the group from race to culture, while racial divisiveness continues to show its frightening durability.

In the current climate of tension it is obvious that the two representations, race and culture, have not yet found a stable coexistence in the social representation of African American. Consequently, African American is itself not yet a stable social representation, but one that is still in the making. As such it possesses a particulary dynamic nature, which often manifests itself in paradoxically conflictual ways. The attack on Affirmative Action by Gingrich and other conservative Republicans, for example, often uses for justification the argument of "reverse discrimination" against white males. Here we see an appeal to quintessentially American values of equality and fairness which at the same time is bound to stir racial animosity (Nosworthy, Lea, & Lindsay, 1995). Or take the trial of O.J. Simpson, accused of murdering his wife and a friend of hers. Aware of the differences in how black Americans and non-black Americans perceive the criminal justice system in general and this trial in particular, the defense lawyers tried to appeal to the jury, in the majority black Americans, by shifting attention from Simpson himself to a racist police conspiracy aimed at framing the former football star. By playing the "race card" so blatantly, the defense attorneys made sure that O.J. Simpson, who used to personify the African American like few others, became the lightning rod for greater division along racial lines.

Yet even though its dynamic quality is very much driven by multidimensional tensions between race and multiculturalism, African American also provides a structure for the articulation of these different dimensions and imposes a synthesis on the polarizing forces contained in the two opposing representations it incorporates. That organizing capacity of African American has to do with its anticipatory nature. The presuppositions contained in the projections of a color blind and multicultural America of the future induce us to redefine black Americans as African Americans today.

Any analysis of African American as an anticipatory social representation must address its lack of a stable central core. As discussed in previous chapters, African American reconceptualizes black Americans anew by supplanting the loaded issue of race with culture. Yet race does not completely dissipate. Rather, it remains present in the dynamic relation African American has to Black. For culture to define and organize the classificatory factors of African American implies that America has already become a multicultural society. Today this reality is still only a tendentious drive, subject to backlashes during which race reasserts its central position. As if hit by a pendulum, the cultural movement of the 1980s, which culminated in Jesse Jackson's Rainbow Coalition, now has to confront the revival (or rebound effect) of race in public discourse.

The modulation of the central core of African American depends on a transformation in the central core of Black—one which reconceptualizes the object and changes its social representation. Such transformation can only come about through a negation of race as the key element of the central core. Pushing aside the divisiveness implied by the social representation of race, African American makes way for the more inclusive images underlying the social representation of multiculturalism. The instability of the central core of African American, besides testifying to the fact that the representation is still in the making, also demonstrates its difference to that of Black, which is an already made and reified representation.

A POSITIVE AND FUTURE-ORIENTED SOCIAL REPRESENTATION

Another interesting aspect of African American as an anticipatory representation is the positive nature of the projections associated with it. This positive redefinition may at first sight appear similar to the positivation of Black in the 1960s. However, one fundamental difference between them is that the redefinition of African American is a broadly based collective effort engaging many groups in America, while the earlier initiative was much more narrowly focused within the black American community. In the case of Black the term was introduced as an alternative to Negro, stressing racial consciousness and pride. The effort at that time centered primarily on changing the self-definition of black Americans by affirming that "Black is Beautiful" and reinforcing the unity of Blacks in their struggle against racism and discrimination.

Indeed, African American, in comparison to Black, points to a redefinition process on the part of black Americans, involving the collective effort of a heterogenous social group in its interactions with the rest of a diverse society. And it is through this intergroup energy that the meaning captured in the new group designation gets elaborated. This new social object has at its consensual core a forward-looking quality that implies at the same time a redefinition of America as a pluralistic, multicultural society. This aspect of the new representation is what makes it so fundamental and so engaging for many Americans. The collective anticipation of a positive future characterized by peaceful coexistence between black and white Americans also impacts on immediate perceptions, images, and attitudes—that is to say, on their social representations of each other.

In its conflict with Black, which is a social representation from the past,

African American is defined as a representation of the future. With two distinct temporal dimensions, they both struggle to shape the representation of black Americans today. Placed within that context, African American is primarily a challenge to the status quo, providing an alternative for the future. As can be seen in the adoption of ego-defensive strategies after being forewarned of an attack (Deaux, 1968; Fitzpatrick and Eagly, 1981; McGuire, 1964; McGuire and Millman, 1965) or in greater ingroup-outgroup evaluative biases while preparing to engage in competition (Doise et al. 1972; Rabbie, Benoist et al., 1974), the anticipation of the future leads to an adjustment in the present.

NAMING, CLASSIFYING, AND FAMILIARIZING

The new social representation in question may be oriented toward the future, but it is anchored in the present. The explicit choice of the new name propels it into the public realm as a new social reality. With some black Americans crystallizing this new name as their social identity, the term gains meaning and acquires a real existence. These proponents of African American are one key source in the process by which the new social object becomes familiarized. Gradually, as those claiming the name for themselves are classified into a distinct subgroup, their demographic features define what African American comes to mean in its contradistinction to Black. They facilitate the objectification of the new object by personifying it.

Blacks, meaning the large majority of disadvantaged black Americans who lack the material basis of education and income to be African Americans, internalize the new social object as representing everything that they are not now, but could be one day in the future. While their exclusion from a less repressive alternative creates pain and anger, the anticipatory qualities of this emerging social representation crystallize for Blacks as a beacon of hope. The fact that some black Americans have been able to overcome marginalization and assume a new identity as African Americans demonstrates in very concrete and tangible fashion the possibility of escape from misery. At a time when the living conditions of many Blacks have clearly worsened, this prospect gives cause for optimism. The name African American can be associated with a better future, precisely because it applies to black Americans as much as Black does. It represents an alternative to Black, both symbolically, repositioning the group as a whole, and materially, as a redefined social object.

For non-black Americans, in particular WASPs (White Anglo-Saxon Protestants) and the ethnic Catholic working-class communities of America's inner cities (e.g., Polish Americans of Chicago, Irish Americans of New York City, Italian Americans of Boston), the emergence of African American provides a source of relief. The social representation of a multicultural America projected by the term contains the promise of a color-blind society freed of racial discrimination. That image makes the term compellingly attractive, because it corresponds to the ideals of the "Just World" (Lerner, 1980) through which Americans of all walks of life define their society.

The virtue of African American, then, is to absolve non-black Americans from having to think about race and all that comes with its social representation. Race obviously does not disappear, just as African Americans do not stop being black Americans. However, it is relocated from its central position, as those calling themselves African American establish around that name a new identity that manages to deemphasize the legacy of racism. Since African American serves at the same time as a new official designation for the entire group, the images produced in this symbolic context are typically the ones held about those identified as African Americans. This dual existence enables non-black Americans to see themselves represented in the term, their interests vested in visions of peaceful coexistence between hitherto divided and antagonistic groups.

Apart from this symbolic significance of the new group designation, non-black Americans also embrace its use by a subgroup of black Americans as proof that the legacy of racism has already been overcome. The very presence of African Americans legitimates a widely held belief among non-black Americans that race is no longer a barrier of exclusion, that black Americans can make it into the mainstream provided they accept the norms and standards of society. Facilitating a collective effort at downplaying the persistence of racism, the association of the new term with a sociodemographically distinct subgroup enables non-black Americans to argue that those black Americans unable to redefine themselves into African Americans have only themselves to blame. The familiarization of African American as a new social representation is thus an exercise in soothing bad conscience and seeking exculpation. These motives make the collective effort at group positivation no less real.

Figure 9.1 illustrates the interconnections between the three components of our triangular model that define the social representation of African American. The line overarching African American shows how this new object combines the reality of black America with that of the mainstream. For Blacks the new representation is fueled with projections of a positive future, and becomes a beacon of hope for them. For non-blacks this representation is structured as a shift from race to culture, supporting the ideals of a "Just World."

As African American becomes familiar, it is assimilated as part of our daily life, as if it has always been there. In the process the term becomes firmly anchored: representing a shift from race to culture, acting as a beacon of hope for a better future, and above all forming an association

Figure 9.1
The Triangular Model of a Social Representation

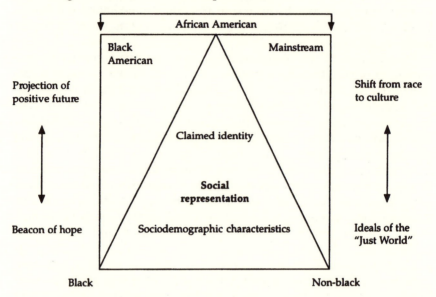

with a distinct subgroup that personifies the term. Because it is composed of projections which by their very nature can only find a concrete existence in the future, African American is not yet fully objectified as an established (reified) social representation. Since African American lacks structural stability, it does not have a clear and consensually shared nucleus of images that could be externalized as real.

OBJECTIFICATION, NATURALIZATION, AND THE MEDIA

Precisely because the term African American is not yet fully objectified and settled, its formation as a social representation is still an active process of domestication. In the absence of a stable central core this process is fluid and multifaceted. While such a nonlinear dynamic makes the process inherently unpredictable and its outcome uncontrollable, we now know that this social representation in the making evolves around two driving forces—finding a name for a thing, and creating a thing for the name.

The term has been claimed as a new identity by about one third of all black Americans. As it is propelled by the prevalent characteristics of this subgroup, the term has become widely associated with young, well-educated, and upwardly mobile black Americans who want their fair share of the American Dream on an equal footing with everone else. These are literally the children of the Civil Rights movement, created by that movement's success in opening the door for a limited number of black Americans to college and to professional careers. The introduction of African American in 1989 completed the process of their emergence as a demographically distinct subgroup by naming that "thing," by giving that new social object its proper name. To the extent that some members of the black community have actually become African Americans, the term is clearly more objectified among black Americans. This personification of the term within the group makes the term a concrete daily reality capable of generating images and directing projections of oneself and one's own group.

For non-black Americans the term lacks such immediacy of personification. Of course, non-black Americans cannot escape the association of the term with the demographically distinct subgroup through which it has become anchored. Nor can they shield themselves from the normative context created by this association, that of transcending race in favor of culture, as the "politically correct" way of thinking. But non-black Americans do not have the prospect of actually being or becoming African Americans. Therefore they cannot bring to bear the same kind of identification with the term that black Americans are capable of. For the new term to mobilize the self-interest of non-black Americans, its projection of images must be more indirect. The name conjures up images of progress toward equality, of a better and more harmonious future in which the legacy of racism will have finally ceased to dominate intergroup relations, of proof that Blacks have only themselves to blame if they cannot become African Americans. As a future-oriented and positive social representation in the making, the term African American materializes among non-black Americans in terms of symbolic expressions projected onto the entire group of black Americans. In contradistinction to Black and Blacks, the term evokes a redefinition of "us versus them" such that, by including part of the "other" in one's own group ("We are all Americans"), it relieves one's own burden of guilt. Both of these dimensions of the term's objectification process among non-black Americans are crucially shaped by the media. The propagation and contextualization of the new term by the press, television, radio, and political leaders provide the framework within which the non-black majority of Americans creates a social object for the name that was presented to them before they had any idea what it was supposed to mean.

In the process of its objectification the social representations of race (from the past) and of a multicultural society (towards the future) battle with each other for the dominant position in the central core of African American. This new group designation, competing with and defining itself in contradistinction to Black, is thus still a dependent and subordinated social representation. As an anticipatory social representation, it allows society to begin shifting the focus from race to culture. A complete objectification of African American would imply that the new term has completely separated from Black, with the two no longer having anything to do with one another, or that the new term has supplanted Black to the point of making the latter dissolve.

Despite its lack of reification, African American finds an existence in the symbolic articulation of intergroup relations in the United States. The term has already infiltrated our conversation and become part of our ordinary language, and the mass media have accelerated this process. While people do not yet perceive the new object figuratively, they are nevertheless compelled to talk about it. During these exchanges the images that are implied come to form a structure, composed of projections of a different future. When we use the term, we envision a representation of black Americans as a culturally defined subgroup in a color-blind America. At this point the materialization of African American as a cultural production is confined to mostly symbolic expressions, referring to the entire group as an integral part of America. This reflects a naturalization process which in the case of African American, rather than being incorporated within the objectification process, is a separate process on its own.

While such a process of objectification may take years to complete, the interest here is not in speculating about final outcomes concerning the social representation of African American. On the contrary, this investigation takes a much more heuristic approach. My primary intent with this research is to understand the cultural phenomenon associated with the emergence of African American as a new group designation. So it is the richness of the phenomenon which must be explored, not its controllability or predictability. I believe that only by studying the phenomenon as a social representation can we really capture its full relevance for contemporary American culture, with all the social psychological dynamics it implies. The study of African American as a cultural phenomenon offers a unique opportunity to look at a new social fabric in its making.

Appendix A

Demographic and Survey Data about the Use of African American

Table A.1
Survey Results for the Choice of Denomination by Black Americans

| Source | N | Date | Preferred Name | | |
			African American	Black	Indifferent
New York Times	165	06-89	9%	36%	46%
ABC/Washington Post	371	09-89	22%	66%	9%
NBC/Wall Street Journal	221	07-90	25%	59%	—
Los Angeles Times	—	09-91	34%	42%	18%

Table A.2
Demographic Distinctiveness and the Use of African American

Demographic		Use of African American
Age	18–29 yrs	28%
	30–49 yrs	19%
	50 yrs +	17%
Education	High school or less	15%
	College +	29%
Gender	Male	28%
	Female	15%
Location	North	28%
	South	15%

Appendix B

Questionnaires
for Black Subjects

Questionnaires B.1 to B.4 are presented here in the same order in which the subjects interviewed received them.

In order to test for a context effect, questionnaires B.1 and B.2 were given to half of the subjects in the sample with the term African Americans being used whenever referring to their own group, while the other half received those same two questionnaires using the term Blacks.

Table B.1
Evaluative Questionnaire (Part 1)

This questionnaire is designed to measure people's perceptions of ethnic identity. There are no right or wrong answers. Use the seven point scale provided below to answer each statement. Please circle the number that best corresponds to your feelings.

-3 = Strongly disagree
-2 = Disagree
-1 = Somewhat disagree
 0 = Undecided, no opinion
+1 = Somewhat agree
+2 = Agree
+3 = Strongly agree

1. There is a lot less racial discrimination now.
   In your opinion.
   | -3 | -2 | -1 | 0 | +1 | +2 | +3 |
   In the opinion of mainstream America.
   | -3 | -2 | -1 | 0 | +1 | +2 | +3 |

2. Racial discrimination will never end in America.
   In your opinion.
   | -3 | -2 | -1 | 0 | +1 | +2 | +3 |
   In the opinion of mainstream America.
   | -3 | -2 | -1 | 0 | +1 | +2 | +3 |

3. It is true that most African Americans should try to be successful within mainstream America.
   In your opinion.
   | -3 | -2 | -1 | 0 | +1 | +2 | +3 |
   In the opinion of mainstream America.
   | -3 | -2 | -1 | 0 | +1 | +2 | +3 |

4. It is true that African Americans are ambitious.
   In your opinion.
   | -3 | -2 | -1 | 0 | +1 | +2 | +3 |
   In the opinion of mainstream America.
   | -3 | -2 | -1 | 0 | +1 | +2 | +3 |

5. It is true that African Americans are arrogant.
   In your opinion.
   | -3 | -2 | -1 | 0 | +1 | +2 | +3 |
   In the opinion of mainstream America.
   | -3 | -2 | -1 | 0 | +1 | +2 | +3 |

Table B.1 (continued)

6. It is true that African Americans are lazy.
    In your opinion.

	-3	-2	-1	0	+1	+2	+3

    In the opinion of mainstream America.

	-3	-2	-1	0	+1	+2	+3

7. It is true that African Americans neglect their families.
    In your opinion.

	-3	-2	-1	0	+1	+2	+3

    In the opinion of mainstream America.

	-3	-2	-1	0	+1	+2	+3

8. It is true that African Americans are often rude.
    In your opinion.

	-3	-2	-1	0	+1	+2	+3

    In the opinion of mainstream America.

	-3	-2	-1	0	+1	+2	+3

9. It is true that African Americans are loud.
    In your opinion.

	-3	-2	-1	0	+1	+2	+3

    In the opinion of mainstream America.

	-3	-2	-1	0	+1	+2	+3

10. It is true that African Americans are talkative.
    In your opinion.

	-3	-2	-1	0	+1	+2	+3

    In the opinion of mainstream America.

	-3	-2	-1	0	+1	+2	+3

11. It is true that African Americans are quick-tempered.
    In your opinion.

	-3	-2	-1	0	+1	+2	+3

    In the opinion of mainstream America.

	-3	-2	-1	0	+1	+2	+3

12. It is true that African Americans are proud of themselves.
    In your opinion.

	-3	-2	-1	0	+1	+2	+3

    In the opinion of mainstream America.

	-3	-2	-1	0	+1	+2	+3

13. It is true that African Americans are intelligent.
    In your opinion.

	-3	-2	-1	0	+1	+2	+3

    In the opinion of mainstream America.

	-3	-2	-1	0	+1	+2	+3

Table B.1 (continued)

14. It is true that most African Americans should strive to be successful outside of mainstream America.

    In your opinion.

    | -3 | -2 | -1 | 0 | +1 | +2 | +3 |

    In the opinion of mainstream America.

    | -3 | -2 | -1 | 0 | +1 | +2 | +3 |

15. It is true that African Americans are suave.

    In your opinion.

    | -3 | -2 | -1 | 0 | +1 | +2 | +3 |

    In the opinion of mainstream America.

    | -3 | -2 | -1 | 0 | +1 | +2 | +3 |

16. It is true that most African Americans have a sense of responsibility towards their own community.

    In your opinion.

    | -3 | -2 | -1 | 0 | +1 | +2 | +3 |

    In the opinion of mainstream America.

    | -3 | -2 | -1 | 0 | +1 | +2 | +3 |

Table B.2
Evaluative Questionnaire (Part 2)

This questionnaire is designed to measure people's perceptions of ethnic identity. There are no right or wrong answers. Use the seven point scale provided below to answer each statement. Please circle the number that best corresponds to your feelings.

-3 = Strongly disagree
-2 = Disagree
-1 = Somewhat disagree
 0 = Undecided, no opinion
+1 = Somewhat agree
+2 = Agree
+3 = Strongly agree

1. African American children should study an African language.
   In your opinion.
   | -3 | -2 | -1 | 0 | +1 | +2 | +3 |
   In the opinion of the African American community.
   | -3 | -2 | -1 | 0 | +1 | +2 | +3 |

2. African Americans should always vote for Black candidates.
   In your opinion.
   | -3 | -2 | -1 | 0 | +1 | +2 | +3 |
   In the opinion of the African American community.
   | -3 | -2 | -1 | 0 | +1 | +2 | +3 |

3. African American women should not date White men.
   In your opinion.
   | -3 | -2 | -1 | 0 | +1 | +2 | +3 |
   In the opinion of the African American community.
   | -3 | -2 | -1 | 0 | +1 | +2 | +3 |

4. African Americans should have a preference for shopping in Black-owned stores.
   In your opinion.
   | -3 | -2 | -1 | 0 | +1 | +2 | +3 |
   In the opinion of the African American community.
   | -3 | -2 | -1 | 0 | +1 | +2 | +3 |

5. African Americans want their rightful share of the American Dream.
   In your opinion.
   | -3 | -2 | -1 | 0 | +1 | +2 | +3 |
   In the opinion of the African American community.
   | -3 | -2 | -1 | 0 | +1 | +2 | +3 |

Table B.2 (continued)

6. African American parents should give their children African names.
   In your opinion.

-3	-2	-1	0	+1	+2	+3

   In the opinion of the African American community.

-3	-2	-1	0	+1	+2	+3

7. African Americans are beginning to have more power in American life and politics.
   In your opinion.

-3	-2	-1	0	+1	+2	+3

   In the opinion of the African American community.

-3	-2	-1	0	+1	+2	+3

8. African Americans are aware of the discrimination against them and will no longer remain an oppressed colony in a rich nation.
   In your opinion.

-3	-2	-1	0	+1	+2	+3

   In the opinion of the African American community.

-3	-2	-1	0	+1	+2	+3

9. There will be more racial discrimination 20 years from now.
   In your opinion.

-3	-2	-1	0	+1	+2	+3

   In the opinion of the African American community.

-3	-2	-1	0	+1	+2	+3

10. Most white people want to see African Americans kept down.
    In your opinion.

-3	-2	-1	0	+1	+2	+3

    In the opinion of the African American community.

-3	-2	-1	0	+1	+2	+3

11. Parents should teach children about what it means to be African American.
    In your opinion.

-3	-2	-1	0	+1	+2	+3

    In the opinion of the African American community.

-3	-2	-1	0	+1	+2	+3

12. Discrimination affects all African Americans, but the best way to handle that problem is for each individual to act like other Americans - to work hard and mind one's own business.
    In your opinion.

-3	-2	-1	0	+1	+2	+3

    In the opinion of the African American community.

-3	-2	-1	0	+1	+2	+3

Table B.2 (continued)

13. Sex discrimination is a real problem for African American women in this country.

    In your opinion.

    | -3 | -2 | -1 | 0 | +1 | +2 | +3 |

    In the opinion of the African American community.

    | -3 | -2 | -1 | 0 | +1 | +2 | +3 |

14. African American women should organize with White women to handle problems of sex discrimination.

    In your opinion.

    | -3 | -2 | -1 | 0 | +1 | +2 | +3 |

    In the opinion of the African American community.

    | -3 | -2 | -1 | 0 | +1 | +2 | +3 |

15. Racial discrimination will never end in America.

    In your opinion.

    | -3 | -2 | -1 | 0 | +1 | +2 | +3 |

    In the opinion of the African American community.

    | -3 | -2 | -1 | 0 | +1 | +2 | +3 |

16. It is more important to be African American than American.

    In your opinion.

    | -3 | -2 | -1 | 0 | +1 | +2 | +3 |

    In the opinion of the African American community.

    | -3 | -2 | -1 | 0 | +1 | +2 | +3 |

17. The non-violent mass disobedience tactics of Dr. Martin Luther King are better suited for social conditions of African Americans today than the "by any means necessary" call to resistance of Malcolm X.

    In your opinion.

    | -3 | -2 | -1 | 0 | +1 | +2 | +3 |

    In the opinion of the African American community.

    | -3 | -2 | -1 | 0 | +1 | +2 | +3 |

18. The creation of the HIV virus, which causes AIDS, is the result of a conspiracy to decimate the African American community.

    In your opinion.

    | -3 | -2 | -1 | 0 | +1 | +2 | +3 |

    In the opinion of the African American community.

    | -3 | -2 | -1 | 0 | +1 | +2 | +3 |

Table B.3
Name Designation Questionnaire

1. What name do you most frequently use to refer to people of your group?
   - (a) African American
   - (b) Afro-American
   - (c) Black
   - (d) Colored
   - (e) Negro
   - (f) People of Color

2. Is there another name that you use some of the time to refer to people of your group?
   - (a) African American
   - (b) Afro-American
   - (c) Black
   - (d) Colored
   - (e) Negro
   - (f) People of Color

3. Under what circumstances will you typically use the second alternative?

   _____
   _____
   _____

4. What name do members of other groups most frequently use to refer to people of your group?
   - (a) African American
   - (b) Afro-American
   - (c) Black
   - (d) Colored
   - (e) Negro
   - (f) People of Color

5. Is there another name members of other groups use some of the time to refer to people of your group?
   - (a) African American
   - (b) Afro-American
   - (c) Black
   - (d) Colored
   - (e) Negro
   - (f) People of Color

6. Under what circumstances do you think they will typically use the second alternative?

   _____
   _____
   _____

Table B.4
Names for Americans of African Descent

1. What do you most prefer to be called by members of another group?
   (Please place in ranking order)
   - (1) African American ( )
   - (2) Afro-American ( )
   - (3) Black ( )
   - (4) Colored ( )
   - (5) Negro ( )
   - (6) People of Color ( )

2. What do you like to be called the least by members of another group?
   (Please place in ranking order)
   - (1) African American ( )
   - (2) Afro-American ( )
   - (3) Black ( )
   - (4) Colored ( )
   - (5) Negro ( )
   - (6) People of Color ( )

3. Which of the following projects the most positive image when used by members of your own group?
   (Please place in ranking order)
   - (1) African American ( )
   - (2) Afro-American ( )
   - (3) Black ( )
   - (4) Colored ( )
   - (5) Negro ( )
   - (6) People of Color ( )

4. Which of the following projects the most negative image when used by members of your own group?
   (Please place in ranking order)
   - (1) African American ( )
   - (2) Afro-American ( )
   - (3) Black ( )
   - (4) Colored ( )
   - (5) Negro ( )
   - (6) People of Color ( )

5. Which of the following projects the most positive image when used by members of another group?
   (Please place in ranking order)
   - (1) African American ( )
   - (2) Afro-American ( )
   - (3) Black ( )

Table B.4 (continued)

      (4) Colored   ( )
      (5) Negro   ( )
      (6) People of Color   ( )

6. Which of the following projects the most negative image when used by members of another group?
   (Please place in ranking order)
         (1) African American   ( )
         (2) Afro-American   ( )
         (3) Black   ( )
         (4) Colored   ( )
         (5) Negro   ( )
         (6) People of Color   ( )

7. What do you think people will use more and more in the future to refer to members of your group?
   (Please place in ranking order)
         (1) African American   ( )
         (2) Afro-American   ( )
         (3) Black   ( )
         (4) Colored   ( )
         (5) Negro   ( )
         (6) People of Color   ( )

8. What do you think people will use less and less in the future to refer to members of your group?
   (Please place in ranking order)
         (1) African American   ( )
         (2) Afro-American   ( )
         (3) Black   ( )
         (4) Colored   ( )
         (5) Negro   ( )
         (6) People of Color   ( )

9. How do you think people of your group will be referred to by others in the future?
   (Please place in ranking order)
         (1) African American   ( )
         (2) Afro-American   ( )
         (3) Black   ( )
         (4) Colored   ( )
         (5) Negro   ( )
         (6) People of Color   ( )

Table B.4 (continued)

10. How do you think people of your group will be referred to by the press in the future?
    (Please place in ranking order)
        (1) African American   ( )
        (2) Afro-American   ( )
        (3) Black   ( )
        (4) Colored   ( )
        (5) Negro   ( )
        (6) People of Color   ( )

11. How do you think people of your group will be referred to by TV commentators in the future?
    (Please place in ranking order)
        (1) African American   ( )
        (2) Afro-American   ( )
        (3) Black   ( )
        (4) Colored   ( )
        (5) Negro   ( )
        (6) People of Color   ( )

12. How do you think people of your group will be referred to by political figures in the future?
    (Please place in ranking order)
        (1) African American   ( )
        (2) Afro-American   ( )
        (3) Black   ( )
        (4) Colored   ( )
        (5) Negro   ( )
        (6) People of Color   ( )

Appendix C

Questionnaires
for Non-black Subjects

Questionnaires C.1 to C.3 are presented here in the same order in which the subjects interviewed received them.

In order to test for a context effect, questionnaire C.1 was given to half of the subjects in the sample with the term African Americans being used whenever referring to Americans of African descent, while the other half received the same questionnaire using the term Blacks.

Table C.1
Evaluative Questionnaire

This questionnaire is designed to measure people's perceptions of ethnic identity. There are no right or wrong answers. Use the seven point scale provided below to answer each statement. Please circle the number that best corresponds to your feelings.

-3 = Strongly disagree
-2 = Disagree
-1 = Somewhat disagree
 0 = Undecided, no opinion
+1 = Somewhat agree
+2 = Agree
+3 = Strongly agree

1. There is a lot less racial discrimination now.
    In your opinion.
        -3   -2   -1   0   +1   +2   +3
    In the opinion of mainstream America.
        -3   -2   -1   0   +1   +2   +3
    In the opinion of the African American community.
        -3   -2   -1   0   +1   +2   +3

2. Racial discrimination will never end in America.
    In your opinion.
        -3   -2   -1   0   +1   +2   +3
    In the opinion of mainstream America.
        -3   -2   -1   0   +1   +2   +3
    In the opinion of the African American community.
        -3   -2   -1   0   +1   +2   +3

3. It is true that most African Americans should try to be successful within mainstream America.
    In your opinion.
        -3   -2   -1   0   +1   +2   +3
    In the opinion of mainstream America.
        -3   -2   -1   0   +1   +2   +3
    In the opinion of the African American community.
        -3   -2   -1   0   +1   +2   +3

4. It is true that African Americans are ambitious.
    In your opinion.
        -3   -2   -1   0   +1   +2   +3
    In the opinion of mainstream America.
        -3   -2   -1   0   +1   +2   +3
    In the opinion of the African American community.
        -3   -2   -1   0   +1   +2   +3

Table C.1 (continued)

5. It is true that African Americans are arrogant.
      In your opinion.

| | -3 | -2 | -1 | 0 | +1 | +2 | +3 |

      In the opinion of mainstream America.

| | -3 | -2 | -1 | 0 | +1 | +2 | +3 |

      In the opinion of the African American community.

| | -3 | -2 | -1 | 0 | +1 | +2 | +3 |

6. It is true that African Americans are lazy.
      In your opinion.

| | -3 | -2 | -1 | 0 | +1 | +2 | +3 |

      In the opinion of mainstream America.

| | -3 | -2 | -1 | 0 | +1 | +2 | +3 |

      In the opinion of the African American community.

| | -3 | -2 | -1 | 0 | +1 | +2 | +3 |

7. It is true that African Americans neglect their families.
      In your opinion.

| | -3 | -2 | -1 | 0 | +1 | +2 | +3 |

      In the opinion of mainstream America.

| | -3 | -2 | -1 | 0 | +1 | +2 | +3 |

      In the opinion of the African American community.

| | -3 | -2 | -1 | 0 | +1 | +2 | +3 |

8. It is true that African Americans are often rude.
      In your opinion.

| | -3 | -2 | -1 | 0 | +1 | +2 | +3 |

      In the opinion of mainstream America.

| | -3 | -2 | -1 | 0 | +1 | +2 | +3 |

      In the opinion of the African American community.

| | -3 | -2 | -1 | 0 | +1 | +2 | +3 |

9. It is true that African Americans are loud.
      In your opinion.

| | -3 | -2 | -1 | 0 | +1 | +2 | +3 |

      In the opinion of mainstream America.

| | -3 | -2 | -1 | 0 | +1 | +2 | +3 |

      In the opinion of the African American community.

| | -3 | -2 | -1 | 0 | +1 | +2 | +3 |

10. It is true that African Americans are talkative.
      In your opinion.

| | -3 | -2 | -1 | 0 | +1 | +2 | +3 |

      In the opinion of mainstream America.

| | -3 | -2 | -1 | 0 | +1 | +2 | +3 |

      In the opinion of the African American community.

| | -3 | -2 | -1 | 0 | +1 | +2 | +3 |

Table C.1 (continued)

11. It is true that African Americans are quick-tempered.
         In your opinion.
                  -3   -2   -1   0   +1   +2   +3
         In the opinion of mainstream America.
                  -3   -2   -1   0   +1   +2   +3
         In the opinion of the African American community.
                  -3   -2   -1   0   +1   +2   +3

12. It is true that African Americans are proud of themselves.
         In your opinion.
                  -3   -2   -1   0   +1   +2   +3
         In the opinion of mainstream America.
                  -3   -2   -1   0   +1   +2   +3
         In the opinion of the African American community.
                  -3   -2   -1   0   +1   +2   +3

13. It is true that African Americans are intelligent.
         In your opinion.
                  -3   -2   -1   0   +1   +2   +3
         In the opinion of mainstream America.
                  -3   -2   -1   0   +1   +2   +3
         In the opinion of the African American community.
                  -3   -2   -1   0   +1   +2   +3

14. It is true that most African Americans should strive to be successful outside of mainstream America.
         In your opinion.
                  -3   -2   -1   0   +1   +2   +3
         In the opinion of mainstream America.
                  -3   -2   -1   0   +1   +2   +3
         In the opinion of the African American community.
                  -3   -2   -1   0   +1   +2   +3

15. It is true that African Americans are suave.
         In your opinion.
                  -3   -2   -1   0   +1   +2   +3
         In the opinion of mainstream America.
                  -3   -2   -1   0   +1   +2   +3
         In the opinion of the African American community.
                  -3   -2   -1   0   +1   +2   +3

16. It is true that most African Americans have a sense of responsibility towards their own community.
         In your opinion.
                  -3   -2   -1   0   +1   +2   +3
         In the opinion of mainstream America.
                  -3   -2   -1   0   +1   +2   +3

Table C.1 (continued)

In the opinion of the African American community.

	-3	-2	-1	0	+1	+2	+3

17. African Americans want their rightful share of the American dream.

In your opinion.

	-3	-2	-1	0	+1	+2	+3

In the opinion of mainstream America.

	-3	-2	-1	0	+1	+2	+3

In the opinion of the African American community.

	-3	-2	-1	0	+1	+2	+3

18. African Americans are beginning to have more power in American life and politics.

In your opinion.

	-3	-2	-1	0	+1	+2	+3

In the opinion of mainstream America.

	-3	-2	-1	0	+1	+2	+3

In the opinion of the African American community.

	-3	-2	-1	0	+1	+2	+3

19. There will be more racial discrimination 20 years from now.

In your opinion.

	-3	-2	-1	0	+1	+2	+3

In the opinion of mainstream America.

	-3	-2	-1	0	+1	+2	+3

In the opinion of the African American community.

	-3	-2	-1	0	+1	+2	+3

20. Discrimination affects all African Americans, but the best way to handle that problem is for each individual to act like other Americans—to work hard and mind one's own business.

In your opinion.

	-3	-2	-1	0	+1	+2	+3

In the opinion of mainstream America.

	-3	-2	-1	0	+1	+2	+3

In the opinion of the African American community.

	-3	-2	-1	0	+1	+2	+3

21. Sex discrimination is a real problem for African American women in this country.

In your opinion.

	-3	-2	-1	0	+1	+2	+3

In the opinion of mainstream America.

	-3	-2	-1	0	+1	+2	+3

In the opinion of the African American community.

	-3	-2	-1	0	+1	+2	+3

Table C.1 (continued)

22. African American women should organize with White women to handle problems of sex discrimination.

      In your opinion.

-3	-2	-1	0	+1	+2	+3

      In the opinion of mainstream America.

-3	-2	-1	0	+1	+2	+3

      In the opinion of the African American community.

-3	-2	-1	0	+1	+2	+3

23. The non-violent mass disobedience tactics of Dr. Martin Luther King are better suited for social conditions of African Americans today than the "by any means necessary" call to resistance of Malcolm X.

      In your opinion.

-3	-2	-1	0	+1	+2	+3

      In the opinion of mainstream America.

-3	-2	-1	0	+1	+2	+3

      In the opinion of the African American community.

-3	-2	-1	0	+1	+2	+3

Table C.2
Name Designation Questionnaire

1. What name do you most frequently use to refer to people of your own group?
   - (a) American
   - (b) (Ancestry)-American, specify: _____
   - (c) Caucasian
   - (d) European
   - (e) White
   - (f) Other: _____

2. What name do you most frequently use to refer to people of African descent?
   - (a) African American
   - (b) Afro-American
   - (c) Black
   - (d) Colored
   - (e) Negro
   - (f) People of Color

3. Is there another name you use some of the time to refer to people of African descent?
   - (a) African American
   - (b) Afro-American
   - (c) Black
   - (d) Colored
   - (e) Negro
   - (f) People of Color

4. Under what circumstances will you typically use the second alternative?

_____

_____

_____

_____

Table C.3
Names for Americans of African Descent

1. What do you most prefer to call people of African descent?
   (Please place in ranking order)
(1) African American	( )
(2) Afro-American	( )
(3) Black	( )
(4) Colored	( )
(5) Negro	( )
(6) People of Color	( )

2. What do you least like to call people of African descent?
   (Please place in ranking order)
(1) African American	( )
(2) Afro-American	( )
(3) Black	( )
(4) Colored	( )
(5) Negro	( )
(6) People of Color	( )

3. Which of the following, in your opinion, project the most positive image?
   (Please place in ranking order)
(1) African American	( )
(2) Afro-American	( )
(3) Black	( )
(4) Colored	( )
(5) Negro	( )
(6) People of Color	( )

4. Which of the following, in your opinion, project the most negative image?
   (Please place in ranking order)
(1) African American	( )
(2) Afro-American	( )
(3) Black	( )
(4) Colored	( )
(5) Negro	( )
(6) People of Color	( )

5. What do you think will be used more and more in the future to refer to people
   of African descent?
   (Please place in ranking order)
(1) African American	( )
(2) Afro-American	( )
(3) Black	( )
(4) Colored	( )
(5) Negro	( )
(6) People of Color	( )

Table C.3 (continued)

6. What do you think will be used less and less in the future to refer to people of African descent?
   (Please place in ranking order)
(1) African American	( )
(2) Afro-American	( )
(3) Black	( )
(4) Colored	( )
(5) Negro	( )
(6) People of Color	( )

7. How do you think people of African descent will be referred to by the press in the future?
   (Please place in ranking order)
(1) African American	( )
(2) Afro-American	( )
(3) Black	( )
(4) Colored	( )
(5) Negro	( )
(6) People of Color	( )

8. How do you think people of African descent will be referred to by TV commentators in the future?
   (Please place in ranking order)
(1) African American	( )
(2) Afro-American	( )
(3) Black	( )
(4) Colored	( )
(5) Negro	( )
(6) People of Color	( )

9. How do you think people of African descent will be referred to by political figures in the future?
   (Please place in ranking order)
(1) African American	( )
(2) Afro-American	( )
(3) Black	( )
(4) Colored	( )
(5) Negro	( )
(6) People of Color	( )

Appendix D

Correlation Tables for Black American Subjects

Table D.1
Correlation Matrix ("your opinion" scale)

Factor	1	2	3	4	5	6
Negative Images						
Cultural Exclusion	.04					
Separation	.13	.48*				
Positive Self-Image	-.16	.06	.06			
Cultural Inclusion	-.15	.09	.12	.37*		
Cultural Participation	.15	.00	.00	.10	.17	

Note: * indicates statistical significance at < .01.

Table D.2
Correlation Matrix ("mainstream opinion" scale)

Factor	1	2	3
Negative Images			
Cultural Integrity	-.34*		
Belief in the "Just World"	.08	.11	

Note: * indicates statistical significance at < .01.

Table D.3
Correlation Matrix ("black Americans' opinion" scale)

Factor	1	2	3
Cultural Exclusion			
Dual Consciousness		.23	
Separation	.20	.30	

Appendix E

Correlation Tables for Non-black American Subjects

Table E.1
Correlation Matrix ("your opinion" scale)

Factor	1	2	3	4	5	6	7	8
Negative Images								
Images of Black Women	-.19							
Integration of Black women	-.10	.06						
Assimilation	.00	.13	.21					
Permanence of Discrimination	-.05	-.03	.07	.06				
Cultural Inclusion	-.02	.30*	.04	.18	-.05			
Separation	-.12	.28*	.01	.00	.09	.24*		
Coping with Discrimination	.18	-.06	.00	-.02	-.04	-.06	.10	

Note: * indicates statistical significance at < .01.

Table E.2
Correction Matrix ("mainstream opinion" scale)

Factor	1	2	3	4	5	6
Negative Images–1						
Negative Images–2	.55*					
Separation–1	-.11	-.29*				
Separation–2	-.06	-.15	.26*			
Civil Rights Legacy	.24*	.22*	-.11	-.13		
Myrdal's Dilemma	.02	.02	.03	-.07	.19	

Note: * indicates statistical significance at < .01.

Table E.3
Correlation Matrix ("black Americans' opinion" scale)

Factor	1	2	3	4	5
Negative Images					
Cultural Inclusion	-.30*				
Welfare	.50*	-.32*			
Declining Significance of Race	.06	-.09	.20		
Perseverance in Integration	-.13	.24*	-.27*	.11	

Note: * indicates statistical significance at < .01.

Analyses of Variance (ANOVA) for Black American Subjects

Table F.1
F Scores for Choice of African American versus Black (your opinion)

Factor	1	2	3	4	5	6
Most used name/ingroup					3.85 (.05)	
Most used name/outgroup	4.60 (.03)					
Preferred name	7.95 (.006)					5.54 (.02)
Positive name/ingroup	9.27 (.003)					
Positive name/outgroup			5.05 (.02)	7.51 (.007)	5.09 (.02)	
Future name			8.44 (.005)		6.80 (.01)	
Type of questionnaire					6.44 (.01)	5.49 (.02)
Most used name/ingroup × Most used name/outgroup						
Most used name/ingroup × Preferred name						
Most used name/ingroup × Positive name/ingroup	3.49 (.03)					
Most used name/ingroup × Positive name/outgroup					5.23 (.02)	

(continued)

Table F.1 (continued)

Factor	1	2	3	4	5	6
Most used name/ingroup × Future name						
Most used name/ingroup × Type of questionnaire						
Most used name/outgroup × Preferred name					4.52 (.03)	
Most used name/outgroup × Positive name/ingroup						
Most used name/outgroup × Positive name/outgroup						
Most used name/outgroup × Future name	4.38 (.01)	2.99 (.05)				
Most used name/outgroup × Type of questionnaire					4.84 (.03)	
Preferred name × Positive name/ingroup						
Preferred name × Positive name/outgroup						
Preferred name × Future name		5.49 (.02)	4.71 (.03)	5.80 (.01)		
Preferred name × Type of questionnaire	3.77 (.05)					5.93 (.01)
Positive name/ingroup × Positive name/outgroup						
Positive name/ingroup × Future name						
Positive name/ingroup × Type of questionnaire						10.17 (.002)
Positive name/outgroup × Future name						
Positive name/outgroup × Type of questionnaire						
Future name × Type of questionnaire						

Note: Factor 1 = Negative Images; Factor 2 = Cultural Exclusion; Factor 3 = Separation; Factor 4 = Positive Self-Image; Factor 5 = Cultural Inclusion; Factor 6 = Cultural Participation.

Table F.2
F Scores for Choice of African American versus Black (mainstream opinion)

Factor	1	2	3
Most used name/ingroup			
Most used name/outgroup			
Preferred name			
Positive name/ingroup			
Positive name/outgroup			
Future name	4.34 (.04)		
Type of questionnaire			
Most used name/ingroup × Most used name/ outgroup	6.34 (.01)		
Most used name/ingroup × Preferred name			
Most used name/ingroup × Positive name/ingroup			
Most used name/ingroup × Positive name/outgroup			4.28 (.04)
Most used name/ingroup × Future name			
Most used name/ingroup × Type of questionnaire			
Most used name/outgroup × Preferred name			
Most used name/outgroup × Positive name/ingroup			3.33 (.04)
Most used name/outgroup × Positive name/outgroup			
Most used name/outgroup × Future name			
Most used name/outgroup × Type of questionnaire			
Preferred name × Positive name/ingroup			
Preferred name × Positive name/outgroup			
Preferred name × Future name			
Preferred name × Type of questionnaire			
Positive name/ingroup × Positive name/outgroup			
Positive name/ingroup × Future name			
Positive name/ingroup × Type of questionnaire			
Positive name/outgroup × Future name			
Positive name/outgroup × Type of questionnaire			
Future name × Type of questionnaire			

Note: Factor 1 = Negative Images; Factor 2 = Cultural Integrity; Factor 3 = Belief in the "Just World."

Table F.3
F Scores for Choice of African American versus Black (black Americans'
opinion)

Factor	1	2	3
Most used name/ingroup		6.12 (.01)	
Most used name/outgroup			
Preferred name		8.42 (.005)	
Positive name/ingroup			4.56 (.03)
Positive name/outgroup	4.04 (.04)	16.94 (.000)	9.02 (.004)
Future name		15.25 (.000)	5.36 (.02)
Type of questionnaire			
Most used name/ingroup × Most used name/outgroup			
Most used name/ingroup × Preferred name			
Most used name/ingroup × Positive name/ingroup			
Most used name/ingroup × Positive name/outgroup			
Most used name/ingroup × Future name			
Most used name/ingroup × Type of questionnaire			
Most used name/outgroup × Preferred name			
Most used name/outgroup × Positive name/ingroup			
Most used name/outgroup × Positive name/outgroup			
Most used name/outgroup × Future name		3.70 (.03)	
Most used name/outgroup × Type of questionnaire			
Preferred name × Positive name/ingroup			
Preferred name × Positive name/outgroup			
Preferred name × Future name			
Preferred name × Type of questionnaire	4.18 (.04)		
Positive name/ingroup × Positive name/outgroup			
Positive name/ingroup × Future name			
Positive name/ingroup × Type of questionnaire			
Positive name/outgroup× Future name			
Positive name/outgroup × Type of questionnaire			
Future name × Type of questionnaire			3.97 (.05)

Note: Factor 1 = Cultural Exclusion; Factor 2 = Dual Consciousness; Factor 3 =
　　Separation.

Appendix G

Analyses of Variance (ANOVA) for Non-black American Subjects

Table G.1
F Scores for Choice of African American versus Black (your opinion)

Factor	1	2	5	6
Most used name		4.22 (.04)		
Preferred name	4.26 (.04)	13.56 (.000)	6.36 (.010)	
Positive name		5.59 (.020)	4.29 (.04)	
Future name		7.18 (.009)		6.89 (.01)
Type of questionnaire			7.20 (.009)	
Most used name × Preferred name				
Most used name × Positive name				
Most used name × Future name			4.39 (.03)	
Most used name × Type of questionnaire				
Preferred name × Positive name				
Preferred name × Future name			3.72 (.05)	
Preferred name × Type of questionnaire				
Positive name × Future name				

(continued)

Table G.1 (continued)

Factor	1	2	5	6
Positive name × Type of questionnaire			4.07 (.04)	
Future name × Type of questionnaire				

Note: Factor 1 = Negative Images; Factor 2 = Image of Black Women; Factor 5 = Permanence of Discrimation; Factor 6 = Coping with Discrimination.

Table G.2
F Scores for Choice of African American versus Black (mainstream opinion)

Factor	2	6
Most used name		
Preferred name		4.97 (.02)
Positive name	4.08 (.04)	
Future name		
Type of questionnaire		
Most used name × Preferred name		
Most used name × Positive name		
Most used name × Future name		
Most used name × Type of questionnaire		
Preferred name × Positive name		
Preferred name × Future name		
Preferred name × Type of questionnaire		
Positive name × Future name		
Positive name × Type of questionnaire		
Future name × Type of questionnaire		

Note: Factor 2 = Negative Images–2; Factor 6 = Myrdal's Dilemma.

Table G.3
F Scores for Choice of African American versus Black (black Americans'
opinion)

Factor	1	4
Most used name		
Preferred name		
Positive name		5.53
		(.02)
Future name	4.46	
	(.03)	
Type of questionnaire		
Most used name × Preferred name		
Most used name × Positive name		
Most used name × Future name		
Most used name × Type of questionnaire		
Preferred name × Positive name		
Preferred name × Future name		
Preferred name × Type of questionnaire		
Positive name × Future name		
Positive name × Type of questionnaire		
Future name × Type of questionnaire		

Note: Factor 1 = Negative Images; Factor 4 = Declining Significance of Race.

Bibliography

Abric, J.C. (1984). A theoretical and experimental approach to the study of social representations in a situation of interaction. In R.M. Farr and S. Moscovici (Eds.), *Social representations*. Cambridge, England: Cambridge University Press.

Abric, J.C. (1987). *Cooperation, competition et représentations sociales*. Cousset, Switzerland: Del Val.

Abric, J.C. (1989). L'étude expérimentale des représentations sociales. In D. Jodelet (Ed.), *Les représentation sociales*. Paris: Presses Universitaires de France.

Abric, J.C. (1994a, September 4). *Nature et fonctionnement du noyau central d'une représentation: La représentation sociale de l'enterprise*. Paper presented at the Second International Conference on Social Representations, Rio de Janeiro.

Abric, J.C. (1994b). Les représentations sociales: Aspects theoriques. In J.C. Abric (Ed.), *Pratiques sociales et représentations*. Paris: Presses Universitaires de France.

Abric, J.C. (1994c). Introduction. In J.C. Abric (Ed.), *Pratiques sociales et représentations*. Paris: Presses Universitaires de France.

Abric, J.C. & Tafani, E. (1994, September 5). *Nature et fonctionnement du noyau central d'une représentation sociale: La représentation de l'entreprise*. Paper presented at the Second International Conference on Social Representations Rio de Janeiro.

Abric J.C. & Vergés, P. (1994). Les représentations sociales de la banque. *Études et Recherches du GIFRESH, 26*, September.

African-American or Black: What's in a name? (1989). *Ebony*, July, 76–80.

Allen, I.L. (1990). *Unkind words: Ethnic labeling from Redskin to WASP*. New York: Bergin & Garvey.

Allen, R.L., Thornton, M.C. & Watkins, S.C. (1995). An African American racial belief system and social structural relationships: A test of invariance. *National Journal of Sociology.*

Allport, G.W. (1935). Attitudes. In C. Murchinson (Ed.), *Handbook of Social Psychology.* Worcester, MA: Clark University Press.

Allport, G.W. (1954). *The nature of prejudice.* Reading, MA: Addison-Wesley.

Amirkhan, J., Betancourt, H., Graham, S., Lopez, S.R. & Weiner, B. (1995). Reflections on Affirmative Action goals in psychology admissions. *Psychological Science, 6,* 140–148.

Bache, R.M. (1895). Reaction time with reference to race. *Psychological Review, 2,* 475–486.

Baldwin, J, (1963). *The fire next time.* New York: Dial.

Baldwin, J. & Mead, M. (1971). *A rap on race.* Philadelphia: J.B. Lippincott.

Banton, M. (1977). *The idea of race.* London: Tavistock.

Banton, M. (1983). *Racial and ethnic competition.* Cambridge, England: Cambridge University Press.

Banton, M. (1988). *Racial consciousness.* London: Longman.

Bardin, L. (1989). *L'analyse de contenu.* Paris: Presses Universitaires de France.

Bell, D. (1992). *Faces at the bottom of the well: The permanence of racism.* New York: Basic Books.

Bellah, R.N., Madse, R., Sullivan, W.M., Swidler, A. & Tipton, S.M. (1985). *Habits of the heart: Individualism and commitment in American life.* New York: Perennial Library.

Bennett, L., Jr. (1970). What's in a name? In P.I. Rose (Ed.), *Americans from Africa: Old memories, new moods.* New York: Atherton Press.

Bernstein, R. (1994). *The dictatorship of virtue: Multiculturalism and the battle for America's future.* New York: Knopf.

Bobo, L. (1983). Whites' opposition to busing: Symbolic racism or realistic group conflict? *Journal of Personality and Social Psychology, 45,* 1196–1210.

Bobo, L. (1987). *Racial attitudes and the status of Black Americans: A social psychological view of change since the 1940s.* Paper prepared for the Committee on the Status of Black Americans. Washington, DC: National Research Council.

Bobo, L. (1989). Memorandum to the Committee on the Status of Black Americans. Washington, DC: National Research Council.

Bradford, W.D. (1987). *Wealth, assets and income of Black households.* Paper prepared for the Committee on the Status of Black Americans. Washington, DC: National Research Council.

Breakwell, G. (1993). Integrating paradigms, methodological implications. In G.M. Breakwell & D.V. Cantor (Eds.), *Empirical approaches to social representations.* Oxford, England: Clarendon Press.

Broad coalition seeks African American name. (1989, January 16). *Jet, 75,* 53.

Campbell, A. (1971). *White attitudes toward Black people.* Ann Arbor, MI: Institute for Social Research.

Carmichael, S. & Hamilton, C.V. (1967). *Black power: The politics of liberation in America.* New York: Random House.

Carson, C. (1986). Paper prepared for the Committee on the Status of Black Americans. Washington, DC: National Research Council.

Carter, S. (1991). *Reflections of an Affirmative Action baby.* New York: Basic Books.

Chomsky, N. (1975). *Reflections on language*. New York: Pantheon Books.

Clark, K.B. (1965). *Dark ghetto*. New York: Harper.

Clark, K.B. & Clark, M.P. (1947). Racial identification and preference in Negro children. In T. Newcomb & E.L. Hartley (Eds.), *Readings in social psychology*. New York: Holt.

Collier, E. (1990). Paradox in paradise: The Black image in Revolutionary America. *The Black Scholar, 21,* 2–9.

Cook, S.W. (1979). Social science and school desegregation: Did we mislead the Supreme Court? *Personality and Social Psychology Bulletin, 5,* 420–437.

Cose, E. (1993). *The rage of a privileged class*. New York: HarperCollins.

Cross, W.E., Jr. (1980). The Negro-to-Black conversion experience: An empirical analysis. In A.W. Boykin et al. (Eds.), *Research directions of Black psychologists*. New York: Russell Sage Foundation.

Dauzat, A. (1956). *Les noms de personnes: Origine et evolution* (4th ed.). Paris: Librairie Delgrave.

Davis, F.J. (1991). *Who is Black? One nation's definition*. University Park, PA: Pennsylvania State University Press.

Davis, J.P. (1966). The Negro in the armed forces of America. In J.P. Davis (Ed.), *The American Negro reference book*. Englewood Cliffs, NJ: Prentice-Hall.

Deaux, K. (1968). Variations in warning, information preference, and anticipatory attitude change. *Journal of Personality and Social Psychology, 9,* 157–161.

Deaux, K. (1992). Personalizing identity and socializing self. In G. Breakwell (Ed.), *Social psychology of identity and the self-concept*. London: Academic Press.

Deaux, K. (1993). Reconstructing social identity. *Personality and Social Psychology Bulletin, 19,* 4–12.

Deaux, K. (1994). Social identification. In T. Higgins & A. Kruglanski (Eds.), *Social psychology: Handbook of basic mechanisms and processes*. New York: Guilford.

Deloria, V. (1981). American Indians, Blacks, Chicanos and Puerto Ricans. *Daedalus,* Spring, 13–27.

Deschamps, J.C. (1977). *L'attribution et la categorisation sociale*. Bern, Switzerland: Peter Lang.

Doise, W. (1984). Social representation, inter-group experiments and level of analysis. In R.M. Farr and S. Moscovici (Eds.), *Social representations*. Cambridge, England: Cambridge University Press.

Doise, W. (1985). Les représentations sociales: Definition d'un concept. *Connexions, 45,* 245–253.

Doise, W. (1986). *Levels of explanations in social psychology*. Cambridge, England: Cambridge University Press.

Doise, W. (1988). Les représentations sociales: Un label de qualité. *Connexions, 51,* 99–113.

Doise, W. (1989). Attitudes et représentations sociales. In D. Jodelet (Ed.), *Les représentations sociales*. Paris: Presses Universitaires de France.

Doise, W. (1992). L'ancrage dans les etudes sur les représentations sociales. *Bulletin de Psychologie, 45,* 189–195.

Doise, W. (1993). Debating social representations. In G.M. Breakwell & D.V. Cantor (Eds.), *Empirical approaches to social representations*. Oxford, England: Clarendon Press.

Doise, W., Clemence, A. & Lorenzo-Cioldi, F. (1993). *Représentations sociales et analyses des données.* Grenoble, France: Presses Universitaires de Grenoble.

Doise, W., Csepeli, G., Cann, H.D., Gouge, C., Larson, K. & Ostell, A. (1972). An experimental investigation into the formation of intergroup representation. *European Journal of Social Psychology, 2,* 202–204.

Dole, A.A. (1995). Why not drop race as a term? *American Psychologist, 60,* 40.

Dovidio, J. & Gaertner, S.L. (1986). *Prejudice, discrimination, and racism.* Orlando, FL: Academic Press.

Du Bois, W.E.B. ([1903] 1965). *The souls of Black folk.* New York: Mentor Books.

Du Bois, W.E.B. ([1928] 1970). Response to Roland Burton: The crisis. Reprinted in L. Bennett, Jr., What's in a name? In P.I. Rose (Ed.), *Americans from Africa: Old memories, new moods.* New York: Atherton Press.

Dunn, L.C. & Dobzhansky, T. (1952). *Heredity, race and society.* New York: Mentor Books.

Durkheim, E. (1953). Individual and collective representations. In E. Durkheim, *Sociology and philosophy.* London: Cohen & West.

Dyson, M. (1993). *Reflecting Black: African-American cultural criticism.* Minneapolis: University of Minnesota Press.

Dyson, M. (1995). A symposium on race and racism. *Social Text, 42,* 12–14. Durham, NC: Duke University Press.

Fairchild, H.H. (1985). Black, Negro, or Afro-American? The differences are crucial. *Journal of Black Studies, 16,* 47–55.

Farr, R.M. (1984). Social representations: Their role in the design and execution of laboratory experiments. In R.M. Farr & S. Moscovici (Eds.), *Social representations.* Cambridge, England: Cambridge University Press.

Farr, R.M. (1987). Social representations: A French tradition of research. *Journal for the Theory of Social Behavior, 17,* 343–369.

Farr, R. (1993). Theory and method in the study of social representations. In G.M. Breakwell & D.V. Cantor (Eds.), *Empirical approaches to social representations.* Oxford, England: Clarendon Press.

Farr, R. (1996). *The roots of modern social psychology 1872–1954.* Oxford, England: Blackwell.

Feagin, J.R. & Feagin, C.B. (1986). *Discrimination American style: Institutional racism and sexism* (2nd ed.). Malabar, FL: Robert Krieger.

Ferguson, G.O. (1916). *The psychology of the Negro: An experimental study.* New York: Science Press.

Festinger, L. (1957). *A theory of cognitive dissonance.* Evanston, IL: Row, Peterson, & Co.

Festinger, L. (1983). *The human legacy.* New York: Columbia University Press.

Festinger, L., Riecken, H.W. & Schachter, S. (1956). *When prophecy fails.* Minneapolis: University of Minnesota Press.

Fitzpatrick, A.R. & Eagly, A.H. (1981). Anticipatory belief polarization as a function of the expertise of a discussion partner. *Personality and Social Psychological Bulletin, 7,* 636–642.

Flament, C. (1987). Pratiques et représentations sociales. In J.L. Beauvois, R.V. Joule & G.M. Monteil (Eds.), *Perspectives cognitives et conduites sociales* (Vol. 1). Couset, Switzerland: Del Val.

Flament, C. (1989). Structure et dynamique des représentations sociales. In D.

Jodelet (Ed.), *Les représentations sociales*. Paris: Presses Universitaires de France.

Flament, C. (1994). Structure, dynamique et transformations des représentations sociales. In J.C. Abric (Ed.), *Pratiques sociales et représentations*. Paris: Presses Universitaires de France.

Flament, C. & Moliner, P. (1989). Contribution expérimentale à la theorie du noyau centrale d'une représentation. In J.L. Beauvois, R.V. Joule, & G.M. Monteil (Eds.), *Perspectives cognitives et conduites sociales* (Vol. 2). Cousset, Switzerland: Del Val.

Fraser, C. (1994). Attitudes, social representations and widespread beliefs. *Textes sur les représentations sociales: Espace de discussion, 3*(1), 13–25.

From "Black" to "African-American"? (1989, January 2). *Newsweek, 113*, p. 28.

Furnham, A. & Procter, E. (1989). Belief in a just world: Review and critique of the individual difference literature. *British Journal of Social Psychology, 28*, 365–384.

Gaertner, S.L. & Dovidio, J. (1983). Racial stereotypes: Associations and ascriptions of positive and negative characteristics. *Social Psychology Quarterly, 46*, 23–30.

Gaines, S.O., Jr. & Reed, E.S. (1995). From Allport to Du Bois. *American Psychologist, 50*, 96–103.

Gaiter, L. (1994, June 26). The revolt of the Black bourgeoisie. *New York Times*.

Gardiner, A.H. (1954). *The theory of proper names: A controversial essay* (2nd ed.). London and New York: Oxford University Press.

Garvey, A.J. ([1925] 1973). Women as leaders. Reprinted in G. Lerner (Ed.), *Black women in White America: A documentary history*. New York: Vintage Books.

Gates, H.L. (1988). *The signifying monkey: A theory of Afro-American literary criticism*. New York: Oxford University Press.

Gilbert, G.M. (1951). Stereotype persistence and change among college students. *Journal of Abnormal and Social Psychology, 46*, 245–254.

Glazer, N. (1995, April 5). Race, not class. *Wall Street Journal*.

Glazer, N. & Moynihan, D.P. (1963). *Beyond the melting pot*. Cambridge, MA: MIT Press.

Golden, T. (1994). *Black male: Representation of masculinity in contemporary American art*. New York: Whitney Museum of American Art.

Gordon, M.M. (1964). *Assimilation in American life: The role of race, religion and national origin*. New York: Oxford University Press.

Gordon, V.V. (1976). The methodologies of Black self-concept research: A critique. *The Journal of Afro-American Issues, 3 & 4*, 372–381.

Gossett, T.F. (1963). *Race: The history of an idea in America*. New York: Schocken Books.

Guinier, L. (1995, January 23). Beyond winner take all: Democracy's conversation. *The Nation*.

Gurin, P., Hatchett, S. & Jackson, J.S. (1988). *Hope and independence: Blacks' struggle in two-party politics*. New York: Russell Sage Foundation.

Hacker, A. (1992). *Two nations: Black and White, separate, hostile, unequal*. New York: Macmillan.

Hacker, A. (1995, July 10). The crackdown on African-Americans. *The Nation*.

Hale, J.E. (1980). De-mythicizing the education of Black children. In R.L. Jones (Ed.), *Black psychology*. New York: Harper & Row.

Harris, O. (1990). The image of the African American in psychological journals. *The Black Scholar, 21*, 25–29.

Hatchett, S. & Schuman, H. (1974). *Black racial attitudes: Trends and complexities*. Ann Arbor, MI: Institute for Social Research.

Hecht, M. & Ribeau, S. (1987). Afro-American identity labels and communicative effectiveness. *Journal of Language and Social Psychology, 6*, 319–326.

Hecht, M. & Ribeau, S. (1991). Sociocultural roots of ethnic identity. A look at Black America. *Journal of Black Studies, 21*, 501–513.

Helms, J.E. (Ed.) (1990). *Black and White racial identity: Theory, research, and practice*. Westport, CT: Greenwood Press.

Herbert, B. (1994, December 4). Who will help the Black man? *New York Times Magazine*.

Hoskins, L. (1992). Eurocentrism vs. Afrocentrism: A geopolitical linkage analysis. *Journal of Black Studies, 23*, 247–257.

Huggins, N.I. (1971). *Harlem Renaissance*. New York: Oxford University Press.

Jackson, J.S. & Gurin, G. (1987). *National survey of Black Americans, 1979–1980*. Ann Arbor, MI: Inter-University Consortium for Political and Social Research.

Jackson, J.S., McCullough, W.R., Gurin, G. & Broman, C.L. (1991). Race identity. In J.S. Jackson (Ed.), *Life in Black America: Findings from a national survey*. Los Angeles: Sage.

Jacobson, C.K. (1985). Resistance to affirmative action: Self-interest or racism? *Journal of Conflict Resolution, 29*, 306–329.

Jarrett, V. (1988, December 22). Redefine "Black" as a positive term. *Chicago Sun-Times*, 39.

Jaspars, J.M.F. & Fraser, C. (1984). Attitudes and social representations. In R.M. Farr & S. Moscovici (Eds.), *Social representations*. Cambridge, England: Cambridge University Press.

Jaynes, G.D. & Williams, R.M., Jr. (Eds.) (1989). *A common destiny: Blacks and American society*. Washington, DC: National Academy Press.

Jennings, G. (1965). *Personalities of language*. London: Victor Gollancz.

Jodelet, D. (1984). The representation of the body and its transformations. In R.M. Farr & S. Moscovici (Eds.), *Social representations*. Cambridge, England: Cambridge University Press.

Jodelet, D. (1989). Représentations sociales: Un domaine en expansion. In D. Jodelet (Ed.), *Les représentations sociales*. Paris: Presses Universitaires de France.

Jodelet, D. (1993). Indigenous psychologies and social representations of the body and self. In U. Kim & J.W. Berry (Eds.), *Indigenous psychologies: Research and experience in cultural context*. Newbury Park, CA: Sage.

Joint Center for Political and Economic Studies (1990). *JCPES survey: Black vs. African American*. Washington, DC.

Jones, E.E. (1989). The framing of competence. *Personality and Social Psychology Bulletin, 15*, 477–492.

Jones, E.E. & Nisbett, R.E. (1972). The actor and the observer: Divergent perceptions of the causes of behavior. In E.E. Jones, D.E. Kanouse, H.H. Kelley,

R.E. Nisbett, S. Valins & B. Weiner (Eds.), *Attribution: Perceiving the causes of behavior*. Morristown, NJ: General Learning Press.

Jones, J. (1986). Racism: A cultural analysis of the problem. In J. Dovidio & S. Gaertner (Eds.), *Prejudice, discrimination, and racism*. Orlando, FL: Academic Press.

Jovchelovitch, S. (1995). Social representations in and of the public sphere: Towards a theoretical articulation. *Journal for the Theory for Social Behavior, 25*, 83–102.

Jovchelovitch, S. (1996). In defence of representations. *Journal for the Theory of Social Behavior, 26*, 121–135.

Joyner, C. (1989). Creolization. In C.R. Wilson & W. Ferris (Eds.), *Encyclopedia of Southern Culture*. Chapel Hill: University of North Carolina Press.

Kallen, H. (1924). *Culture and democracy in America*. New York: Boni & Liveright.

Karlins, M., Coffman, T.L. & Walters, G. (1969). On the fading of social stereotypes: Studies in three generations of college students. *Journal of Personality and Social Psychology, 13*, 1–16.

Katz, D. & Braly, K. (1933). Racial stereotypes of one hundred college students. *Journal of Abnormal and Social Psychology, 28*, 280–290.

Kelly, H.H. & Thibaut, J.W. (1969). Group problem-solving. In G. Lindzey & E. Aronson (Eds.), *Handbook of social psychology* (Vol. 4). Reading, MA: Addison-Wesley.

Kelves, D.J. (1985). *In the name of Eugenics: Genetics and the uses of human heredity*. New York: Knopf.

Kinder, D.R. & Sanders, L.M. (1990). Mimicking political debate with survey questions: The case of white opinion on affirmative action for blacks. *Social Cognition, 8*, 73–103.

Kinder, D.R. & Sears, D.O. (1981). Prejudice and politics: Symbolic racism versus racial threats to the good life. *Journal of Personality and Social Psychology, 40*, 414–431.

King, M.L., Jr. (1964). *Why we can't wait*. New York: Signet Books.

Kleinpfenning, G. & Hagendoorn, L. (1993). Forms of racism and the cumulative dimension of ethnic attitudes. *Social Psychology Quarterly, 56*, 21–36.

Kluegel, J.R. & Smith, E.R. (1983). Affirmative action attitudes: Effects of self-interest, racial affect, and stratification beliefs on whites' views. *Social Forces, 61*, 797–824.

Kovel, J. (1984). *White racism*. New York: Columbia University Press.

Kozulin, A. (1990). *Vygotsky's psychology*. Cambridge, MA: Harvard University Press.

Kripke, S. (1972). *Naming and necessity*. Oxford, England: Oxford University Press.

Kripke, S. (1980). *Naming and necessity* (2nd ed.). Oxford, England: Oxford University Press.

Larkey, L.K., Hecht, M.L. & Martin, J. (1993). What's in a name? African American ethnic identity terms and self-determination. *Journal of Language and Social Psychology, 12*, 302–317.

Lawrence, C. (1987). The id, the ego, and equal protection: Reckoning with unconscious racism. *Stanford Law Review, 39*, 317–388.

Lee, Y.T. (1993). Ingroup preference and homogeneity among African American and Chinese American students. *Journal of Social Psychology, 133*, 225–235.

Lerner, G. (Ed.). (1973). *Black women in White America: A documentary history*. New York: Vintage Books.

Lerner, M.J. (1980). *The belief in a just world: A fundamental delusion*. New York: Plenum.

Levine, L.W. (1977). *Black culture and Black consciousness: Afro American folk thought from slavery to freedom*. New York: Oxford University Press.

Levi-Strauss, C. (1966). *The savage mind*. London: Weidenfeld & Nicholson.

Lewin, K. (1935). *A dynamic theory of personality*. New York: McGraw-Hill.

Lewin, K. (1948). *Resolving social conflict*. New York: Harper.

Lipset, S.M. & Schneider, W. (1978). The Bakke case: How would it be decided at the bar of public opinion? *Public Opinion, 1*, 38–44.

Malcolm X. (1965). *The autobiography of Malcolm X*. New York: Grove Press.

Marrow, A.J. (1969). *The practical theorist: The life and work of Kurt Lewin*. New York: Basic Books.

McCauley, C.R. & Segal, M.E. (1987). Social psychology of terrorist groups. In C. Hendrick (Ed.), *Group processes and intergroup: Review of personality and social psychology* (Vol. 9). Newbury Park, CA: Sage.

McConahay, J.B. (1982). Self-interest versus racial attitudes as correlates of anti-busing attitudes in Louisville: Is it the buses or the Blacks? *Journal of Politics, 44*, 692–720.

McDougal, W. (1923). *Introduction to social psychology*. Boston: John W. Luce & Co.

McGuire, W.J. (1964). Inducing resistance to persuasion. In L. Berkowitz (Ed.), *Advances in experimental social psychology* (Vol. 1). New York: Academic Press.

McGuire, W.J. & Millman, S. (1965). Anticipatory belief lowering following forewarning of a persuasive attack. *Journal of Personality and Social Psychology, 2*, 471–479.

Mill, J.S. (1879), *A system of logic* (10th ed.). London: Longmans, Green & Co.

Miller, K. (1937). Negroes or Colored People? *Opportunity*, May, 142–146.

Moliner, P. (1989). Validation expérimentale de l'hypothese du noyau central de représentation sociale. *Bulletin de psychologie, 41*, 759–762.

Moliner, P. (1995). A two-dimensional model of social representations. *European Journal of Social Psychology, 25*, 27–40.

Moscovici, S. (1961). *La psychanalyse: Son image et son public*. Paris: Presses Universitaires de France.

Moscovici, S. (1963). Attitudes and opinions. *Annual Review of Psychology, 14*, 231–260.

Moscovici, S. (1973). Foreword. In C. Herzlich, *Health and illness: A social psychological analysis*. London: Academic Press.

Moscovici, S. (1976a). *La psychanalyse: Son image et son public* (2nd ed.). Paris: Presses Universitaires de France.

Moscovici, S. (1976b). *Psychologie des minorités actives*. Paris: Presses Universitaires de France.

Moscovici, S. (1980). Toward a theory of conversion behavior. In L. Berkowitz (Ed.), *Advances in experimental social psychology* (Vol. 13). New York: Academic Press.

Moscovici, S. (1981). On social representations. In J.P. Forgas (Ed.), *Social cognition: Perspectives on everyday understanding.* London: Academic Press.

Moscovici, S. (1982). The coming era of social representation. In J.P. Codol and J.P. Leyens (Eds.), *Cognitive approaches to social behaviour.* The Hague, Netherlands: Nijhoff.

Moscovici, S. (1984). The phenomenon of social representations. In R.M. Farr & S. Moscovici (Eds.), *Social representations.* Cambridge, England: Cambridge University Press.

Moscovici, S. (1985). Social influence and conformity. In G. Lindzey & E. Aronson (Eds.), *Handbook of social psychology* (Vol. 2). New York: Random House.

Moscovici, S. (1987). Answers and questions. *Journal for the Theory of Social Behavior, 17,* 513–529.

Moscovici, S. (1988a). *La machine à faire des dieux.* Paris: Fayard.

Moscovici, S. (1988b). Notes towards a description of social representations. *European Journal of Social Psychology, 18,* 211–250.

Moscovici, S. (1989). Des représentations collectives aux représentations sociales: Elements pour une histoire. In D. Jodelet (Ed.), *Les représentations sociales.* Paris: Presses Universitaires de France.

Moscovici, S. (1994). Social representations and pragmatic communication. *Social Science Information, 33,* 163–177.

Moscovici, S. & Doise, W. (1992). *Conflict and consensus: A general theory of collective decisions.* London: Sage.

Moscovici, S. & Faucheux, C. (1972). Social influence, conformity bias, and the study of active minorities. In L. Berkowitz (Ed.), *Advances in experimental social psychology* (Vol. 16). New York: Academic Press.

Moscovici, S., Lage, E. & Naffrechoux, M. (1969). Influence of a consistent minority on the responses of a majority in a color perception task. *Sociometry, 32,* 365–379.

Moscovici, S. & Personnaz, B. (1980). Studies in social influence V: Minority influence and conversion behavior in perceptual task. *Journal of Experimental Social Psychology, 16,* 270–282.

Moscovici, S. & Personnaz, B. (1991). Studies in social influence VI: Is Lenin orange or red? Imagery and social influence. *European Journal of Social Psychology, 21,* 101–118.

Moscovici, S. & Zavalloni, M. (1968). The group as a polarizer of attitudes. *Journal of Personality and Social Psychology, 12,* 125–135.

Mugny, G., Kaiser, C., Papastamou, S. & Perez, J.A. (1984). Intergroup relations, identification and social influence. *British Journal of Social Psychology, 23,* 317–322.

Myrdal, G. (1944). *An American dilemma.* New York: Harper & Row.

Neuberg, S.L. & Fiske, S.T. (1987). Motivational influences on impression formation: Outcomes dependency, accuracy-driven attention, and individuating processes. *Journal of Personality and Social Psychology, 53,* 431–444.

Nosworthy, G.J., Lea, J.A. & Lindsay, R.C. (1995). Opposition to Affirmative Action: Racial affect and traditional value predictors across four programs. *Journal of Applied Social Psychology, 25,* 314–337.

Omi, M. & Winant, H. (1986). *Racial formation in the United States: From the 1960's to the 1980's.* New York: Routledge.

Oyserman, D. (1993). The lens of personhood: Viewing the self, others, and conflict in a multicultural society. *Journal of Personality and Social Psychology*, 65, 993–1009.

Oyserman, D. & Markus, H.R. (1995). Das Selbst als soziale Repräsentation. In U. Flick (Ed.), *Psychologie des Sozialen: Repräsentationen in Wissen und Sprache*. Hamburg, Germany: Rowohlt.

Paicheler, G. (1976). Norm and attitude change. I: Polarization and styles of behaviour. *European Journal of Social Psychology*, 6, 405–427.

Park, R.E. (1950). *Race and culture* (Vol. 1). Glencoe, IL: Free Press.

Parker, I. (1987). Social representations: Social psychology's (mis)use of sociology. *Journal for the Theory of Social Behavior*, 17, 447–457.

Peirce, C.S. (1932). *Collected Papers* (Vol. 2). Cambridge, MA: Harvard University Press.

Pettigrew, T.F. (1979). Racial change and social policy. *Annals of the American Association of Political and Social Science*, 441, 114–131.

Pettigrew, T.F. & Meertens, R.H. (1995). Subtle and blatant prejudice in Western Europe. *European Journal of Social Psychology*, 25, 57–75.

Philogène, G. (1994), African American as a new social representation. *Journal for the Theory of Social Behavior*, 24, 89–109.

Philogène, G. (1995, August 24). *The naturalization of an anticipatory representation.* Paper delivered at the Symposium on Social Representations in the Northern Context, Mustio, Finland.

Plous, S. & Williams, T. (1995). Racial stereotypes from the days of American slavery: A continuing legacy. *Journal of Applied Social Psychology*, 25, 795–817.

Potter, J. & Litton, J. (1985). Some problems underlying the theory of social representations. *British Journal of Social Psychology*, 24, 81–90.

Poussaint, A. (1966). The Negro American: His self-image and integration. *Journal of the National Medical Association*, 58, 419–423.

Pratkanis, A.R. & Greenwall, A.G. (1989). A sociocognitive model of attitude structure and function. *Advances in Experimental Social Psychology*, 22, 245–285.

Proshansky, H. & Newton, P. (1968). The nature and meaning of Negro self-identity. In M. Deutsch, I. Katz & A.R. Jensen (Eds.), *Social class, race, and psychological development*. New York: Holt, Rinehart, & Winston.

Purkhardt, C. (1993). *Transforming social representations*. London: Routledge.

Putnam, H. (1975). The meaning of "meaning." In K. Gunderson (Ed.), *Language, Mind and Knowledge*. Minnesota Studies in the Philosophy of Science (Vol. 7). Minneapolis: University of Minnesota Press.

Putnam, H. (1983). *Realism and reason*. Philosophical Papers (Vol. 3). Cambridge, England: Cambridge University Press.

Quine, W.V. (1973). *The roots of reference*. LaSalle, IL: Open Court.

Rabbie, J.M., Benoist, F., Oosterbaan, H. & Visser, L. (1974). Differential power and effect of expected competitive and cooperative intergroup interaction on intragroup and outgroup attitudes. *Journal of Personality and Social Psychology*, 30, 46–56.

Rasinski, K.A. (1987). What's fair is fair—or is it? Value differences underlying public views about justice. *Journal of Personality and Social Psychology, 53,* 201–211.

Roberts, J.V. (1985). The attitude-memory relationship after 40 years: A meta-analysis of the literature. *Basic and Applied Social Psychology, 6,* 221–241.

Rodriguez, R. (1982). *Hunger of memory: The education of Richard Rodriguez.* New York: Bentham Books.

Rokeach, M. (1960). *The open and closed mind.* New York: Basic Books.

Rose, P. (1968). *The subject is race.* New York: Oxford University Press.

Rose, P. (1981). *They and we: Racial and ethnic relations in the United States.* New York: Random House.

Rosenthal, R. (1985). From unconscious experimenter bias to teacher expectancy effects. In J.B. Dusek, V.C. Hall & W.J. Meyer (Eds.), *Teacher expectancies.* Hillsdale, NJ: Erlbaum.

Rosenthal, R. (1991). Teacher expectancy effects: A brief update 25 years after the Pygmalion experiment. *Journal of Research in Education, 1,* 3–12.

Rowan, C.T. (1989, January 18). Saying "African American" ain't where it's at. *Chicago Sun-Times,* 21.

Rubin, Z. & Peplau, L.A. (1975). Who believes in a just world? *Journal of Social Issues, 31,* 65–87.

Sanders Thompson, V. (1992). A multifaceted approach to the conceptualization of African American identification. *Journal of Black Studies, 23,* 75–85.

Sanders Thompson, V. (1995). Sociocultural influences on African-American racial identification. *Journal of Applied Social Psychology, 25,* 1411–1429.

Schlesinger, A., Jr. (1992). *The disuniting of America: Reflections on a multicultural society.* New York: Norton.

Schuman, H. & Hatchett, S. (1974). *Black racial attitudes: Trends and complexities.* Ann Arbor, MI: Institute for Social Research.

Schuman, H., Steeh, C. & Bobo, L. (1985). *Racial attitudes in America: Trends and interpretations.* Cambridge, MA: Harvard University Press.

Sears, D.O. (1988). Symbolic racism. In P.A. Katz & D.A. Taylor (Eds.), *Eliminating racism: Profiles in controversy.* New York: Plenum.

Sherif, M. (1966). *In common predicament: Social psychology of intergroup conflict and cooperation.* Boston: Houghton Mifflin.

Sherif, M. (1967). *Social interaction: Process and products.* Chicago: Aldine.

Sherif M., Harvey, O.J., White, B.J., Hood, W.R. & Sherif, C.W. (1961). *Intergroup conflict and cooperation: The robber's cave experiment.* Norman: University of Oklahoma Press.

Simmel, G. (1950). *The sociology of Georg Simmel.* (K.M. Wolf, Trans.). New York: Free Press.

Simmel, G. (1955). *Conflict and the web of group affiliations.* (K.M. Wolf & R. Benhix, Trans.) New York: Free Press.

Simpson, G.E. & Yinger, M.J. (1972). *Racial and cultural minorities: An analysis of prejudice and discrimination* (4th ed.). New York: Harper & Row.

Smith, R. (1981). Black power and the transformation from protest to politics. *Political Sciences Quarterly, 96,* 431–443.

Smith, T.W. (1992). Changing racial labels: From "Colored" to "Negro" to "Black" to "African American." *Public Opinion Quarterly, 56,* 496–514.

Smitherman, G. (1977). *Talkin' and testifyin': The language of Black America*. Boston: Houghton Mifflin Company.

Squire, C. (1994). Empowering women: The Oprah Winfrey show. In Kum-Kum Bhavnani & Ann Phoenix (Eds.), *Shifting identities, shifting racisms: A feminism & psychology reader*. Thousand Oaks, CA: Sage.

Staples, B. (1994). *Parallel time: Growing up in Black and White*. New York: Pantheon Books.

Stephan, W.G., Stephan, C.W., Stefanenko, T., Ageyev, V., Abalakina, M. & Coates-Shrider, L. (1993). Measuring stereotypes: A comparison of methods using Russian and American samples. *Social Psychological Quarterly, 56,* 54–64.

Tajfel, H. (1982). Social psychology of intergroup relations. *Annual Review of Psychology, 33,* 1–39.

Terkel, S. (1992). *Race: How Blacks and Whites think and feel about the American obsession*. New York: New Press.

Thernstorm, S. (Ed.) (1980). *Harvard encyclopedia of American ethnic groups*. Cambridge, MA: Harvard University Press.

Thomas, W.I. & Znaniecki, F. (1918–20). *The Polish peasant in Europe and America* (2 vols.). Chicago: University of Chicago Press.

Tocqueville, A. de. ([1869] 1966). *Democracy in America*. New York: Harper & Row.

Torrance, C. (1990). Blacks and the American ethos: A reevaluation of existing theories. *Journal of Black Studies, 21,* 72–86.

Turner, J.C. (1981). The experimental social psychology of intergroup behaviour. In J.C. Turner & H. Gilles (Eds.), *Intergroup Behaviour*. Oxford, England: Basil Blackwell.

Vergès, P. (1992). L'evocation de l'argent: Une methode pour la définition du noyau central d'une représentation. *Bulletin de Psychologie, 45,* 203–209.

Vygotsky, L.S. ([1931] 1978). *Mind in society: Development of higher psychological processes*. Cambridge, MA: Harvard University Press.

Wagner, W. (1994). Fields of research and socio-genesis of social representations: A discussion of criteria and diagnostics. *Social Science Information, 33,* 199–228.

Walczak, L. (1995, March 13). The new populism. *Business Week.*

Walzer, M. (1990). What does it mean to be an "American"? *Social Research, 57,* 591–614.

Weber, M. ([1925] 1976). Grundriss der Sozialökonomik. Reprinted as *Wirtschaft und Gesellschaft* (5th ed.). Tübingen, Germany: J. Winckelmann.

Weber, M. (1968). *Economy and society: An outline of interpretative sociology*. New York: Bedminster Press.

Wegner, D.M. (1989). *White bears and other unwanted thoughts*. New York: Viking Press.

Wegner, D.M. & Schneider, D.J. (1989). Mental control: The war of the ghosts in the machine. In J. Uleman & J. Bargh (Eds.), *Unintended thought*. New York: Guilford Press.

Wegner, D.M., Schneider, D.J., Carter, S. & White, T. (1987). Paradoxical effects of thought suppression. *Journal of Personality and Social Psychology, 55,* 1–9.

Wegner, D.M., Schneider, D.J., Knutson, B. & McMahon, S.R. (1991). Polluting the stream of consciousness: The effect of thought suppression on the mind's environment. *Cognitive Therapy and Research, 15,* 141–152.

Wegner, D.M., Shortt, J.W., Blake, A.W. & Page, M.S. (1990). The suppression of exciting thoughts. *Journal of Personality and Social Psychology, 58,* 409–418.

West, C. (1992, August 2). Learning to talk of race. *New York Times Magazine.*

West, C. (1994). *Race matters.* New York: Vintage Books.

Wilkins, R. (1995, March 27). Racism has its privileges. *The Nation,* 409–416.

Wilkinson, D. (1990). Americans of African identity. *Society, 27,* May/June, 14–18.

Williams, J.E. (1964). Connotations of color names among Negroes and Caucasians. *Perceptual and Motor Skills, 18,* 121–131.

Williams, J.E. (1966). Connotation of racial concepts and color names. *Journal of Personality and Social Psychology, 3,* 531–540.

Williams, J.E., Tucker, R. & Dunham, F. (1971). Changes in the connotations of color names among Negroes and Caucasians, 1963–1969. *Journal of Personality and Social Psychology, 19,* 222–228.

Williams, L. (1988, December 20). Black: Call us African American. *Chicago Sun-Times,* 4.

Wilson, W.J. (1978). *The declining significance of race.* Chicago: University of Chicago Press.

Wilson, W.J. (1988). The ghetto underclass and the social transformation of the inner city. *Black Scholar, 19,* 10–17.

Winant, H. (1994). *Racial conditions: Politics, theory, comparisons.* Minneapolis: University of Minnesota Press.

Wittgenstein, L. (1958). *Philosophical investigations.* Oxford, England: Basil Blackwell.

Yaroshevsky, M. (1989). *Lev Vygotsky.* Moscow: Progress Publishers.

Yee, A.H., Fairchild, H.H., Weizman, F. & Wyatt, G.E. (1993). Addressing psychology's problem with race. *American Psychologist, 48,* 1132–1140.

Yee, A.H., Fairchild, H.H., Wyatt, G.E. & Weizman, F. (1995). Readdressing psychology's problem with race. *American Psychologist, 50,* 46–47.

Index

About the Author

GINA PHILOGÈNE is Assistant Professor of Psychology at Sarah Lawrence College in Bronxville, New York.

ISBN 0-275-96284-9

EAN

9 780275 962845

HARDCOVER BAR CODE